Crossroads of Heritage and Religion

Crossroads of Heritage and Religion

Legacy and Sustainability of World Heritage Site Moravian Christiansfeld

Edited by
Tine Damsholt, Marie Riegels Melchior,
Christina Petterson, and Tine Reeh

berghahn
NEW YORK · OXFORD
www.berghahnbooks.com

First published in 2022 by
Berghahn Books
www.berghahnbooks.com

Library of Congress Cataloging-in-Publication Data

Names: Damsholt, Tine, editor, author. | Melchior, Marie Riegels, 1974- editor,
author. | Petterson, Christina, editor, author. | Reeh, Tine, editor, author.
Title: Crossroads of heritage and religion : legacy and sustainability of world
heritage site Moravian Christiansfeld / edited by Tine Damsholt, Marie
Riegels Melchior, Christina Petterson, and Tine Reeh.
Description: New York ; Oxford : Berghahn Books, 2022. | Includes
bibliographical references and index.
Identifiers: LCCN 2022004811 (print) | LCCN 2022004812 (ebook) | ISBN
9781800735491 (hardback) | ISBN 9781800735507 (ebook)
Subjects: LCSH: Christiansfeld (Denmark)--History. | Christiansfeld (Denmark)--
Social life and customs. | Moravian Church--Denmark--History. | World
Heritage areas--Denmark--Christiansfeld.
Classification: LCC DL291.C5 C76 2022 (print) | LCC DL291.C5 (ebook) | DDC
948.9/52--dc23/eng/20220505
LC record available at https://lccn.loc.gov/2022004811
LC ebook record available at https://lccn.loc.gov/2022004812

British Library Cataloguing in Publication Data

A catalogue record for this book is available from the British Library

ISBN 978-1-80073-549-1 hardback
ISBN 978-1-80073-550-7 ebook

https://doi.org/10.3167/9781800735491

Contents

Illustrations

Figures

Table

Acknowledgments

This book is the product of a network grant from the Independent Research Fund Denmark — Humanities (2018–2020) to examine from a cross-disciplinary perspective what has been titled "Religion, Modernity and Cultural Heritage: Inquiries in the Legacy and Sustainability of Moravian Christiansfeld." Over three years we had a number of inspiring and challenging seminars and meetings, and we would like to thank each and every participant in these seminars and network activities. The editors would also like to thank the University of Copenhagen, especially the Section of Church History, Faculty of Theology, and the Section of European Ethnology at the Saxo-Institute, Faculty of Humanities, who have been gracious and supportive hosts. We would also like to thank the Moravian congregation in Christiansfeld for granting us access to archival materials and answering all our questions and the Christiansfeld Center for giving us access to the lived experiences of Moravian Christiansfeld. Finally, we would like to thank the anonymous reviewers for their helpful suggestions and extend our thanks to the editors at Berghahn Books for their support and encouragement.

Introduction

Tine Damsholt, Marie Riegels Melchior, Christina Petterson, and Tine Reeh

The present anthology deals with the crossroads between heritage and religion through the case study of Moravian Christiansfeld's listing as a World Heritage site. The anthology reaches back to the eighteenth century when the church settlement was founded, assesses its importance for Danish culture, and brings this history into its UNESCO heritage listing on 4 July 2015. Finally, it explores the consequences of the listing for the everyday life of a religious community in a UNESCO World Heritage site.

Christiansfeld, a small Moravian Church settlement, began as a utopian town on the periphery of European civilization during the blossoming of the Enlightenment period. It was founded by a radical international religious network, the Moravians, at the invitation of the liberal *Geheimekabinetsminister*, or de facto prime minister of Denmark, Johann Friedrich Struensee (1737–1772) and his brother, finance minister Carl August Struensee (1735–1804).[1] The society's founding process shows a bringing together of seemingly incompatible elements and thus challenges dominant popular views and theories on a number of issues regarding the relationship between religion, everyday practices, and the shaping of modern European secular cultures.[2]

While many religious minority societies are characterized by voluntary isolation, the Moravians generally—and in Christiansfeld in particular—have enjoyed a dynamic, open relationship with the surrounding society from their foundation. Moravian communities influenced and interacted with their local national cultures, but at the same time, their members understood themselves as part of a larger, closely knit, transnational society. With the original town of Christiansfeld and the living cultural heritage of the place declared a UNESCO World Heritage site, this particular religious take on life and society has been legitimized and emphasized as important for our common awareness and care.

The present book reflects the debates and knowledge exchange concerned with understanding the history, religion, and sustainability of a community such as Christiansfeld. What are the effects of the World Heritage inscription? How may Christiansfeld live up to the UNESCO ideals? What are some possible ways to strengthen and ensure care for the site into the future?

Christiansfeld is a suitable site for studying ongoing processes of "heritagization," meaning the processes by which heritage is socially constructed and culturally practiced.[3] Questions of the past and its relationship with the present have been increasingly problematized in scholarly debate in recent decades, as scholars investigate how pasts are selectively recalled and used in the present and how they are performed and lived.[4] Through the case of Christiansfeld's designation as a UNESCO World Heritage site, this book does not investigate heritage as something stable or a well-defined object, or as something to be taken for granted or possessed by a limited group. Instead, we consider heritage as continuously created and re-created owing to all those actors engaged in heritagization processes and in what Sharon Macdonald calls past presencing: "the ways in which people variously draw on, experience, negotiate, reconstruct, and perform the past in their ongoing lives."[5] We regard the uses of Moravian heritage in the past as well as in present everyday practices as a particular way to mediate between the religious and the secular in constituting Christiansfeld in practice—as crossroads of secularization and sacralization of heritage-making and place-making since the origin of the church settlement.[6]

As all of the book's chapters will demonstrate, Christiansfeld represents a unique opportunity to study the unfolding, continuous, and complex entanglement of religion and the formation of modern European cultures, the everyday life and modeling forms of social and individual subjectivity, the aesthetics and materialization of such ways of living, and not least the processes and effects of continuous heritagization processes. In the remainder of this introduction, we briefly present the context of the formation of Christiansfeld and the theological background of the Moravian congregation, including its organizational structure and specific titles and vocabulary, in order to define its particularity and self-perception.

Moravians' Historical and Theological Background

The renewed Moravian Brethren are part of the general Pietist movement that swept across Germany and northern Europe after the Thirty Years' War (1618–48) and advocated social and educational reform and, above all, individual piety. The Moravian Brethren trace their origins further back, namely to the Reformation movement led by Jan Hus (1372–1415) in Moravia and Bohemia in the fifteenth century. After Hus was burned at the stake for heresy, many of his followers went underground and, after the Thirty Years' War, sought refuge in the neighboring Protestant states. So, in 1722, thirty Moravian refugees arrived in the Oberlausitz region at the estate of Count Nikolaus Ludwig von Zinzendorf und Pottendorf (1700–1760) in Berthelsdorf and founded the village of Herrnhut.

Herrnhut soon attracted seekers from all over the German states, and Moravians also kept coming in a steady stream. Count Zinzendorf, a known Pietist, had, after ending his law studies in Wittenberg (1716–1719), settled in Dresden and was appointed councilor to the court of the Elector of Saxony. It was during this time, in 1722, that he bought the estate in Berthelsdorf and granted, through his estate manager, the Moravians permission to settle. Zinzendorf, however, remained mostly in his position in Dresden for the next five years, while the village was taking shape. He traveled back and forth but did not engage himself fully in the goings-on in Herrnhut before 1727, when he left Dresden, arrived in the Oberlausitz, and took charge. By 1727 the population of Herrnhut had grown to around three hundred members, who had different ideas about what it was and was to be. Out of the ongoing conflicts in Herrnhut, Zinzendorf and other leaders managed to create a community, whose spiritual birth is dated 13 August 1727. This was confirmed in the signing of the Seigneurial Precepts and Prohibitions (Herrschaftliche Gebote und Verbote) and the Statutes of the Brotherly Agreement (Statuten des Brüderlichen Vereins und Willkür in Herrnhut). The first was a legal document, binding for all residents of Herrnhut; this agreement placed them under Zinzendorf's protection and granted them free subject status. The second document was more constitutional for the community as such.[7]

The mobility afforded by free subject status was a crucial part of the mission of the Moravians not only in Europe but also in the colonies. After Herrnhut, other settlements followed in the eighteenth century, including twelve in counties, states, and dutchies later to be part of the German realm, one in the Netherlands, two in the United States, and four in England and Northern Ireland.

The theological background and profile of the Moravians is complex and unique.[8] As they understand themselves to be descendants of the pre-Reformation Protestant church of Bohemia, they share some of the theological traits of that movement. They see the church as subject to the norms of the praxis of Christ and the early Christians as witnessed in the scriptures. In other words, lifestyle as evidence of faith is important. They did not adapt the distinction made by reformers such as John Wycliff or Martin Luther between visible and invisible church. However, other central issues of the Reformation left their mark, and although Orthodox Lutherans contested Moravians' observance, they share core Protestant beliefs. Christocentrism—that is, the emphasis on Christ as the only way of redemption and salvation—as well as a strong focus on the relation between the individual and God/Christ are at the center of Moravian faith and religious praxis. This facilitated the so-called blood and wounds devotion prevalent in eighteenth-century Moravianism, with a strong focus on the life, suffering, and sacrificial death of Christ as the instrument of redemption of the Christian individual. Thus, the violent blood and wounds of Christ were conceived of as an entry point or access to salvation and interpreted as refuge and consolation to the human being.[9]

Whereas Hallensian pietists stressed the penitential struggle as the way to rebirth, Zinzendorf asserted that rebirth occurs when the believers realize in their heart that they are already saved by Christ's suffering and death. In other words, the Christian can appropriate the atonement of Christ through faith, which is stimulated by contemplation of the aspects of the humanity and passion of Christ. This idea produces meditations, hymns, liturgies, and images with a dominant and sometimes graphic focus on Christ's passion. At the same time, it leads to a joyous character of playful relief, since all work is done and salvation secured through the death and resurrection of Christ. Although the more explicit blood and wounds devotion was dismissed in the nineteenth century, the Christocentrism, passion-symbolism, and personal surrender to Christ remained strong. The classical soteriological theme of the Christian believer's union with Christ, sometimes depicted with a bridal mysticism, is another, related prominent characteristic of Moravian beliefs during Zinzendorf's leadership.[10]

The Moravian Church did not issue an independent confession but regarded the Apostles' Creed, the first twenty-one articles of the Lutheran *Confessio Augustana*, and Luther's Shorter Catechism as their platform. Nevertheless, doctrine was not attributed a strong role; rather, an ecumenical sense of community was promoted. In fact, the early congregation in Herrnhut could be perceived as a super-confessional community, including various traditions and orders of worship, all sharing a "communal idea" of a community in Christ. A synod in Herrnhaag in 1745 decided that the church should not have an independent confession

but consist of three "tropes": a Lutheran, a Reformed, and one in accordance to the Bohemian branch. This would, in time, allow congregations in
Copenhagen and Christiansfeld to blend into the Lutheran state church.
However, Moravians can be said to differ from mainstream Lutherans
in questions related to both the sanctified life of the believer and the
doctrine of the Lord's Supper. They tend to interpret the latter with more
emphasis on a mystic element and to define the presence of Christ as a
spiritual presence.

The Moravian Communities and Lifestyles as Evidence of Faith

During Zinzendorf's life, the leadership consisted of an idiosyncratic
mixture of feudal lordship and Moravian village administration. From
1739 the various leaders from the communities met regularly in synods.
There had been one synod earlier, in 1736, but none further until the 1739
synod in Ebersdorf, after which it became regular practice. The synods
were gatherings where the leaders discussed all manner of problems,
ranging from troublesome members to finances, missions, and industry.
    After Zinzendorf's death in 1760, there was some expectation that
Johannes von Watteville, Zinzendorf's charismatic son-in-law, would
take over. Instead, it was decided by senior members that the community
would be governed by council and elders between the general synods,
and the Unitäts Ältesten Conferenz (UAC), or Unity Elders Conference,
was established at the founding General Synod in Marienborn in 1764.
    One of the ways in which the leaders of Herrnhut successfully man-
aged the social schisms of the 1720s was by dividing the community up
into smaller groups in which personal issues and conflicts were talked
through. These early groups were called *Banden* (bonded groups) and/
or *Gesellschaften* (associations) and were informally structured and led by
one of the members. This structure had been more or less discarded by the
late 1730s and early 1740s, replaced by what is called the choir structure,
where the community is divided into larger overarching groups known
as choirs according to sex and marital status (adult choirs) and sex and
maturity/age (children's choirs). The basic choirs were organized as follows: Children's choir, Boys' choir and Girls' choir (sometimes divided
into younger and older children), Single Brothers, Single Sisters, Married
choir, Widowers, and Widows. The only two choirs that contained both
sexes were the Married choir and the Children's choir.[11]
    Each choir had a leader and an office that was eventually divided into
two offices, the *Pfleger* and the *Vorsteher*.[12] Each choir also had several
helpers, members who helped the other members to transition into their

new choir (for example, after the death of a spouse the transition into the Widows' or Widowers' choir) or prepared them for the next one (when a Single Brother or Sister was to be married, or a child about to move into either the Boys' or Girls' choir). The choirs served as both pastoral groups and social structures and would have frequent meetings where they were addressed and instructed according to their particular choir status. These gatherings are called *Chor-viertelstunden*, which translates as "choir quarter-hours." In most communities the Single Brothers and Single Sisters' choirs lived in large communal houses, and in many communities the Widows also had a communal house. Herrnhut had communal houses for all six unmarried choirs, and Christiansfeld had them for the Single Sisters, Single Brothers, and Widows.[13]

In Moravian communities like Christiansfeld, everyday life was and is liturgical, or part of the (public) Christian worship.[14] As such, it is permeated with specific ideals about the true Christian life that organize the community as a whole and define every individual's place and tasks to be practiced every day. The religious choir system and its gender and age segregation, along with communal dwellings, were manifest in the urban layout, in institutions, buildings, and interiors, in clothing and tools, industry and housework, music and literature, meals and sleeping practices, and even in the *Gudsager*—the cemetery.[15] The religious discourse was, and still is, not just an overarching structure but rather performed, embodied, and negotiated in daily micropractices by the inhabitants. Thus, it saturates everyday life in the ways it is practiced and materializes in rituals and routines from the overall design to the tiny details.

One of the distinct Moravian ritual practices is the *Liebesmahl* (Lovefeast), which is a small gathering at which refreshments are served and a song or hymn is sung. These were commonly held in connection with an annual occasion, such as a birthday, where the member whose birthday it was gave a Lovefeast for his or her nearest.

In the course of a week, a Moravian community had a number of liturgical events. Apart from morning and evening prayers, choir meetings, Lovefeasts, and community gatherings (or Sunday service), there was also the weekly *Singstunde*, literally an hour of singing, a song service, where the verses were topically ordered.[16]

Finally, there is the *Lebenslauf*, the memoir, which several of the chapters in this volume mention or discuss.[17] The memoir became a traditional Moravian practice in the 1740s. Members would write about their life and faith, which would later be complemented by an account of death added by a choir Brother or Sister, to be read at the person's funeral.[18] If, say, a Single Sister had not left anything in writing, the choir Sisters would compose a memoir based on what they knew of her life. Thus, the

Moravian archives hold thousands of memoirs dating back to the mid-eighteenth century, narrating the life, conversion, sometimes profession, life in the congregation, and then death of a vast amount of Moravian Brothers and Sisters.

The Moravian Brethren in the Danish Context

Moravian thought was introduced in Denmark in the late 1720s.[19] In the eighteenth century, the conglomerate state of Denmark-Norway was made up of Denmark, Norway, Iceland, Greenland, the Faroe Islands, the duchies of Schleswig and Holstein, and finally the colonies. It was a mono-confessional state, considered by many a very powerful Lutheran stronghold. It was one of the largest, and possibly *the* largest, Protestant kingdoms of that time. It was an absolutist state with a Lutheran Protestant state church as the only legitimate religion.

The king, Christian VI ([b. 1699] 1730–1746), was married to Sophie Magdalene of Brandenburg Kulmbach. Her mother's second cousin was the aforementioned Count Zinzendorf. The crown prince Christian met Zinzendorf as early as 1728, and when Frederik IV ([b. 1671] 1699–1730) died, Zinzendorf was invited along with the rest of the new queen's family to take part in the anointment ceremony in 1731. He appears to have made a splendid impression, and Zinzendorf and the Moravian missionaries were subsequently granted access to the Danish colonies. Apart from the Danish West Indies (1732) and Greenland (1733), they also went to the Danish Gold Coast (1737) and Tranquebar (1759). In 1736, Zinzendorf asked the Danish king for permission to build a new colony in the Holstein. The king gave his permission and in 1737, the Moravian Church established Pilgerruh between Lübeck and Hamburg. In 1739 a society of Moravians was established in Copenhagen under the name "Brødresocietetet," or "The Fraternal Society."[20]

However, the presumably pious king and perhaps some of his administrative staff gradually became suspicious of "sectarianism" and feared separatism. Therefore, they took initiatives to slow down or obstruct religious ideas and societies that may challenge the monolithic Lutheran state church—at the time, in the late 1730s, dominated by Hallensian pietism.[21] In January 1741, the king banned religious gatherings, or *Konventikler*, without the presence of an official clergyman. On 20 November 1744, he gave a decree directed specifically at the Moravian influence, stating that one could not hold an office in the Danish state church if one had visited Herrnhut or any other Moravian colony, had sent one's children to be educated in a Moravian colony, or had had any dealings with the

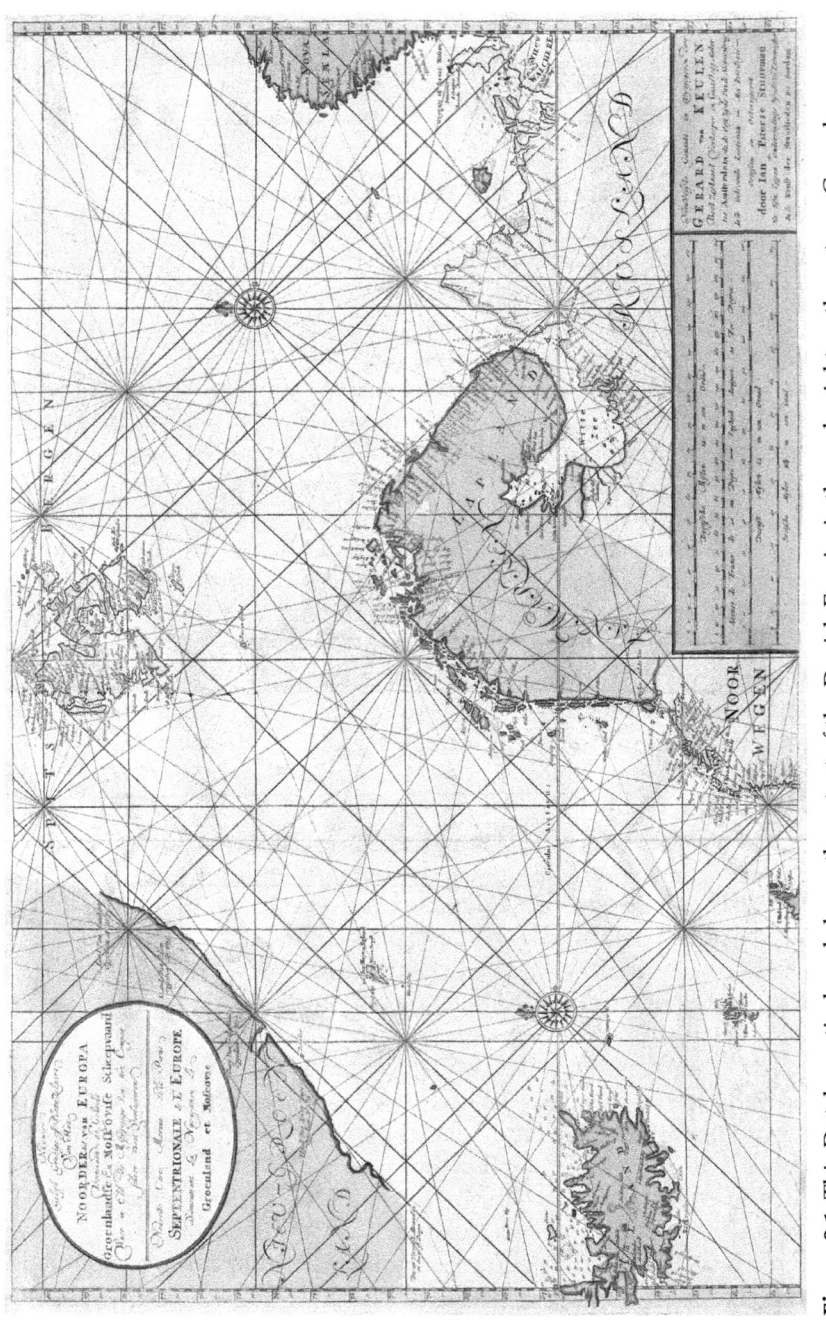

Figure 0.1. This Dutch nautical card shows the extent of the Danish Empire in the early eighteenth century. Gerard van Keulen (1668–1726), c.1722. From the collection of the Royal Danish Library.

Moravian Church. A few months later, on 29 January 1745, the king found need for another decree, which stated that any citizen immigrating to a Moravian colony would lose all civil rights, along with rights to property and inheritance. This illustrates the new attitude toward Moravians by the regime, but the very need for the decrees also indirectly proves their impact or the seriousness of their threat.

Two decades later, in 1766, the grandson of Sophia Magdalene, Christian VII, became king at the age of fifteen. In 1768, he and his entourage visited the Moravian colony of Zeist. The high level of industrial and commercial development impressed the king and his company. This inspired Christian VII and his close adviser, Johan Friedrich Struensee, along with his brother Carl August Struensee, to try to "import" the Moravian phenomenon and, in particular, their industrious know-how and modern spirit.[22] They approached the Justice Councellor, Lorenz Prætorius (1708–1781), who was also a prominent member of the Moravian Society in Copenhagen. After having assured the leadership in Herrnhut that the hostile decrees of 1744 and 1745 would be annulled, they began negotiations. In December 1771, a concession was signed to secure the colony. In June 1772, the king confirmed the purchase of Tyrstrupgaard, where the new Moravian colony was to be established. On 1 April 1773 the first foundation stone of the town was laid.[23] Lorenz Prætorius was appointed the pastor of the town, and the chairman of the Society in Copenhagen, Jonathan Briant (1726–1810), became the first chairperson of the settlement. The concession of the town secured for the congregation a number of privileges to stimulate its development and success. Thus, the Moravian colony in Christiansfeld represents a rupture with the previous religious politics of the Danish state and the advent of a new, more liberal or modern standard.

Moravians lived in and influenced life in not only the settlement of Christiansfeld but also the so-called diaspora, that is, Moravian circles outside the town itself. Up until the founding of Christiansfeld, this had been the organizational form in which the Moravians tended to operate in the northern countries of Denmark, Norway, Sweden, and Finland. Known as a societies, these were congregations of Brethren in larger towns, who met according to the liturgical and organizational structure of the Moravian congregations (i.e., gender segregation and choirs), but were not settlements. These were more or less well defined societies or communities of *auswärtige Geschwister*, Brothers and Sisters living scattered in "The World." The work and principles of these people were highly regarded, and after the founding of Christiansfeld the diaspora grew to include groups in the countryside, especially in Jutland and on Funen. Also, during the last decades of the eighteenth century, the

Moravian Society in Copenhagen flourished and a number of theological students, later to become pastors, were thereby influenced by Moravian ideas. With the intention of vitalizing the congregations rather than creating a new religion, the Moravians published and distributed numerous pamphlets for laymen, many of which were translations of German prototypes.

Activities of the diaspora sparked debates over whether these represented a foreign or new religion or simply new energy for the existing Christianity of the area. In principle, the work in the diaspora was directed centrally from Herrnhut, but in reality, it was largely orchestrated from local settlements like Christiansfeld. Emissaries were appointed from Herrnhut but often recruited locally and sent out to perform missions and share their ardent Christian love through humble and modest living, often as craftsmen. They sought to integrate into the surrounding local communities and families and, through conversation as well as by showing mercy, patience, and love to the people there, to perform the work of God. The emissaries created networks and communities that later would constitute epicenters of the broader religious awakenings in the nineteenth century.

Christiansfeld between German and Danish: A Religious Island in a Sea of Nationalism

In 1817, the tercentenary of the Lutheran Reformation was celebrated in Schleswig-Holstein, including Moravian Christiansfeld. The three days of celebrations concluded with a prayer for the congregation, for land and people, for ministers and king, for all Catholic, Orthodox, Reformed, and Lutheran Christians, for all the smaller denominations of the church, and for all humankind. This clearly signals a type of Christianity that perceives itself as universal.[24] Of course, the congregation paid its respect to the Danish king, Frederik VI, as the members were good patriots and nationalism in its nineteenth-century version did not play any significant role—yet.[25] In Schleswig the daily use of German as well as Danish, along with numerous blends in local dialects, had long been the case. In towns, the official language in court, churches, and schools was more often German than Danish, and German-speaking Moravians were by no means considered strange.[26] However, from the 1830s onward, issues of nationality increasingly set the agenda in the Danish king's realm and especially in Schleswig—or Southern Jutland, as it was renamed by the "Danish" side in the conflict. Language, in particular, became politicized.

In 1829 a Danish-speaking preacher was appointed to the Brothers' House in Christiansfeld, to provide services in Danish for local people outside the congregation as a supplement to the main German-language services. These Danish services became popular and gathered people from the southern part of Jutland, where religious lay awakening movements were flourishing as part of a general awakening.[27] However, the leaders of the congregation were, in terms of religious questions, oriented toward Herrnhut and Germany and considered questions of language and nationality as worldly matters and thus of minor importance. Gradually, resentment grew against the engagements with Danish-speaking participants and other new and more politically oriented institutions and initiatives in the duchy.[28] The leaders shared what a newly appointed Danish-speaking preacher in 1846 characterized as "Antiphatie für Alles, was Dänisch heist" (antipathy toward everything that is Danish).[29]

Because national issues—and especially the question of whether Schleswig and Holstein should be part of Denmark or Germany—were entangled with claims for a democratic constitution, civil war broke out in 1848. Conflicting national moods as well as patriotic loyalty to the Danish king pervaded Christiansfeld. However, incensed by the Danish removal of German-speaking civil servants—including clergymen—the German vicar Roentgen made a sudden about-face and saluted the German army. After international pressure brought the war to an end in 1851, the Danish government continued the new line toward civil servants. German-speaking pastors and officials who had supported the insurgents in even the slightest way were mercilessly dismissed. In Christiansfeld a number of teachers at the boarding schools were dismissed, including the warden of the Brothers' House, and the vicar Roentgen was silently relocated to a position in Königsberg.[30]

The Danish government—elected after a new democratic constitution, Grundloven (1849), granted freedom of religion to all citizens—considered the population of Schleswig to be Danish by heritage. The contemporary inhabitants had simply forgotten their "true language." Thus, they would have to learn it anew and, by means of directives, Danish became the official language in church and school. Christiansfeld did not receive a new concession and kept to its former rights as much as possible, but the German religious orientation and language at assemblies were a problem. The Danish national movements condemned Christiansfeld for being part of the institutions for "Germanification." In retrospect, some regretted that the town and congregation had not chosen a more neutral strategy in the national conflict. However, during the 1850s the boarding schools regained some of their influence and attraction with many pupils coming from Southern Jutland and the Scandinavian countries.[31]

After a new war and a Danish defeat in 1864, both duchies became part of Prussia. A new national border was drawn only three kilometers north of Christiansfeld, and the town became peripheral and isolated from its surrounding rural area. Also, the traffic and trade between south and north was noticeably diminished.[32] The issues of language and religious orientation were turned upside down. In 1865 the UAC in Berthelsdorf dismissed the Danish co-pastor of Christiansfeld under accusation of anti-German activities. This was the beginning of a struggle between Danish members of the congregation and their German leaders.[33]

From 1864 to 1920, when a plebiscite again made Christiansfeld part of Denmark, the Moravian congregation played a minor role in the German modernization and development of Schleswig. Several new religious institutions were founded in the region, among them the Evangelical Lutheran Deaconess Institution in Flensburg (1874), which soon became the leading institution, with affiliated institutions in towns and villages throughout Schleswig. Also, the *Innere Mission*, or Home Mission—with both German and Danish orientation and recruitment—had many activities in the region. In Northern Schleswig, the Moravians of Christiansfeld chose to join the work of the Home Mission and the Bible and Treaty Society. However, the aggressive project of Germanizing Schleswig from 1898 to 1903, when more than nine hundred persons were expelled from Northern Schleswig, also had consequences. The policy proved to be counterproductive, as it led to a political awakening—and also an awakening of the old religious movements. By the first decade of the twentieth century it was obvious that the majority of the population of Northern Schleswig was in favor of Denmark.

It was impossible for Christiansfeld and the Moravians, with their international views and contacts, to join this struggle. They remained an island in a sea of nationalism and, unable to compete with the new, efficient institutions of the modern, dynamic German Empire, Christiansfeld became insignificant.[34] The town turned silently into a relic; an interesting old-fashioned model of a church and society. Still, many people from the surrounding area gathered for the Mission Bazaar and meetings in support of the Moravians' foreign mission work. The early twentieth century was in fact an era of optimism; "the evangelization of the world in our time" was the motto in 1910.[35] As a result of nationalism, Christiansfeld was considered a German outpost in Northern Schleswig. After the plebiscite and its reincorporation in Denmark, a gradual process of Danification accelerated. In 1920, there were 301 members of the congregation, 126 of whom were living outside Christiansfeld. At the plebiscite there was a Danish majority of 247 Danish against 124 German votes in the town. The council of elders, which now had a Danish majority, urged German members to stay in the town—referring to the international character of the Moravian settlement and organization.[36] Starting in 1920, Danish services were initiated in turns; the German minister remained in office, but the congregation was supplied with an assistant Danish minister until 1924. Since the Second World War the language of the congregation has gradually shifted to Danish—with Moravian concepts in German, like *Liebesmahl* (Lovefeast), *Singstunde* (hour of singing), and *Gottesacker* (God's acre, i.e., cemetery), integrated naturally.[37]

As this brief history of Christiansfeld demonstrates, its location in the border region of southern Denmark and Germany meant that Christiansfeld was never entirely Danish, nor was it entirely German. It was both and perhaps neither. It was a community of a universalistic character in a region permeated by nationalism, and with practices of unique internationalism in an age of distinct confessionalism.[38] With the UNESCO World Heritage designation, this universalistic character of Moravian Christiansfeld was further legitimized.

Outline of the Book

The book consists of eleven chapters, which express the interdisciplinary profile of the publication and the broad interest from many academic disciplines in a topic such as the Moravian Church settlement of Christiansfeld and its UNESCO World Heritage status. Further, the authors of two of the chapters are scholars who belong to the Moravian community, namely two ministers of the Moravian congregations in Herrnhut, Germany, and in Christiansfeld. The chapters are divided into two sections reflecting the book's two overarching topics: first, religion and everyday practices and their legacy in modern Danish society; and second, processes of heritagization and sustainability. The two sections are concerned with these topics as they unfold in the case of the Moravian Brethren, and of Christiansfeld in particular.

The first section—on religion and its legacy within modern society— examines the complexity of the mutual entanglement of Moravian religious practices and broader society. Exploring historical material, these chapters focus on the specific values ascribed to Moravian Brethren within Danish traditions of church and music history and discuss how everyday practices of the eighteenth-century Brethren were intertwined with new expressions of both civic and religious selfhood. The second section—on heritage and sustainability—explores the processes of heritagization. The chapters discuss whether these processes have the potential to make the site and the congregation sustainable beyond the immediate attention given Christiansfeld when it became a UNESCO World Heritage site.

Part I: Religion and Its Legacy within Modern Society

Church historian Tine Reeh opens the collection with an outline of the standard works on Christiansfeld from the field of Danish church history. She examines how their representation of Christiansfeld and its legacy are, on the one hand, defined by the authors' theological outlook and, on the other hand, a potential resource for non-theologians' secular claims of significance of religious sites and movements. In the case of Christiansfeld, Reeh suggests that the Danish Grundtvigian concepts of church and Christianity stimulated a historiographical focus on the life of the congregation in the vernacular that facilitated the assessment of the surrounding Christiansfeld as valuable cultural heritage.

In chapter 2, church historian Sigrid Nielsby Christensen investigates the arrival of Moravians as well as the construction of individuality and community in the early Moravian Society in eighteenth-century Copenhagen. Based on a study of the diary of the Single Brothers' choir in 1746 and the practice of so-called watchwords (biblical words of guidance), the chapter demonstrates how the Moravian Society introduced new, individualized ideas of Christianity that coexisted with a strong sense of congregational community, which would be an inspiration for the later Danish Grundtvigian awakening movement.

The legacy of Christiansfeld within a broader Danish context is also discussed in ethnologist Tine Damsholt's contribution. Taking examples from *Instructions for the Moravian Choir Helpers* (1785–86) and the memoirs of Norwegian author Camilla Collett on her stay in Christiansfeld, Damsholt examines how everyday practices shaped a distinctive and emotional self. The overall objective is to demonstrate that religious and political discourses were not separate spheres; instead, they were deeply entangled in the development of a new form of emotional and civic selfhood in the late eighteenth century and onward.

From the very beginning, Christiansfeld was a tourist attraction with wider implications for Danish-Norwegian society. In chapter 4, music historian Peter Hauge demonstrates how the Moravian approach to music, as well as the aesthetic values, led to important discussions among Danish music-cultural intellectuals, reformers, and educators. By employing Countess Anna Sybille's description of an outing to Christiansfeld in 1796, Hauge takes a closer look at the music as a cultural practice within and outside the Moravian Church as represented through the music archives of Christiansfeld. The daily routines and musical education of the community constitute an important legacy through contemporary debates on how to improve hymn singing, music aesthetics, and education in Danish society at large.

Part II: Heritage and Sustainability

Opening the second part of the book, sociologist of religion Margit Warburg examines the sustainability of the Moravian congregation historically and, in particular, in Christiansfeld. She discusses the Moravian Brethren within the framework of another transnational minority religion, the Baha'is, and the similarities with regard to their establishment, spreading, and consolidation. With a global outlook, the Christiansfeld community must balance inclusiveness and exclusiveness in order to remain sustainable.

Anthropologist Rasmus Rask Poulsen examines in chapter 6 the responses of local Moravians in Christiansfeld to the increasing external interpretations and valuations of their identity and heritage. Based on fieldwork conducted in 2016 and 2017, Poulsen demonstrates that the increase in tourism that resulted from the World Heritage listing has given rise to negotiations and struggles over the authority of knowledge on Moravian heritage between the Moravians and the non-Moravian tour guides.

In chapter 7, ethnologist Marie Riegels Melchior explores how the local tradition of making honey cakes—and the ways this tradition is narrated and practiced in the everyday life of the place—is part of Christiansfeld both being heritage and becoming World Heritage. Melchior argues that in the larger scale of things the seemingly insignificant honey cakes are, so to speak, the "sweet glue" that connects past and present for both the visitors to Christiansfeld and its local community. In short, she shows how the honey cakes are past presencing acts and, as such, are part of sustaining Christiansfeld as an acknowledged heritage and religious community.

As co-minister of the Moravian congregation in Herrnhut, Jill Vogt describes in chapter 8 the activity and tradition of writing one's memoir, the so-called *Lebenslauf*. Here, Vogt offers a very rare inside view into religious community practices as she explores the tradition of the *Lebenslauf* and the question of the sustainability of this living tradition among the Moravians. She argues that this tradition is an important part of the cultural heritage of the Moravian community, as it continues not only a testimony of members' lives in connection with the larger Moravian community but also their narration of the story of God within the community.

In chapter 9, minister Jørgen Bøytler further explores the situation of Christiansfeld in terms of the legacy and sustainability of the settlement, in light of the Moravian Church congregation being included on the UNESCO World Heritage list. He focuses on the concepts of tangible and intangible heritage and argues that even though Christiansfeld is inscribed as tangible World Heritage, intangible perspectives are important for a thorough understanding of the site. This leads Bøytler to discuss the very differentiation between tangible and intangible when talking about cultural and religious lifestyles and the challenges of remaining sustainable.

From an interdisciplinary perspective, Christina Petterson's chapter examines the local archives in Christiansfeld. Petterson demonstrates how the organization of the local archival material is parallel to the communal structure of Christiansfeld and to global Moravian aspects, analyzing how the epistemological structures are embedded in community organization and vice versa. This leads to a discussion of whether the processes of heritagization and their implied understanding of history can adequately grasp and represent this complexity.

In the last chapter, Katherine Faull explores contemporary issues in research methods and, more specifically, how the digital medium affects the experience of heritage and what ethical responsibilities fall to the digital creator as well as the critic of digital heritage. Drawing on her extensive experience as leader of "Moravian Lives," the digital humanities project on Moravian *Lebensläufe* (memoirs), Faull investigates the intersection of the digital and archival and asks the following questions: What happens when personal documents are instrumentalized by different readers? How does the digital research affect the different parties involved as well as heritage productions?

Finally, some concluding remarks wrap up some of the perspectives and discussions that cut across the chapters and reflect on the future sustainability of Christiansfeld as a religious and historic heritage site.

Tine Damsholt is professor of European ethnology at the University of Copenhagen. She has written extensively on national and patriotic discourses in eighteenth- and nineteenth-century Denmark and political rituals in contemporary Western countries based on cultural history and ethnographic fieldwork. Subjectivity, materiality, temporality, emotions, body, and gender are recurrent themes in her research. She is currently investigating the transformed everyday life during the COVID-19 pandemic and how it affects the ways we understand and practice pasts, present, and futures in daily life.

Marie Riegels Melchior is an associate professor in European ethnology at the University of Copenhagen. Her research interests concern mainly fashion and design culture, cultural history from the nineteenth century onward, and heritage and museum studies. She has written extensively on Danish fashion and design history in the twentieth- and twenty-first centuries as well as on museological issues when fashion enters museums. She is on the editorial board of the journal *Ethnologia Scandinavica: Journal of Scandinavian Ethnology.*

Christina Petterson is a visiting research fellow at the Australian National University and at the Department of Church History, University of Copenhagen. Her background is in theology (M.Th.) and cultural studies (PhD) and her research interests concern the relationship between Christianity and social history in the eighteenth century both in the colonies and Europe. She is on the editorial board of the *Journal of Moravian History* and recently published *The Moravian Brethren in a Time of Transition: A Socio-Economic Analysis of a Religious Community in Eighteenth-Century Saxony* (2021).

Tine Reeh is an associate professor in church history at the University of Copenhagen. Her scholarly focus has been on the nexus between religion and society in the Nordic countries. She has also worked with historiography, Luther reception, and secularization, and she is currently leading the interdisciplinary research project "Managing Melancholy: Dynamics of Theology and Medicine in 18th-Century Denmark-Norway," funded by the VELUX Foundations.

Notes

1. Thyssen, "Det store og det lille herrnhutersamfund," 42–43; Berg, Marcussen, and Stoklund, "Christiansfeld," 89.
2. Pagden, *Enlightenment*.
3. See Harrison, *Heritage*; Kuutma, "Between Arbitration."
4. Macdonald, "Presencing."
5. Macdonald, 234.
6. See chapters by Bøytler, Poulsen, Melchior, and Faull in this volume.
7. On early Herrnhut, see Uttendörfer, *Alt-Herrnhut*; Wollstadt, *Geordnetes Dienen*; see also Peucker, *Herrnhut*.
8. See chapter 9 in this volume.
9. Peucker, *Herrnhut*, 26–28.
10. Principal figures such as Bernard of Clairvaux, Johannes Tauler, and Martin Luther influenced Zinzendorf in this regard.
11. See Petterson, *Moravian Brethren*.
12. For the Sisters' choir in Herrnhut, this happened in 1747, when Maria Henrietta von Pustar took up office as the "business manager." See Homburg, "Glaube," 56–57.

13. See chapter 10 in this volume.
14. See chapters by Hauge and Bøytler in this volume.
15. *Gudsager* is the Danish word for God's Acre. Both are translations from the German *Gottesacker*, which was a common German term for cemeteries. In its translated forms, it is connected with the Moravians.
16. See Hauge's chapter in this volume.
17. See the chapters in this volume by Bøytler, Damsholt, Faull, Reeh, and Vogt.
18. McCullough, "Most Memorable."
19. See Christensen's chapter in this volume.
20. See Christensen's chapter.
21. For an overview of the line of Pietism developed within Halle with August Hermann Francke as one of the key figures, see Shantz, *Introduction to German Pietism*, chap. 5. See also the section "Herrnhut and Halle" in Peucker, *Time of Sifting*, 17–19. For an analysis of the situation in Denmark, see Engelhardt, "Pietismus und Krise," 341–69.
22. This was a well-known strategy in the Danish-Norwegian absolutist state. In the seventeenth century, Dutch peasants were invited to the island of Amager to produce vegetables for Copenhagen, and in 1719 the provincial town of Fredericia welcomed French Huguenots in order to improve local commercial life.
23. This accounts for the fact that some articles refer to Christiansfeld's founding in 1772 and others in 1773.
24. Some of these sections come from Bach-Nielsen, "Christiansfeld 1864–1920," an unpublished paper generously made available to the editors in place of a contribution.
25. On Danish-Norwegian patriotism, see chapter 3.
26. The question of language was by the mid-nineteenth century already politicized and all accounts, investigations, and cartographies already part of the conflict. Daily language often did not follow the official language. In the northern part of Schleswig, Danish church language was more frequent, but there were differences between towns (more German speaking) and the countryside (more Danish speaking). On a map by German cartographer Frans Geerz from 1838, Christiansfeld is marked as having German church language; see "Franz Geerz's kort over sprogforhold i Sønderjylland 1838," danmarkshistorien.dk, accessed 20 February 2022. https://danmarkshistorien.dk/lek sikon-og-kilder/vis/materiale/franz-geerzs-kort-over-sprogforhold-i-soenderjylland-1838/.
27. See chapter 1.
28. By the mid-nineteenth century the popular religious lay movements had gradually become affiliated with *grundtvigianism* (see chapter 1), Home Mission, and other church organizations inspired by English, American, and Swedish religious movements.
29. Thyssen, "Det store og det lille herrnhutersamfund," 81–82.
30. Bach-Nielsen, "Christiansfeld," 2; Thyssen, "Det store og det lille herrnhutersamfund," 84.
31. Thyssen, 84–86
32. Regarding the development of commerce, see also chapter 7.
33. Bach-Nielsen, "Christiansfeld," 4.
34. Bach-Nielsen, 5–6.
35. Bach-Nielsen, 8.
36. Thyssen, "Det store og det lille herrnhutersamfund," 92.
37. Thyssen, 90, 95.
38. Bach-Nielsen, "Christiansfeld," 9.

Bibliography

Bach-Nielsen, Carsten. "Christiansfeld 1864–1920." Unpublished paper presented at the seminar *Religion and the Formation of Modern Society*, University of Copenhagen, 30 January 2018.

Berg, Annemette Løkke Borg, Lene Lindberg Marcussen, and Karen Stoklund, eds. *Christiansfeld: A Danish Moravian Settlement*. Kolding: Kolding kommune, 2013.

Engelhardt, Juliane. "Pietismus und Krise. Der Hallesche und der Radikale Pietismus im Dänischen Gesamtstaat" [Pietism and crisis: Hallensian and radical Pietism in the Danish conglomerate state]. *Historische Zeitschrift* 307, no. 2 (2018): 341–69.

Harrison, Rodney. *Heritage: Critical Approaches*. 1st edn. London: Routledge, 2013.

Homburg, Heidrun. "Glaube—Arbeit—Geschlecht: Frauen in der Ökonomie der Herrnhuter Ortsgemeine von den 1720er Jahren bis zur Jahrhundertwende. Ein Werkstattbericht" [Faith—work—gender: Women in the economy of the Moravian settlement from the 1720s to the end of the century; A workshop report]. In *Gender im Pietismus. Netzwerke und Geschlechterkonstruktionen* [Gender in Pietism: Networks and gender constructions], edited by Pia Schmid, 43–62. Franckeschen Stiftungen Halle: Harrassowitz Verlag, 2015.

Kuutma, Kristin. "Between Arbitration and Engineering: Concepts and Contingencies in the Shaping of Heritage Regimes." In *Heritage Regimes and the State*, edited by Regina Bendix, Aditya Eggert, and Arnika Peselmann, 21–38. Göttingen: Universitätverlag, 2013.

McCullough, Thomas J. "The Most Memorable Circumstances: Instructions for the Collection of Personal Data from Church Members, circa 1752." *Journal of Moravian History* 15, no. 2 (2015): 158–76.

Macdonald, Sharon. "Presencing Europe's Pasts." In *A Companion to the Anthropology of Europe*, edited by Ullrich Kockel, Máiréad Nic Craith, and Jonas Frykman, 233–52. Oxford: Wiley-Blackwell, 2012.

Pagden, Anthony, ed. *The Enlightenment: And Why It Still Matters*. 1st edn. New York: Random House, 2013.

Petterson, Christina. *The Moravian Brethren in a Time of Transition:A Socio-Economic Analysis of a Religious Community in Eighteenth-Century Saxony*. Historical Materialism Book Series, vol. 231. Leiden: Brill, 2021.

Peucker, Paul. *Herrnhut: The Formation of a Moravian Community, 1722–1732*. Pietist, Moravian, and Anabaptist Studies series. University Park: Penn State University Press, 2021.

Peucker, Paul. *A Time of Sifting: Mystical Marriage and the Crisis of Moravian Piety in the Eighteenth Century*. University Park: Penn State University Press, 2015.

Shantz, Douglas H. *An Introduction to German Pietism: Protestant Renewal at the Dawn of Modern Europe*. Baltimore: John Hopkins University Press, 2013.

Thyssen, Anders Pontoppidan. "Det store og det lille herrnhutersamfund" [The universal and particular Moravian community]. In *Herrnhuter-samfundet i Christiansfeld* [The Moravian community of Christiansfeld], edited by Anders Pontoppidan Thyssen, 11–101. Aabenraa: Historisk Samfund for Sønderjylland, 1984.

Uttendörfer, Otto. *Alt-Herrnhut. Wirtschaftsgeschichte und Religionssoziologie Herrnhuts während seiner ersten Zwanzig Jahre (1722–1742)* [Old Herrnhut: Herrnhut's economic history and sociology of religion during its first twenty years]. Herrnhut: Verlag Missionsbuchhandlung, 1925.

Wollstadt, Hanns-Joachim. *Geordnetes Dienen in der Christlichen Gemeinde* [Ordered service in the Christian congregation]. Göttingen: Vandenhoeck and Ruprecht, 1966.

Chapter 1

How a *Hyggeligt* Home Became Cultural Heritage

On the Church Historiography of Moravian Christiansfeld

Tine Reeh

To qualify for the prestigious UNESCO World Heritage list, Moravian Christiansfeld had to be assessed by the surrounding non-Moravian society as being of specific significance. More precisely, it had to be judged to be of universal value and to meet at least one of ten fixed selection criteria. According to UNESCO's evaluation, Christiansfeld meets the third and fourth criteria: that is, it bears "a unique or at least exceptional testimony to a cultural tradition or to a civilization which is living or which has disappeared" and is "an outstanding example of a type of building, architectural or technological ensemble or landscape which illustrates (a) significant stage(s) in human history."[1]

UNESCO required evidence in order to reach its conclusion; in producing this evidence, narrations or interpretations of Christiansfeld and, not least, its importance became of vital use. The documentation, as well as the application itself, was produced and supported by a conglomerate of Danish state and local municipality.[2] However, one could ask why this group of representatives from twenty-first-century mainstream secularized Danish society found itself investing in and struggling for a religious minority establishment with a substantial German element.

In this chapter, I examine a line of Danish church historiography that may explain how a general appreciation of Christiansfeld came to be, as well as explaining part of the argumentation of the UNESCO application documents. In doing so, my aim is threefold: first, to briefly present the standard historical literature on Moravian Christiansfeld; second, to illustrate the importance of context and the criteria of relevance embedded in these representations of the past; and third, to argue that a particular Grundtvigian theological point of departure, along with its concordant historiography, facilitated interpretations of Christiansfeld and its past that have contributed to its recognition as valuable cultural heritage.

N. F. S. Grundtvig's Concept of Church and the Living Word

From the nineteenth century until the present, N. F. S. Grundtvig (1783–1872) has been one of the most significant influences on Danish Christianity and culture. Unlike his contemporaries Hans Christian Andersen and Søren Kierkegaard, Grundtvig is known only sporadically outside the Nordic countries. Because his followers split into several parties, and his impact was not only on theology and church but also on education, politics, and popular culture, perceptions of Grundtvig and his influence have been debated ardently. Nevertheless, in this context it may be both judicious and useful to point to a few agreed-upon elements of his oeuvre and legacy.[3]

Although Grundtvig was in his own time already a public and political figure—one may even say an institution—his base and background were in his ideas of Christianity. In a time of increasing use of historical biblical criticism and rationalistic theology, he felt the need to oppose these trends and propound alternative ideas concerning the foundation of Christianity and the church. In contrast to many of his contemporaries, Grundtvig did not consider dogma a useful foundation for a Christian church. He also became a strong antagonist of those who took refuge in a literal or fundamentalist use of biblical texts. In some respects, Grundtvig gradually disagreed with orthodox Lutheran viewpoints as he developed his objections against classical ideas of a scriptural base for the church.

Instead, he developed his teaching on the "living word."[4] He considered the church itself and its tradition, as expressed in the congregation's confession of the apostolic creed, as the basis of Christianity and the church. For Grundtvig a true Christian community, or church of Christ, had existed before the texts of the Bible. Thus, the church was—and still is—created and supported by the living word, not a later "dead" or mummified text, dogmas, or ecclesiastical institutions.[5] For Grundtvig, the concept of Christianity and the church is intimately connected with the "living word," which he regarded as created by God, carried by and within the Christian congregation, and renewed by the presence of Christ at the sacraments. To quote from one of his most influential theological texts,

Not until we have discovered the living expression of the Christian Faith in the profession of the Creed at Baptism, and the living expression of Christian Hope in the Lord's Prayer, both at Baptism and Holy Communion, and the living expression of Christian Love in Christ's words of affection to his believers, or his declaration of love to his Bride at Holy Communion—not until then can we, in congregational life, boast a Christian profession, preaching and praise which are the peculiar and unmistakable life-signs of Christian Faith, Christian Hope and Christian Love.[6]

The above is sometimes called Grundtvig's "ecclesiastical view" (*den kirkelige anskuelse*), and it may be his most distinctive and influential contribution to Danish theology. Grundtvig's concept of Christianity was considered world- and life-affirming, and a group of people soon started gathering around him. He gave impetus not only to explicitly Grundtvigian communities but also to a broad awakening of a different character than the previous Pietism and the later Home Mission.[7] This movement grew rapidly in nineteenth-century Denmark, extending well beyond explicitly religious spheres.[8] As we shall see, it can be argued that Grundtvig's ideas also had an impact on mainstream society's assessment of Moravian Christiansfeld well into the twenty-first century.

The Moravian Congregation as a *Hyggeligt* Home

One of the first scholars outside Moravian circles to study and write about Christiansfeld was the high-profile Danish Grundtvigian Ludvig Schrøder (1836–1908).[9] In 1902, Schrøder published a book on the significance of Moravians for religious life in Denmark.[10] In many ways, his work anticipates or shapes key points of orientation for some of the later and more advanced academic studies. His book is based on a sharp distinction between Pietists and Moravians, and his sympathy is unequivocally with the latter. This mirrors Schrøder's contemporary situation, where two parties dominated the religious landscape: the Grundtvigian awakening movement and the Pietistic awakening of the Home Mission.

In Schrøder's narrative, the Pietists won a stronghold within the Danish church organization and the government. He indirectly depicts Moravians as a minority, but the minority issue is not his primary interest. Instead, he points to theological consequences of Pietistic dominance within the powerful state church:

But in one matter the Moravians had better chances of winning the simple-minded Christians than their pietist rivals. They strongly emphasized the basic Lutheran testimonial of justification by faith. Therefore, to them Christianity

was a Gospel, a joyous message—while their opponents, who always stressed
sanctification, were tempted to reduce Christianity to Law.[11]

For Schrøder, this theological quality, and its significant consequences
for one's way of life, is in essence why the influential Danish lay
revival movements of the nineteenth century are forever indebted to
the Moravians. He also accentuates the Moravians' limited emphasis on
dogma, of which he, as a Grundtvigian, strongly approves. Schrøder
demonstrates how the—in his view—"genuine Lutheran" Moravians, as
opposed to the crypto-reformed Pietists, did not emphasize outer modes
of behavior such as asceticism, prohibition of dancing and theater, and
so on. Instead, the Moravians' social life and culture, their optimistic
spirit, music, and song are attractive to Schrøder, and he even sees this as
proof of their true concept of Christianity. So too their sense of equality
and community, which he holds in high regard. In other words, it is
the theological characteristics of Moravians in Denmark—namely, that
they did not make Christianity into Law without Gospel—that Schrøder
promotes as worth of attention.

It is not only Schrøder's perception of Christianity but also his ecclesiology (concept of the church) that is of key importance in his aspiration
to describe the impact of the Moravians in Denmark. For Schrøder, a
true Christian congregation is comparable to a guest, and the church as
an institution is like a guesthouse; again, we see how the church as an
institution and its dogmas are not given importance. Schrøder's use of
"guest" and "guesthouse" in relation to the Moravians are Grundtvigian
metaphors, in contrast to the majority who would consider the Moravians
as an odd minority. Instead, Schrøder sees the Moravians as proper guests
and part of the true Christian congregation.[12]

This point relates to another key issue within Schrøder's book, namely
the conviction that in measuring or estimating the value a religious movement, one should give credence neither to their formal or official church
statements nor to their leaders. This allows Schrøder to discard Count
Nikolaus Ludwig von Zinzendorf and his controversial statements, as
well as the debate over whether Moravians could be considered Lutherans
from a strictly dogmatic standpoint. Instead, "the living word" and the
vigor of the congregation is key, which is why Schrøder investigates
personal statements, testimonials, and memoirs as his preferred source
material.[13] One of Schrøder's sources is the testimony of Niels Blicher,
the father of popular Danish poet and pastor Steen Steensen Blicher.
Niels Blicher was not himself a Moravian, but he was closely acquainted
with Christiansfeld from his youth, and during his retirement, he gave
a description of the congregation. Blicher's testimony defended the

Moravians in Christiansfeld against accusations of hypocrisy, separatism, and religious fanaticism; instead, he claimed that they were "in close agreement with our own evangelical beliefs."[14] Both Blicher and Schrøder highlight the shared daily rhythm and vitality of the congregation, with its morning prayers, grace, evening prayers, Bible studies, and singing. There is no swearing, slander, or inappropriate joking; instead, there is decency, diligence, mildness, and cheerfulness. Music is plentiful and excellent, and the hospitality outstanding. In their material production, Moravians in Christiansfeld strive for perfection, and their leaders are pleasant and learned people. "In this way they endeavor, in mentality and behavior, to carry out Christian teaching."[15] Blicher's narrative, as well as Schrøder's summary, serves at least two purposes. First, it shows the Moravian community as a true guest, a true Christian congregation in the face of all dogmatic criticism and suspicion from the state church and its suspicions of dangerous separatism. Second, it becomes an opportunity to highlight an example of a happy, joyous type of awakened Christianity, in deep contrast to the contemporary Home Mission's pietistic awakening and its focus on penitence, synergism, and law.[16]

In his conclusion, Schrøder sums up the importance and impact of the Moravians in Denmark: the congregation of Moravian Brethren — particularly in Christiansfeld — has been a "*hyggeligt*"[17] home to true Christians as displayed in their exemplary congregational life.[18]

Moravian Lay Christianity as a Helping Hand to Danish Religious Life

The first academic work on the archival material from Christiansfeld was published in 1903 by theologian Jørgen Lundbye. Lundbye prefers the more German-sounding term "Herrnhutism," and the subtitle of his book reveals the research questions and criteria of relevance. The book's title, translated, is *Herrnhutism in Denmark: The Home Mission of the Eighteenth Century*.[19]

Lundbye himself was from a family of pastors and grew up in an area strongly marked by the Home Mission. Nevertheless, he expresses sympathy for the Grundtvigians and seems to have regarded himself as such,[20] even though his work deviates from shared traits of this religious faction. This ambivalence is also present in his basic point of view that Moravians are a product of Pietism and forerunners of the Home Mission in Denmark. It is somewhat contradictory for a person with Grundtvigian sympathies to write a book depicting the excellent qualities of the Moravians based on the Moravian legacy within the Home Mission.

Lundbye's work is an academic and more classical piece of church history than that of Schrøder, and as such Lundbye pays attention to theology and dogmatic questions as well as the role of leading persons and significant events. The question of the Moravians' genuine Lutheran qualities is a recurrent theme, and it is theologically characteristic that Lundbye on numerous occasions defends Moravian morality, albeit as a signifier of the Home Mission perspective. He sees the role of Moravian laypeople in the diaspora outside Christiansfeld as an important renewal of the state church, which was to spread all over the country, and his use of the expression "the Herrnhut Home Mission"[21] clearly expresses this view. This emphasis not only supports his central thesis but also allows him to argue that Christiansfeld—despite the fact that it is to a large degree a German-speaking religious minority and, at the time, even located south of the Danish border *in* Germany— could have contributed significantly to the Lutheran-majority church in Denmark.

Lundbye concludes his book by observing that the Moravians are to be considered true evangelical Lutherans, but also that this is more evident in their way of life and structure of the congregation than in their formal theology. According to Lundbye, the Moravians taught laypeople to think for themselves. Subsequently, the impulse for laypeople to take on authority or personal responsibility and congregate is regarded as the most important Moravian legacy.[22]

It took forty years and a reunification with Denmark of the region that included Christiansfeld before the next study within this classical church historical paradigm was published, now by the Danish right-wing Grundtvigian Jens Holdt.[23] Holdt builds on material from the Danish administrative archives as well as material found in Christiansfeld and Herrnhut, but his attention is focused exclusively on Christiansfeld. Holdt lived in Brede, in the southern part of Jutland, and initiated the work less than a decade after the reunification. Meanwhile, the emerging threat from expanding Nazi Germany can be detected in his tendency to downplay the German cultural traits of the settlement. Instead, he finds that Christiansfeld differs from Herrnhut in many ways, most importantly in that Herrnhut continued as an isolated *Konventikel* (community).[24] For Holdt, Christiansfeld interacted with the surrounding society as a "sourdough," whereby he clearly meant that it had raised the spirit of this society.[25]

In contrast to Lundbye, Holdt makes a clear distinction between Pietism and Moravianism, but he sees them as related "twins." However, his main interest is not in theological labels but rather in themes such as freedom of religious communities and the relation between state and church. He gives a detailed account of the sources documenting the founding of Christiansfeld, illustrating the interests of the state, the Moravians, and the different players in the process. Legal documents and considerations such as the royal concession from 10 December 1771 are meticulously presented, as are the consequences for the developments of the later Danish model of legislation regarding church and state. Holdt presents the reader with the prevalent debate on the relation between church and state in Lutheran theology in the interwar period. The question clearly has urgency for him, as not only a Grundtvigian and as a Dane in Northern Schleswig but also dangerously close to the new order of state and church in Nazi Germany.

As mentioned, Holdt does not give much weight to the teachings of Moravians, preferring to focus on the daily religious life and the life forms of the community in the settlement. This is evident in the section "The Community,"[26] where both the wording and the values in Holdt's description bear an unmistakable likeness to classical Grundtvigian ideals. His exposition of the life of the community is followed by a lengthy section on the formal framework, with the subtitle "The Constitution." Here, an account of the documents and organization of the religious life and community is clearly oriented against the current societal and political developments. At the end of the section, the contemporary relevance of his historical studies comes to the fore, with Holdt concluding that in a time when "the demonic powers of the state are worshipped" the study of organization of Moravians in Christiansfeld is of particular interest. He closes his exposition with this statement: "Only the Church of Christ can defeat the dictator-deamon."[27]

As in much mainstream historiography from this period, the narrative is influenced by events, and personal agency is considered of significance. Holdt even includes a whole section devoted to miniature biographies of pastors, various administrative leaders,[28] and more than thirty distinguished members of the congregation.[29] In Holdt's view, the impact of the Moravian settlement in Christiansfeld was not primarily in terms of the industrial and economic fields (as intended by the Danish state) but in terms of novel and valuable ideas within church life and schools. In this context, one may add that Holdt holds the origin of the Moravians as Czech and not German, and this allows him to emphasize that "our present concept of church congregation and school [in Denmark in general] is more evangelical-Moravian than German-Lutheran."[30] Holdt concludes that the Moravians have been "a helping hand" to the Danish school system of his day, not least in terms of a religious congregational culture of laymen.[31]

Religion and Society

In postwar Denmark one can observe a pronounced renewal in church historiography, and this was also of consequence for research on Moravians
and Christiansfeld. One of the first signs of change was an extensive
and programmatic article by Hans Jensen, political and social historian,
in the dominant journal for church history, *Kirkehistoriske Samlinger*.
Jensen explores links between religious and societal developments in
eighteenth-century Denmark.[32]

A connection between, on the one hand, the development of church
and dogma and, on the other, the surrounding society had since the
Reformation been part of the narrative of the church's past.[33] In his article,
Jensen widens the scope to include social or societal aspects of broader
religious movements, as well as interaction between the research fields of
social, political, and church history. Unfortunately, Jensen died only two
years after his groundbreaking work, but it did not pass unnoticed. A few
years later, church historian P. G. Lindhardt sought to develop Jensen's
perspective to support his own views on the awakening movements and
their impact on the shaping of Nordic societies in the nineteenth century.[34] In Lindhardt's understanding, awakening was a rupture of the
old life not only in relation to religion but also with regard to society,
economics, and politics.[35] The highly polemical character of Lindhardt's
work created much attention, but it was another church historian, Hal
Koch, who paved the way for a more thorough methodological and paradigmatic change.

In the late 1950s, Koch gathered a group of talented young church
historians at the department of Danish Church History at the University
of Copenhagen to work on novel questions within church history and to
experiment with the use of methods developed in other disciplines. One
of their innovations was the use of teamwork to provide more adequate
answers to larger and more complex questions, and from this group
a number of pioneering studies emerged.[36] One of the larger works to
emerge from this collaboration was the multivolume *opus magnum* on the
origin and early development of the religious awakening in Denmark.[37]
The editor in chief, the young Anders Pontoppidan Thyssen, had
Grundtvigian sympathies, and the monumental project was financed
by the National Science Foundation. The work emphasized not only
religious but also—and to a high degree—social, political, and cultural
perspectives on the developments. It is precisely these research interests
that made Christiansfeld prime source material.

Thyssen opens the lengthy introduction to the complete opus with
an introduction to the Danish constitution of 1849. This is telling, as it

reveals a fundamental interest behind the work—namely, in a time of rapid secularization, to explore whether religious awakening stimulated the shaping of modern Denmark.

In the fourth volume of *Vækkelsernes Frembrud i Danmark*, we find Thyssen's thorough and comprehensive account of Christiansfeld and its significance. This book also represents the most extensive and detailed source-based historical work on Christiansfeld.[38] Thyssen not only found and organized an immense amount of unpublished source material in the archives of Danish state administration, church institutions, and private persons with relevance for the history of Christiansfeld, but he also made extensive pioneering studies in the Moravian society's own archival material from Copenhagen, Christiansfeld, and Herrnhut. This allowed him to give a detailed account of Christiansfeld's background, including the antecedent strong pietistic movement in the southern part of Jutland and Northern Schleswig—notably, Thyssen differentiates between Pietism and Moravian Christianity—and the founding of the settlement. He describes the construction and development of the congregation, the liturgy, the choirs, and the life therein, as well as the diaspora and emissaries. The formal structure, numbers, and social and sociological aspects are in the foreground, but the theological basis of the practical arrangements is evident throughout. One could say that Thyssen's text aims to show the manifestation of Moravian Christianity in the tangible life of the individuals as well as in the community.

As mentioned, one of Thyssen's overall goals was to bring forth hitherto unnoticed source material, but the extensive and heterogeneous material does not make him lose his focus. Characteristic of his focused and balanced account is his use of two small books from the 1820s by the Moravian defector or apostate Johannes Hansen.[39] Thyssen used classical historical methods and found information on Hansen in the Moravians' own archives to check all possible information from other sources, and he remarks on discrepancies in footnotes. He then lets Hansen voice a description of life in the settlement in Christiansfeld that focuses on theological as well as sociological aspects, in a way that not only is critical of the Moravians but also potentially disrupts Thyssen's own thesis.

Hansen was born the son of a baker in Husum in 1797. He lived in Christiansfeld from 1804 until he left the congregation in 1817. He later reapplied for membership in Christiansfeld and then the Netherlands, most likely in Zeist.[40] After a few years, he finally broke with the community, began to study theology in Leipzig, and wrote a book on his experiences and why he did not consider Moravianism as true Christianity.[41] He declares that he does not wish to pass a unilateral judgment, but his indignation grows steadily over the course of the text. In particular, he

opposes the element of subordination throughout the system, the surveil-
lance, the means of social discipline, and the use of the lot—according
to Hansen, a powerful tool of the leadership—as well as the frequent
transfer of people to weaken relations of importance and break down
any potential threat to the leaders' authority. For Hansen, the celebrated
Moravian education only transforms young persons into uniform characters or machines, and he describes how the system created weak-willed,
self-denying, and dependent individuals.[42] The religious teaching supported the idea of subordination through emphasis on numerous won-
ders rather than individual studies of the Bible, and Lutheran dogmas
clearly played a most subordinate role. He sees life in Christiansfeld as
life in a secluded, "secret" society, which led to hypocrisy and turned
the instinct or inclination of the heart into an idol. In Hansen's view, true
Christian life was to be lived not in an isolated structure but in the world,
and the Gospel was meant as a message to be preached to all people. He
therefore concludes his first book with a strong attack on the statutes and
structures of the Moravian congregations and settlements.

Hansen's book provoked a sharp anonymous refutation in 1822,[43]
which led him to publish a new book in 1823.[44] Hansen now gave a
more detailed account of the refined means of subordination in use in
Christiansfeld. Three years later, however, Hansen became a pastor in his
hometown of Husum, not far from Christiansfeld, and—by request—he
sent out a recantation, stating that he had written the previous books at a
time when he was unable to judge dispassionately.

Thyssen refrains from drawing explicit conclusions from the affair and
Hansen's books, but he mentions apologetically that much of the criticism Hansen raised was met in the following years by more unrestricted
forms, openness, and publicity in all areas by the Moravians. In particular, the lot was abandoned and a rapprochement with the Danish state
church took place. Nevertheless, Hansen's descriptions of Christiansfeld
disrupt the narrative of the religious awakening movements as enabling
independence of mind and personal authority and thereby facilitating
political awakening and modern European democracy.

However, many of the elements Hansen accentuates as problematic
may also be identified in modern "totalitarian" societies or as drawbacks
of modernity. In this sense, Hansen's criticism confirms Thyssen's connection between the religious ideas of awakening and the development
of a modern European political system.

In the conclusion of the project in the seventh volume, Thyssen states
that the results have not been able to confirm a definite association
between religious awakening and economic circumstances.[45] However,
the project confirms a connection between religious and later political

awakening. Also, it became evident during the project that the material from Christiansfeld was particularly well suited for a study of the nexus between religion and society.

Christianity and Culture

As a theologian with a center of gravity in studies of Grundtvig, Thyssen was one of the most ardent and penetrating critics of the fashionable contemporary attempts to secularize Grundtvig's ideas and his awakening.[46] In the postwar period, Thyssen was strongly opposed to a group of theologians and people from the *Folkehøjskole* (folk high schools) who emphasized a divide between Christianity and human life in Grundtvig's thinking and legacy.[47] Instead, the formula "Christianity *and* culture" was at the core of Thyssen's work, and his basic viewpoints in theological debates are reflected in his project designs and also in a second large work on the Moravians from 1984.

This publication was the product of a large multidisciplinary project sponsored by the Danish Research Council,[48] and to some extent it continues the previous project led by Thyssen. While the authors of the first project on awakening were all theologians whose methods were drawn from the social sciences and economic history, the second project narrows the focus to Christiansfeld but is developed by researchers drawn from different fields in the humanities. This illustrates a shift in interest from the relations of religion and society to religion and social or cultural history.

The book's preface, which describes the project, opens by highlighting the singular character of Christiansfeld in a Danish context. This is followed by an underlining of the strong global connections and quality of the congregation, all of which makes it special in terms of "mode of life, religious exercise and social system."[49] It further states that this extraordinary religiously based society founded a particular and functionalistic material culture and production, including crafts and trade, small-scale industry, and farming, as well as cultural production, which is why the Danish Research Council agreed to support an interdisciplinary exploration of Christiansfeld and its connections to social and cultural history.

The two volumes are organized thematically, with one author for each chapter. This approach presents a bouquet of different disciplines tied together by the fact that the chapters cover different perspectives and material. In contrast to the earlier collective work on awakenings, there is no overarching thesis or research question. Except for Thyssen's lengthy first chapter, the theologically informed church history is abandoned;

instead, the first volume comprises social history in terms of demography and poor relief combined with economic perspectives in the cases of crafts, industry, and farming. The second volume opens with explorations of architecture, followed by three chapters on pedagogy and the boarding schools, before reaching music, song, and finally liturgy.

One could say that the two volumes mirror a general turn in historiography toward social and cultural history, although it is hard to find explicit historiographical statements. Rather, the volumes illustrate how scholars from different fields in the humanities began to show renewed attention to material produced in an explicitly religious context. One could also say that the volumes illustrate how Moravian Christianity in Christiansfeld is now analyzed as creator of what a decade later would be labeled "cultural heritage."

Thyssen's interdisciplinary project from the 1980s is the last academic investigation of Christiansfeld per se. However, a number of specialized studies using Moravian material have flourished since the 1990s, and in this aspect, Danish developments resemble those on an international level.[50] Also, material produced by the mission has been used in cultural, colonial, and global studies, thereby producing new knowledge in relation to the Moravians in Christiansfeld.[51]

Nevertheless, Moravians—and subsequently Christiansfeld—still play only a small part in the standard narratives of Danish history, and there are no international academic studies of Christiansfeld in existence.[52]

Concluding Remarks

In this chapter, I have focused on the ways in which previous studies have represented the Moravians in Christiansfeld and how deeply dependent their representations have been on the outlook of the researcher and debates in society at the time. This approach has resulted in a range of different assessments of not only the material itself but also the value of working with Christiansfeld and the character of its impact or its heritage.

The first Moravian outsiders to write on Christiansfeld were theologians, who were occupied with the theological qualities of the life and Christianity encountered there. Thus, Schrøder explored how this theology was distributed by individuals from the particular minority congregations to the majority or mainstream awakenings, especially the Grundtvigian wing of the awakenings. Lundbye, in contrast, who carried out the first classical academic study, saw a connection between the Moravians and the later pietistic awakening in the Home Mission—the opponents of the Grundtvigians. Later, in the shadow of Nazi Germany, the right-wing Grundtvigian theologian Holdt emphasized the true evangelical character of the Czech Moravians as opposed to the German Lutherans. He stressed Christiansfeld's legacy in broader religious life in Denmark, as he found it had supported the construction of the special Danish arrangement regarding the nation-state, on one side, and a substantial space or freedom for church and schools within the state framework, on the other.

In the postwar period, Thyssen conducted the most thorough and comprehensive church historical studies of Christiansfeld thus far. This was in the 1960s as part of a collective project by theologians aiming to examine the influence of religion on the development of modern societies and, in particular, the consequence of awakening movements with regard to political developments. Here, Christiansfeld constituted a first class material, and Thyssen's in-depth analysis displayed how Moravian Christianity was manifested in the tangible lives of the individuals and permeated the structure and life of the community at large. Further, Thyssen's project highlights how life in Moravian Christiansfeld carried traits that could be identified as essential for twentieth-century modern European society, such as individuality and independence from family structures, differentiation of labor, equality between sexes and age groups, functionalistic designs of the social organization and material framework of the life in the settlement, and not least the development of the ability and inclination of individuals from outside the ruling class to take on management and political responsibility. One may characterize the theologians' quest for a religious debt in modern society as an apologetic project in a time of advancing secularization.

The second collective research project was headed by Thyssen a decade later. This was carried out by a different type of scholar, namely researchers from the humanities. Thyssen's contemporary theological opposition toward disrupting the connection between Christianity and vernacular life in Grundtvig's thought is mirrored in his project design. He now invited colleagues from different disciplines to explore the social and cultural history of Christiansfeld. At the same time, the social and cultural turn in the humanities made Christiansfeld a source of relevant material for non-theological disciplines. Since this project was not held together by a shared thesis, the contributions illustrated how different disciplines are able to use the material from Christiansfeld in their respective fields, rather than proving a general point concerning Christianity and culture. Nevertheless, the project as a whole strengthened attention toward what would later be called Christiansfeld's cultural heritage.

The case of Christiansfeld illustrates developments in church historiography as well as in the process of European secularization. It is also evident that the Grundtvigian ideas of church and Christianity have facilitated a historiographical focus on the life lived in the vernacular congregation, as well as an intimate nexus between religion and society. In addition, the latter was seen as not only a natural but also a most positive dynamic interaction. One may draw a straight line from the Grundtvigian ideas illustrated by Schrøder's slogan "Christianity is not teaching but life"[53] to the non-Moravian and even non-religious agency that supported and contributed to Christiansfeld's prominent heritage status.

At the same time, both historiography and the documentation from the heritage application omit critical and conflictual evidence (such as the books of Hansen), obvious dogmatic discrepancies and debates, a most ambiguous sense of nationality, and tensions between minority and majority religion. This allows an almost unconditional positive narrative of Moravian Christiansfeld's past and an uncontested positive heritage.[54]

The argument that research always carries the mark of the researcher's person, discipline, and cultural context is neither new nor original. But it may be worth bearing in mind, when we engage in debates on religion and culture, the identification of singular qualities or uniqueness and what we consider heritage—and the agency of research in the heritage process.

Tine Reeh is an associate professor in church history at the University of Copenhagen. Her scholarly focus has been on the nexus between religion and society in the Nordic countries. She has also worked with historiography, Luther reception, and secularization, and she is currently leading the interdisciplinary research project "Managing Melancholy: Dynamics of Theology and Medicine in 18th-Century Denmark-Norway," funded by the VELUX foundations.

Notes

1. "The Criteria for Selection," UNESCO, accessed [11 August 2020], https://whc.unesco. org/en/criteria/; "Christiansfeld, a Moravian Church Settlement," UNESCO, accessed [11 August 2020], https://whc.unesco.org/en/list/1468/.
2. See chapter 9 in this collection.
3. For a brief introduction in English, see Schjørring, "Grundtvig, Nikolaj Frederik Severin." For a broader general introduction to his work and legacy, in English, see Holm, *Essential N.F.S. Grundtvig;* for an introduction to Grundtvig's thought and

impact with regards to society and societal developments, see Hall, Korsgaard, and Pedersen, *Building the Nation*.

4. For a more detailed account of the concept in English, see Bradley, *N. F. S. Grundtvig*, 517–18; Holm, "N. F. S. Grundtvig," 106–10. On the role of the "living word" in Grundtvig's thinking and later developments, see Thyssen, "Grundtvig's Ideas ... up to 1824"; "Grundtvig's Ideas ... 1825–1847"; Thodberg, "Importance of Baptism."

5. S. A. J. Bradley translates a key quote from Grundtvig: "The church of Christ is founded upon and with the loud and living word of God in the mouth of man, long before a Christian book was penned." Bradley, *N. F. S. Grundtvig*, 517. In his thoughts on the biblical text, Grundtvig refers to a Pauline and Augustinian tradition.

6. This famous quote is from Grundtvig's account of his perception of Christianity; translation is from Bradley, *N. F. S. Grundtvig*, 518.

7. The Danish term "Indre Mission" has been translated as Inner Mission, Inland Mission, Homeland Mission, and Home Mission. It is an independent Danish pietistic revival organization but not an independent church, and its members belong to the Danish Lutheran Church. It was founded in 1861 with the purpose of conducting "missions" or evangelization within the framework of the local Lutheran Protestant Church. The initiative in many ways resembles the work of Johann Hinrich Wichern in Germany, but in Denmark it also had a substantial footing in the rural parishes. It soon became one of the largest Danish revival movements, with a strong rivalry with—and pietistic opposition to—the Grundtvigians, as it accentuated rebirth and renunciation of the sinful modern world.

8. Most obviously, the areas of school and education, the co-operative movement, and political culture in Denmark have been impacted by Grundtvig's thought and the activism of his followers. See Bugge, "School for Life"; Broadbridge, *School for Life*; Korsgaard, "Grundtvig's Idea"; Damsholt, "'Hand of King.'"

9. Ludvig Schrøder was the principal of one of the first new folk high schools in Rødding and later the school in Askov. He was one of the leading figures among the influential Danish Grundtvigians, followers of the ideas of N. F. S. Grundtvig. Schrøder was a most successful and innovative principal at Askov. See Hjermitslev, "Windmills, Butter and Bacon."

10. Schrøder, *Om Brødremenighedens Betydning*.

11. Schrøder, 26. Author's translation.

12. According to Schrøder, the first Moravian leader, Zinzendorf, had abused the hospitality of Copenhagen (and thus shown himself as a false guest), but the subsequent Moravian society in Copenhagen, as well as the community in Christiansfeld, showed themselves as real guests or part of the true congregation of Christ. One should note that Grundtvig in his world chronicle from 1812 labels Zinzendorf as "ungodly." However, Schrøder claims to recall a personal conversation he had with Grundtvig in 1864, where Grundtvig praised the Moravian Luther reception and how their *folkelige*, or vernacular community spirit, facilitated the ground for folk high schools and a Grundvigian awakening. According to Schrøder, this opinion offered by Grundtvig himself says it all, or constitutes all the authority needed.

13. Some of the recollections used as testimony were those of Niels Blicher, the father of St. St. Blicher; Camilla Collett, daughter of Norwegian clergyman N. Wergeland; and professor of church history Frederik Hammerich; as well as artisans and craftsmen such as Hans Hansen from Broager and Hans Kaspar Brandt from Svendborg.

14. Blicher, "Nogle Ord," 290. For Schrøder's abstract of Blicher's text, see Schrøder, *Om Brødremenighedens Betydning*, 30–31.

15. Blicher, "Nogle Ord," 291; Schrøder, *Om Brødremenighedens Betydning*, 31.

16. Schrøder moves on to numerous other more or less famous peoples' testimonials and memories to prove the impact of Moravians not only from Christiansfeld but

also from the society in Copenhagen. A distinct tendency throughout the choir of different voices is the indirect opposition to, or even protest against, rationalism and rationalistic religion—a viewpoint shared by Schrøder; see *Om Brødremenighedens Betydning*, 40. Also, the element of strong and competent laymen as the foundation for a Christian congregation is in line with Schrøder's own agenda.

17. The term *"hygge"* has been seen as a particularly Danish or Nordic concept and cultural trait, referring to a state of being cozy, relaxed, cheerful, and pleasant. More recently it has also been used as a selling point in a variety of cultural contexts; see, for example, "What Is Hygge?," VisitDenmark.com, accessed 21 September 2021, https://www.visitdenmark.com/denmark/highlights/hygge/what-hygge.

18. Schrøder, *Om Brødremenighedens Betydning*, 71.

19. Lundbye, *Herrnhutismen*. Lundbye's studies started as a prize-winning dissertation at the University of Copenhagen, and subsequently he received a grant to go to Herrnhut to work on the material with a connection to Denmark.

20. See the interview with Lundbye on the occation of his pension in April 1949: https://www.hammel-voldby-ladingkirker.dk/fileadmin/group/928/04_Kirker_og_byg ninger/Artikler_Hammel/A_001.pdf (accessed 21 September 2021).

21. Lundbye, *Herrnhutismen*, 201.

22. Lundbye, 211, 213. See also chapter 3 in the present volume.

23. Holdt, "Brødrekolonien Christiansfeld." He later followed up this work with a substantial work on the schools in Christiansfeld: Holdt, "Kostskolerne i Christiansfeld"; "Elevfortegnelse."

24. This type of ecclesiology that is often ascribed to Phillipp Jakob Spener considers two types of church, namely (1) the large church with (2) a smaller assembly of Christians within it, or *ecclesiola in ecclesia*. See Wallmann, "Spener, Philipp Jakob."

25. In the New Testament, sourdough is used as a negative metaphor referring to pollution and the need for a new "dough" (Matt. 16:6, Mark 8:15, Luke 12:1, 1 Cor. 5:6–7, Gal. 5:9), and the same interpretation of the metaphor can be seen in the work from 1736 of the Danish pietistic theologian Erik Pontoppidan, *Fejekost*. However, Zinzendorf and different veins of the awakening movements used it as description of the positive impact of true Christians and Christianity within church and society.

26. Holdt, *Brødrekolonien Christiansfeld*, 81–86.

27. Holdt, 92. It must be noted that even though Jens Holdt opposed Nazism he did not unequivocally support democracy in the interwar period, and on several occasions he criticized democracy as decadent and "un-Danish." However, the developments of the Second World War seem to have altered his views in this regard. Steenbæk, *Præsternes Forening*, 156–58.

28. See chapter 10 in the present volume.

29. Holdt, *Brødrekolonien Christiansfeld*, 165–77; all pages densely written with denser typography.

30. Holdt, 178.

31. Holdt, 178–79. As mentioned above in note 24, Holdt followed this line with further work focused on the schools in Christiansfeld.

32. Jensen, "Brud og Sammenhæng."

33. Reeh, "On the Development."

34. Lindhardt, *Vækkelser og kirkelige retninger*. This first edition of the book is a collection of fifteen articles and three lectures broadcast on the radio and as such is not a systematic scientific opus. The second and thoroughly revised edition from 1959 benefited from not only Lindhardt's own revision but also the many pioneering studies of the subject in the 1950s, and it is in many ways a different book but in support of the same thesis.

35. Lindhardt, 8. Lindhardt developed his viewpoint from neither a Marxist nor a Weberian point of departure but rather by advancing the liberal church historiography's

preoccupation with the religious personality of leading figures and by adding to the equation the background that shaped these personalities. In doing so, Lindhardt combated any attempt at hagiography of the main characters from religious awakening, as well as the view of the Holy Spirit as a possible agent in religious developments. He thereby deliberately offended a number of persons from the contemporary revival movements and the Home Mission, the latter of which constituted part of his own Pietistic upbringing and background.

36. See, for instance, the programmatic introduction in Koch, *Et kirkeskifte*, 11. Their first goal was to examine changes in the appearance, function, and self-understanding of the church in nineteenth-century Denmark and how this transformation was connected to changes of life forms within politics, work life, school, and education—in short, the life of ordinary people.

37. Thyssen, *Vækkelsernes Frembrud*. Especially volumes 1, 4, and 5 include lengthy parts on the Moravians.

38. Thyssen, *Vækkelsernes Frembrud*, 4:11–175. Thyssen's later texts on the subject can be considered a summary of these almost two hundred densely informed pages.

39. Thyssen, 4:162–65. The author is also found under the name Hans, and Thyssen has found information on him and verified some of his accounts in the Moravian archives; see his note 29.

40. Thyssen, 4:162.

41. Hansen, *Kann die herrnhutische Gemeine*.

42. This ambiguous character is also raised in chapter 3 in this volume.

43. Anon. *Unpartheiische Beurtheilung*.

44. Hansen, *Ein ernstes Wort wieder die Herrnhuter*.

45. Thyssen, *Vækkelsernes Frembrud*, 7:389–402, esp. 392–93.

46. This was stimulated by the work of Kaj Thaning and a theological school named Tidehvervsgrundtvigianere. See also Schjørring, "Grundtvig, Nikolaj Frederik Severin."

47. See Pedersen, "Anders Pontoppidan Thyssen," 4–13.

48. Thyssen, *Herrnhuter-samfundet*. This is what other articles refer to as "the yellow Bible."

49. Sørensen, "Projekt og bog," 5.

50. Mai, "Mit eget hjertes forhold"; "Heart-stories"; Hauge, *Works*; "Honningkager og motetter."

51. Cf. Sebro, *Mellem afrikaner og kreol*; Henningsen, "On Difference"; Jensz and Petterson, *Legacies of David Cranz*.

52. On Christiansfeld's role and representation in history in general, see Sanders, "Herrnhutisme i Danmark."

53. "Kristendommen er ikke Lære men Liv." Schrøder, *Om Brødremenighedens Betydning*, 72.

54. See chapter 11 in the present volume.

Bibliography

Anon. *Unpartheiische Beurtheilung und Berichtigung der Hansenshen Schrift* [Impartial assessment and correction of the Hansen publication]. Leipzig: P. G. Kummer, 1822.

Blicher, Niels. "Nogle Ord i Anledning af Dagens literaire Tvistigheder" [Some words occasioned by the literary feud of the day]. *Theologisk Maanedsskrift* (1825): 287–92.

Bradley, S. A. J. *N. F. S. Grundtvig: A Life Recalled*. Aarhus: Aarhus University Press, 2008.

Broadbridge, Edward, Uffe Jonas, and Clay Warren, eds. *The School for Life: N. F. S. Grundtvig on Education for the People*. Aarhus: Aarhus University Press, 2011.

Bugge, K. E. "The School for Life: Basic Ideas of Grundtvig's Educational Thinking." In *Heritage and Prophecy: Grundtvig and the English-Speaking World*, edited by A. M Allchin, David Jasper, Jens Holger Schjørring, and Kenneth Stevenson, 271– 82. Aarhus: Aarhus University Press, 1993.

Damsholt, Tine. "'Hand of King and Voice of People': Grundtvig on Democracy and the Responsibility of the Self." In Hall, Korsgaard, and Pedersen, *Building the Nation*, 151–68.

Hall, John A., Ove Korsgaard, and Ove K. Pedersen, eds. *Building the Nation: N. F. S. Grundtvig and Danish National Identity*. Montreal and Kingston: McGill-Queen's University Press, 2015.

Hansen, Johannes. *Ein ernstes Wort wieder die Herrnhuter: Beantwortung einger sogenannten unpartheyischen Beurtheilung und Berichtigung* [A serious word against the Moravians: A response to the so-called impartial asssessment and correction]. Kiel and Hamburg, 1823.

Hansen, Johannes. *Kann die herrnhutische Gemeine eine wahrhaft evangelisch-christliche genannt werden?* [Can the Moravian congregation be called genuinely Protestant Christian?]. Leipzig, 1821.

Hauge, Peter. "Honningkager og motetter: Musiklivet i Christiansfeld i slutningen af 1700-Tallet" [Honey cakes and motets: Musical life in Christiansfeld in the late eighteenth century]. *Magasin* 29, no. 1 (2016): 65–74.

Hauge, Peter. *Works from the Music Collection of the Moravian Society, Christiansfeld*. Copenhagen: Dansk Center for Musikudgivelse, 2015.

Henningsen, Anne Folke. "On Difference, Sameness and Doublebinds: Ambiguous Discourses, Failed Aspirations." In *Protestant Missions and Local Encounters in the Nineteenth and Twentieth Centuries: Unto the Ends of the World*, edited by Hilde Nielssen, Inger Marie Okkenhaug, and Karina Hestad Skeie, 131–55. Leiden: Brill, 2011.

Hjermitslev, Hans Henrik. "Windmills, Butter and Bacon: The Circulation of Scientific Knowledge among Grundtvigians in the Decades around 1900." In Hall, Korsgaard, and Pedersen, *Building the Nation*, 362–80.

Holdt, Jens. "Brødrekolonien Christiansfeld indtil Aar 1800" [The Moravian colony of Christiansfeld until 1800]. *Sønderjyske Aarbøger* 3 (1940): 53–187.

Holdt, Jens. "Kostskolerne i Christiansfeld" [The bording schools in Christiansfeld]. *Sønderjydske Aarbøger* 1 (1943): 1–49.

Holdt, Jens. "Elevfortegnelse fra Christiansfelds kostskoler 1775–1891" [Record of students at the Christiansfeld boarding schools, 1775–1891]. *Sønderjydske Aarbøger* 2 (1944): 92–129.

Holm, Anders. "N. F. S. Grundtvig: The Matchless Giant." In *Kierkegaard and his Danish Contemporaries*, edited by John Stewart, vol. 7, tome II, 95–151. Burlington: Ashgate, 2009.

Holm, Anders. *The Essential N. F. S. Grundtvig*. Aarhus: Filo, 2019.

Jensen, Hans. "Brud og Sammenhæng i dansk Aandsliv efter 1864" [Rupture and continuation in Danish intellectual life after 1864]. *Kirkehistoriske Samlinger* (1943): 270–349.

Jensz, Felicity, and Christina Petterson, eds. *Legacies of David Cranz's "Historie Von Grönland" (1765): Christianities in the Trans-Atlantic World*. Cham: Springer/ Palgrave Macmillan, 2021.

Koch, Hal, ed. *Et kirkeskifte: Studier over brydninger i dansk kirke- og menighedsliv i det 19. århundrede* [A change of church: Studies on struggles within the Danish church and congregational life in the nineteenth century]. Copenhagen: G. E. C. Gads Forlag, 1960.

Korsgaard, Ove. "Grundtvig's Idea of a Peoples's High School and Its Historical Influence." In Hall, Korsgaard, and Pedersen, *Building the Nation*, 315–30.

Lindhardt, P. G. *Vækkelser og kirkelige retninger i Danmark* [Revival movements and religious parties in Denmark]. Copenhagen: Det danske Forlag, 1951.

Lundbye, Jørgen. *Herrnhutismen i Danmark: Det attende Århundredes Indre Mission* [Herrnhutism in Denmark: The Home Mission of the eighteenth century]. Copenhagen: Karl Schønbergs Forlag, 1903.

Mai, Anne-Marie. "'Mit eget hjertes forhold til Gud Herren': Memoirer af Herrnhuterkvinder læst som oplysningstekster" ["My own heart's relationship to the Lord God": Moravian women's memoirs read as Enlightenment texts]. *Religionsvitenskapelig Tidsskrift* 2007, no. 2 (2007): 48–62.

Mai, Anne-Marie. "Heart-stories: Christiansfeld—an International German-Danish City." In *German-Danish Cultural Relations in the 18th Century*, edited by Stefanie Stockhorst and Søren Peter Hansen, 11–25. Potsdam: V&H Unipress, 2019.

Pedersen, Kim Arne. "Anders Pontoppidan Thyssen in Memoriam." *Grundtvig studier* (2004): 4–13.

Pontoppidan, Erik. *Fejekost til at udfeje den gamle surdej eller de i Danske Lande tiloversblevne og her for Dagen bragte Levninger af saavel Hedenskab som Papisme* [Broom with which to sweep away the old sourdough or those surviving relics of paganism and papism in the Danish realms]. Copenhagen: Det Schønbergske Forlag, 1923.

Reeh, Tine. "On the Development of History of Dogma in Denmark." In *Differenz und Wahrheit: Theologische Transformationen konfessioneller Glaubensreflexion im 19. Jahrhundert* [Difference and truth: Theological transformations of confessional reflexions of faith in the nineteenth century], edited by Markus Wriedt and Frederikke Geers. Tübingen: Mohr Siebeck, forthcoming.

Sanders, Hanne. "Herrnhutisme i Danmark: et religiøst og globalt fænomen" [Moravianism in Denmark: A religious and global phenomenon]. In *Den glömda kyrkan: Om Herrnhutismen i Skandinavien* [The forgotten church: On Moravianism in Scandinavia], edited by Christer Ahlberger and Per von Wachenfeldt, 29–59. Skellefteå: Artos, 2016.

Schjørring, Jens Holger. "Grundtvig, Nikolaj Frederik Severin." In *Religion Past and Present Online*. Accessed 21 September 2021. https://referenceworks.brillonline. com/entries/religion-past-and-present/grundtvig-nikolaj-frederik-severin-SIM_09092?s.num=0&s.f.s2_parent=s.f.book.religion-past-and-present&s. q=grundtvig.

Schrøder, Ludvig. _Om Brødremenighedens Betydning for Kirkelivet i Danmark_ [On the significance of the Moravians for the religious life in Denmark]. Kolding: Lehman og Stange, 1902.

Sebro, Louise. _Mellem afrikaner og kreol: Etnisk identitet og social navigation i Dansk Vestindien 1730–1770_ [Between African and Creole: Ethnic identity and social navigation in the Danish Virgin Islands]. Lund: Lund University Press, 2010.

Stenbæk, Jørgen. _Præsternes Forening gennem 100 år_ [One hundred years of the pastors' union]. Copenhagen: Præsteforeningens Forlag, 1999.

Sørensen, Søren. "Projekt og bog" [Project and book]. In _Herrnhuter-samfundet i Christiansfeld_ [The Moravian community of Christiansfeld], edited by Anders Pontoppidan Thyssen, 4–5. Aabenraa: Historisk Samfund for Sønderjylland, 1984.

Thodberg, Christian. "The Importance of Baptism in Grundtvig's View of Christianity." In _Heritage and Prophecy: Grundtvig and the English-Speaking World_, edited by A. M Allchin, David Jasper, Jens Holger Schjørring, and Kenneth Stevenson, 133–51. Aarhus: Aarhus University Press, 1993.

Thyssen, Anders Pontoppidan. "Grundtvig's Ideas on the Church and the People up to 1824." In _N. F. S. Grundtvig: Tradition and Renewal_, edited by Christian Thodberg and Anders Pontoppidan Thyssen, 87–121. Copenhagen: Det danske selskab, 1983.

Thyssen, Anders Pontoppidan. "Grundtvig's Ideas on the Church and the People, 1825–1847." In _N. F. S. Grundtvig: Tradition and Renewal_, edited by Christian Thodberg and Anders Pontoppidan Thyssen, 226–93. Copenhagen: Det danske selskab, 1983.

Thyssen, Anders Pontoppidan, ed. _Herrnhuter-samfundet i Christiansfeld_ [The Moravian community of Christiansfeld]. Vols. 1–2. Aabenraa: Historisk Samfund for Sønderjylland, 1984.

Thyssen, Anders Pontoppidan, ed. _Vækkelsernes Frembrud i Danmark_ [The outbreak of the revival movements in Denmark]. Vols. 1–7. Copenhagen: G. E. C. Gads Forlag, 1964–1977.

Wallmann, Johannes. "Spener, Philipp Jakob." In _Religion Past and Present Online_. Accessed 11 August 2020. http://dx.doi.org.ep.fjernadgang.kb.dk/ 10.1163/1877-5888_rpp_SIM_025667.

Chapter 2

"We Held a Quite Blessed Communion, the Lamb Was Unusually Close to Me"

Individual and Community in the Moravian Society in Eighteenth-Century Copenhagen

Sigrid Nielsby Christensen

Church historians who have given accounts of the Moravian heritage or legacy in Denmark have traditionally considered the Moravians as a catalyst for the awakening movements in the nineteenth century.[1] Danish theologian Ludvig Schrøder (1836–1908) and Danish pastor Kaj Baagø (1926–1987) both emphasized the link between the Moravian Society in Copenhagen and the beginning of the Grundtvigian awakening movement.[2] Further, Poul Georg Lindhardt (1910–1988) broadened the scope in connecting the religious awakening movements in eighteenth-century Denmark to social and economic processes of change in the nineteenth century.[3]

In contrast to Lindhardt's position, church historian Anders Pontoppidan Thyssen (1921–2004) argues that the development of the awakening movements depended on several factors, such as community and the religious authority of the individual.[4] Thyssen's perspective is in accordance with that of church historian Hal Koch (1904–1963) and literary scholar Thomas Bredsdorff (b. 1937).[5] Koch and Bredsdorff have not conducted specific studies of the Moravians, but in connection to their work on related topics, they consider the Moravian Society in Copenhagen (hereafter, the Copenhagen Society) as the first mover in developing the modern concept of the individual's religious authority independent from the Lutheran state church.[6] Recent studies of connections between religious currents and Enlightenment thought have only strengthened the potential of this approach.[7]

While ecclesiastical and sociological heritage has hitherto been the point of departure for most previous studies of Moravians in the context of

Danish church history, this chapter explores their focus on the individual, or ideas of religious individualization. At the same time, these theological concepts of the individual were embedded in a strong congregational community. The chapter will use the Moravian practice of "watchwords" from the Copenhagen Society as a prism, to investigate the dynamics and developments of concepts of an individualized Christianity as well as the concurrent renewal of the congregational community. At the same time, the archival material regarding this practice may also provide a window into the world and life of eighteenth-century Moravians in Denmark.

Moravian Diaries

On 20 December 1740, the synod at Marienborn instructed every choir within the Moravian congregations to write diaries (*Diarium*) to testify to important events, such as arrivals or departures of traveling Moravian Brethren, resolutions, and religious activities in the congregations.[8] In contrast to the growth of personal diaries in the eighteenth century,[9] the Moravian diaries were "a record of the events of the day as an on-going narrative of the religious development of the community,"[10] according to Paul Peucker, who is director and archivist at the Moravian Archives in Bethlehem, Pennsylvania. The Moravian movement considered life as a service to God, and the diaries interpret this religiously perceived existence of the congregation as a living liturgy.[11]

To testify to the religious development in the communities, Moravian congregations sent the diaries to the "mother-congregation" in Herrnhut, Germany, where they were edited, distributed to other congregations, and stored.[12] The Moravian writers of the diaries were strictly cognizant both of the diaries' "public nature" and of the editing process.[13] In accordance with the synod's instruction of December 1740, the Unitätsarchiv (Unity Archive) in Herrnhut today preserves diaries of the Copenhagen Society dating back to 1741.[14]

Even though the purpose of the Moravian diaries was to report the work of God in the congregations and societies, the diaries of the Copenhagen Society also occasionally reveal an individualized Christianity and self-reflection within the society. Precisely because of these fragmentary appearances, the diaries essentially illustrate and exemplify how themes of individualization were entangled with a strong congregational community.

Historical research has neglected the diaries of the Copenhagen Society thus far. They are a rich source material, however, as will be illustrated by examples from the diary of the Single Brethren's choir in Copenhagen written in July 1746 by the recently arrived Brother Michael Cröger (1714–1800). It is not made explicit in the diary that Cröger was called to write the diary of the Single Brethren's choir in Copenhagen; however, it is documented in records from the Moravian Synod in Zeist on 20 May 1746 and in Cröger's own *Lebenslauf* (memoir).[15] Even though the identification of the writer was not decisive for the purpose of the diaries,[16] it can be of interest for an examination of individualized Christianity within a congregational community, especially because the 1746 diary of the Copenhagen Society implicitly describes Cröger's integration and religious identity.

The remainder of this chapter will, first, examine the relation between individuality and a congregational community and, second, examine through the Moravian practice of watchwords the dynamics between individualized Christianity and the congregational framework.

Individualized Experience of Faith within a Congregational Community

Although it may seem counterintuitive, the congregational community appears to be an evident starting point for the examination of individualized Christianity practiced in the Copenhagen Society. It was significant for the Moravian movement in the eighteenth century that individual Christianity and the congregational community were not opposites but two dimensions mutually entangled.[17] In other words, the community constitutes a vital framework for the shaping of individualized Christianity in Moravian congregations.[18] Individuals constructed their religious identities through the established identity of the congregation as developed by religious routines and practices, just as the individuals helped in shaping the congregations.[19]

The diary of the Copenhagen Society from July 1746 illustrates this mutual entanglement in the case of Michael Cröger. Cröger arrives in Copenhagen on 9 July 1746 with another Single Brother, Christen Kjær, who is from Stepping, near the later settlement of Christiansfeld. The archival material shows that the arrival of these two Brethren had been anticipated and carefully organized, specifically in terms of their immediate reception and accommodation. Cröger wrote, "I was immediately assigned my lodging with Brothers Brodersen, Braadt and Korn at Rosengaarden, the dear hearts [have] received me with much affection and tenderness, and we have rejoiced in each other like children."[20] German historian Gisela Mettele accentuates how the feeling of inner joy often signifies that an action is in agreement with God's will.[21] Hence, the

Brethren's inner joy, narrated in a Moravian vocabulary, can be seen as related to the two new Brethren's inclusion into the Copenhagen Society. At the same time, it underscores that this occurrence is an expression of God's will.

Furthermore, it is grammatically notable how Cröger arrives at the congregation as a singular subject but transforms into a plural subject at the congregational reception, demonstrating at a grammatical level that he has become part of the congregation. The singular subject is not absorbed into a plural subject but constantly changes throughout the diary from 1746. The changing of the grammatical subjects *"ich"* and *"wir"* reflects the reciprocal relation between individual and community within the Copenhagen Society.

Three days after his arrival, Cröger is introduced to the choir, a divided social group based on age, gender, and marital status. The Moravians assumed the choirs to be "nurseries of the Holy Spirit,"[22] which represented a specific aspect of Jesus's life.[23] The aim of the Single Brethren's choir was to develop a deep empathy with Jesus in regard to his "life, suffering and death."[24] After Cröger had become part of the Single Brethren's choir, as he notes on 12 July 1746, he was assigned to the work of the Single Brothers:

> I was introduced to their choir and assigned the work of the Single Brothers, all this took place with grace and legitimation of the Lambkin's presence, my heart was quite soft and melted thereby. Then we, Brother Prætorius, Brodersen and I, spoke with each Brother, separately in Brother Lund's parlor. Brother Braadt was appointed as my right hand and closest helper in the matter of the Single Brothers.[25]

Cröger emphasizes the mutual obligation within the society. The individuals have their duties in the choir, and similarly the choir has a responsibility to each individual of the choir, which appears (in the quotation) in terms of selecting of a choir helper for the newly arrived Brother, Cröger.

In spite of the fact that principles for the choir helper were formulated much later,[26] the diary of the Moravian Society reveals that each member of the choir in Copenhagen was related to a choir helper, whose function was to assist the member in his inner development, just as the member was required to speak and confess to his helper.[27] Moreover, Cröger accentuates how the introduction happened in accordance with God's will, because it was legitimized through the proximity of the Lamb, Christ, which in turn brings about a mollification of Cröger's heart. The mollification implies that at the moment of his introduction to the choir, Cröger already gains a deeper recognition of his sinfulness, which is part of the basic principle for the choir.[28] Likewise, the proximity of the Lamb expresses a strong desire for union with Christ similar to other Moravian congregations at that time.[29]

The proximity of the Lamb is a topic to which Cröger returns in the diary. On Sunday, 17 July 1746, he reports that the choir had a conference in the house of Brother Prætorius in the proximity of the Lamb:

> We held a very important conference at Br. Prætorius, the Lambkin's presence was with me in an impressionable and respectable way. In [this meeting] occurred: 1) the good Lamb allowed us to hold Communion 2) the Lambkin permitted that the Single Brothers henceforth can be treated and dealt with separately by their own choir-worker. I took this as a special grace for us, and I have immediately kissed the feet of the Savior with shame and bowing.[30]

First, Cröger narrates the occurrences from the meeting, succeeded by his individual religious experience of the occurrences. In addition, he underlines the proximity of the Lamb during communion on Friday, 29 July:

> We held a quite blessed communion, the Lamb was unusually close to me and palpable and perceptible in its martyr-appearance. Yes, I have seen, kissed and with tears eaten the slaughtered sheep J[esus] X[Christ].[31]

Cröger describes vividly in Moravian terms his individual religious experience, which is evoked by the congregational community in the Single Brethren's choir. Similar to other Moravian congregations in the "Sifting Time,"[32] the diary demonstrates that the Copenhagen Society was devoted to the blood and wounds of Christ.[33] The diary of the Copenhagen Society characteristically presents individualized experiences of religious occurrences as taking place only within the congregational community, which may be seen as a specific instance of the general assumption that the congregational community is the constituted framework for individualized Christianity in the Moravian Church.

In general, Moravian life in the Copenhagen Society—specifically in terms of activities that contributed to shaping a religious culture—resembled the life in Moravian towns, though it was less structured. As we will see in the diary of the Copenhagen Society, some global religious activities also contained local modifications and peculiarities. The diary reveals how the choir of Single Brethren met three times a week: on Tuesdays and on two other days, which varied.

Among the choir's activities that sought to strengthen the congregational community, Cröger mentions meetings, "quarter-hours," singing, communion, foot washing, and the Lovefeast. Another Moravian practice was the use of watchwords, which were essential to the diary of the Moravian Brethren in Copenhagen; the practice demonstrates the particular self-perception within the society. This takes us to the next section, which addresses how the practice of watchwords in the Copenhagen Society can be contemplated as an individualized Christianity entangled in a strong congregational community.

Practice of Watchwords

The Moravian faith was a matter of the heart rather than the head;[34] therefore, Moravians emphasized the individual experience of Christ over the study of scripture.[35] During the 1740s, religious opponents claimed that Moravians did not use the Bible but instead based their sermons on hymn texts.[36] Peucker perceives the antibiblical statements of the Moravians as not only provocative behavior against the Pietists but also a consequence of Moravian theology concerning the subjective experience of God's love.[37]

In regard to development of the individual's relationship with God, the Moravians had meditated upon daily watchwords since 1729.[38] Watchwords were extracts from the Bible combined with a stanza of a Moravian hymn, printed in devotional booklets. Yearly editions of watchwords have been published every year since 1731.[39] The same watchword for meditation was read every day in all Moravian congregations, a practice that helped in establishing a sense of global community over great distances.[40]

The leader of the Moravian Church, Nicolaus Ludwig von Zinzendorf (1700–1760), intended to grant laymen access to the scriptures, and by using watchwords the scriptures entered lives and understanding—so much so that the congregation was seen to become a living Bible.[41] In other words, the global Moravian practice of watchwords was collectively founded. However, the local diaries from the Moravian Society in Copenhagen illustrate another peculiar practice of watchwords.

The diaries of the Copenhagen Society reveal frequent use of watchwords, and every instance of watchwords is underlined in the diaries.[42] Moravians were to some extent in opposition to Hallensian Pietism, especially in terms of scripture and penitential struggle[43]—an individual conscious act, strongly endorsed by the German Pietist August Hermann Francke (1764–1727), to constantly fight the inner and outer sin and deduce whether the religious individual was an elect.[44] At the same time, Peucker clarifies that, while ideas of the penitential struggle influenced the Moravians, in the theological development of the 1740s they turned to the notion of redemption as taking place solely through the suffering of Christ.[45] In other words, it is not that the Copenhagen Society diluted concepts like inner development and consciousness of sin in the development of Moravian theology, but rather that they emphasized redemption instead of penitential struggle.

In the diary entry of 12 July 1746, Cröger reports the selection of his choir helper, whose function was precisely to assist the Brother's inner development, including confession of sin.[46] A further topic for consideration is whether the practice of watchwords is a Moravian development of the Pietist devotional practice of self-examination.

The Practice of Watchwords and Self-Examination in Copenhagen

In Denmark, self-examination was a crucial subject of the Hallensian Pietistic devotional literature during the reign of Christian VI (1730–1746). It was considered a method for raising the consciousness of sin, whereby the individual gained insight into his or her spiritual condition and became able to decide his or her actual relationship with God.[47] The orphanage (*Vajsenshuset*) in Copenhagen distributed the idea of Hallensian self-examination through devotional literature, pamphlets, hymns, and sermons.[48]

Even though the Moravians in Copenhagen turned away from the Hallensian idea of penitential struggle because it occasioned confusion and melancholy,[49] there are indications that the Copenhagen Society practiced self-examination. According to Danish theologian Knud Heiberg, the Moravian Society for decades used the booklet *De otte Saligheder* (*The Eight Beatitudes*) as a means for self-examination and introspection.[50] The booklet was written by a Moravian, Christian David (1692–1751), who had great influence on the early Moravian movement in Copenhagen.[51]

What characterized self-examination within the Danish pietistic state church was a typological reading of the Bible to describe spiritual conditions, most frequently in three contrasting categories. Thus, each person could determine his or her individual spiritual condition through identification with one of the categorized situations and thereby decide whether he or she had a valid covenant of baptism.[52]

To avoid the possibility that self-examination might lead to self-deception regarding redemption, the pastor within the absolutist state church had a great responsibility for supervision and guidance.[53] In spite of the fact that the Moravians did not find it necessary to determine their spiritual condition through Bible studies, since the assurance of an individual relation to God was given by the heart and expressed through inner feelings, the Moravians in Copenhagen used the booklet by David to examine their individual progression in faith.[54]

Self-examination was to David not in conflict with the Moravian practice of watchwords. In fact, he regarded self-examination partly as the aim of watchwords. In the 1735 publication *Beschreibung und zuverlässige Nachricht von Herrnhut,* he describes the practice and purpose of the Moravian watchwords:

> The manner of our watchword procedure is the following: we select either a verse from the Bible or a stanza of a hymn that is best suited to our condition or our guidance. This verse or stanza for the day is first explained, the previous evening after the service of song, by the Count himself or some other Brother, and, on the following morning, carried from house to house in all of Herrnhut by a Brother appointed so to serve, and this on all days. Then throughout the day, wherever Brethren or Sisters meet in their several callings, there is conversation about the watchword, in order that we may continue in the spirit of true self-control and self-examination. Hence if someone is not of our disposition and does not strive consistently this is soon manifest, since the verses and the stanzas are ever directed to our condition.[55]

The watchwords, or biblical meditations, served to guide an actual situation and to acknowledge the individual's spiritual condition. In addition, the quotations expose another dynamic of individualized Christianity within the congregational community. When the practice of watchwords strengthened the individual's life in Jesus, it prevented the congregational community from sin and thereby strengthened the congregation.

Another record from 1742 that exemplifies a kind of self-examination within the Copenhagen Society is Henrik Gerner's (1701–1786) defense of the Moravian Society against Christian VI. Gerner was archdeacon in Copenhagen, and he assumed the responsibility of invigilating the Moravian assemblies in accordance to the royal restriction, or *Konventikelplakaten,* of 13 January 1741. Besides being a supervisory state authority, Gerner also secretly sympathized with and protected the Copenhagen Society, before he and his family went to a Moravian congregation in Schlesien in 1748 after several conflicts with the absolutist state church in relation to his dual capacity.[56]

In the document from 1742, Gerner explains how the Moravian assemblies, which the Copenhagen Society held in Gerner's house, were a great blessing because of the society's strengthening and consolidation in grace. In addition, Gerner emphasizes that the devotional progression occurred after individuals of the congregation "were examined by either me, a Catechist, a Student or another, who had been in position so to serve."[57] Thus, Gerner describes a variety of self-examinations partly in contrast to the Hallensian self-examination within the absolutist state church, delineated above.

Further, he reports that individuals do not examine themselves, but rather that someone, who apparently has a connection to the clergy, undertakes the examination. That someone connected to the state clergy should have examined individuals of the Moravian Society in Copenhagen seems inconsistent with the Moravian organization. However, Gerner protects the activities of the Moravian Society by noting the participation by someone linked to the state authorities. The quotation closes with a very veiled formulation, because the expression "position so to serve" may refer to a position in the clergy or in the order of the Moravian organization, where it may refer to another authority from the congregation, called to this purpose, which would imply laymen. The last reading of the quotation involves a displacement of the clergy and state authority to a new congregational authority.

Dynamics of the Individualized and Congregational Practice of Watchwords

Christian David's description of certain elements in the practice of Moravian watchwords, as well as Gerner's indication of a new congregational authority, are also characteristic of the diary of the Copenhagen Society. Thus, there are implications for the dynamics of an individualized Christianity entangled in a congregational community.

The Moravian practice of watchwords, described in the diaries of the Copenhagen Society, is similar to self-examination through a biblical meditation on an actual situation. Right after Cröger has arrived in Copenhagen, in July 1746, he uses a watchword on his actual situation:

> When I saw the town, I threw a lot in regard to my plans, which said (9 July 1746) *One shall say: I am the Lord's, and another shall call himself by Jacob's Name, and another with his hand shall subscribe unto the Lord, and surname himself by Israel's name. Isaiah 44,5.*[58]

The watchword confirms that Cröger's entry into the Copenhagen Society is in accordance with God's will, because he is about to be designated Israel and to be part of the chosen people. Even though the watchword in this case reflects Cröger's individual situation, it also expresses the self-perception of the Moravian Society in Copenhagen: that they are

God's chosen people and thereby a fulfillment of the scripture. The public nature of the diaries and the edifying process strongly indicates that these comprehensions were current in the Copenhagen Society and not just an expression of Cröger's interpretation.

That the Moravian Society regarded themselves as God's chosen people and an ongoing fulfillment of the scripture is corroborated in another use of a watchword in the diary, from 19 July 1746:

> The watchword: *God went* 2 Sam 7,23 *to make him a blessed people in times to report*. The watchword is also here in Copenhagen more fulfilled from year to year[.] The blessed people is already there, and it is making progress to report. For that reason we, the Single Brothers, are divided into a separate choir and class by the Lambkin, and with each other we are pointed towards his first wound, so that we are even more prepared and [able to] enjoy the separated choir-grace and blessing, which he has earned for us, until we are decorated by the blood and mind of the Lamb and are prepared to become his true disciples.[59]

In agreement with the daily watchword, the hopeful Moravian Society regards itself as a people of benediction, and Cröger emphasizes how this watchword is fulfilled year after year. In Cröger's meditation of the watchword in respect to the actual situation of the society, he highlights the dynamics of individualized Christianity entangled in the congregational community by explaining how the individual is embedded in the congregational community, in the same way that, concerning redemption, each individual is mutually obliged to the blood and wound.

The blood and wound devotion within the Moravian Society is perceived as a fulfillment of scripture, and the congregational community becomes a foretaste of the redemption. With reference to Moravian wound theology, German theologian Peter Vogt describes how the Moravians regarded the side wound as a "matrix," whence the individual believer was spiritually born.[60]

The diary of the Copenhagen Society has already confirmed that the congregational community and its structure shaped and developed individual religious identity. In relation to the selection of a choir helper, Cröger completes the diary on 12 July 1746 with the daily watchword:

> The watchword said: *though your sins are as red as crimson, they shall be as white as snow, and though they be* red like crimson, *they shall be as wool, Isaiah* 1:18. *Nobody is as holy as a sinner, who has grace.*[61]

Through assistance from the choir helper, the individual develops his religious identity and faith. The watchword underlines how the

Brethren are regarded as sinners, but those who experience the grace of God are sanctified in a way that is similar to Gerner's explanation in his defense from 1742. In the July 1746 diary it is clear that every experience of God, or proximity of the Lamb, happens within the Moravian congregational community. Just like Gerner's indication of a new congregational authority in his defense of Moravian activities, the practice of watchwords within the Moravian Society in Copenhagen reveals a new emphasis on the religious authority of the individual. In contrast to the Danish absolutist state church, it was no longer the pastor who ensured the correct theological understanding of the scripture, or religious development of the individual, but the congregation. In that way, the Moravian practice of watchwords can be considered an extension of Martin Luther's idea of the universal priesthood of the baptized.

Even though Cröger represents the choir of the Single Brethren, his use of the watchwords shows an individual meditation on scripture in relation to the actual situation, whereby the practice of watchwords can be perceived as an individualization of Christianity entangled in a congregational community.

Conclusion

The diary of the Moravian Society in Copenhagen from July 1746 is an essential source for illustrating the dynamics of the entanglement of individualized Christianity with the strong congregational community. The diaries emphasize mutual obligations within the Moravian Society in Copenhagen among the individuals and the choir, and the diary shows that individual religious experiences of the proximity of Christ take place only within the congregational community.

The Moravian organization, routines, and practices helped in shaping individualized Christianity, including the practice of watchwords. The practice of watchwords within the Copenhagen Society can in some aspects be perceived as a further Moravian development of self-examination within the Danish absolutist state church in terms of biblical meditation on actual human existence. More specifically, the individualized practice differs from the general comprehension of the Moravian practice of watchwords, pointing to a local peculiarity of a global Moravian practice. In contrast to the practice of self-examination within the Danish absolutist state church, records on the practice of watchwords within the Copenhagen Society indicate a new extension of the layman's authority within the congregational community.

The practice of watchwords within the Copenhagen Society reveals different perspectives of the dynamics between individualized Christianity and the congregational community. First, the diary exposes an individualized practice of watchwords, when Cröger uses the daily watchword as a meditation on his actual individual human existence. Second, the practice of watchwords reflects the self-perception of the Moravian Society as God's chosen people and a fulfillment of scripture. Finally, through meditation on the watchwords, Cröger emphasizes the individual as anchored within the congregational community.

In other words, the diary of the Moravian Society in July 1746 illustrates how the establishment of the Copenhagen Society in 1739 introduced new individualized ideas of Christianity and at the same time a renewal of concepts of congregation and solidarity. Also, even though the Moravian Society was not separated from the absolutist state church of the mono-confessional kingdom, the question of the autonomy of the religious subject along with congregational freedom was embedded in the Copenhagen Society. The development of this Moravian variety of individualized Christianity required a strong congregational community. The foundation of the settlement Christiansfeld corroborated the strong congregational community, which became an invaluable source of inspiration for the later Grundtvigian awakening movement.

Sigrid Nielsby Christensen is a PhD fellow at the Section of Church History at the University of Copenhagen, working on a project on the Moravian Society of Copenhagen between 1739 and 1771. In 2019 she received a gold medal for her dissertation from the University of Copenhagen, and she published the article "Enevold Ewalds selvprøvelsesprogram" (*Kirkehistoriske Samlinger* 2020) on the Danish Pietists' practice of self-examination and ideas of subjectivity.

Notes

1. For a detailed presentation and evaluation of the different positions in studies of the Moravian movement in Denmark, see chapter 1, by Tine Reeh, in the present volume.
2. Schrøder, *Om Brødremenighedens Betydning*, 4; Baagø, *Vækkelsernes Frembrud*, 21. See also chapter 1.
3. Lindhardt, *Vækkelser og kirkelige Retninger*, 105. For further information on the awakening movements in Denmark, see chapter 1.

4. Thyssen, *Vækkelsernes Frembrud*, 296–400. In addition to Thyssen, theologian Jørgen Lundbye also points, in 1903, to the individual's authority; see Lundbye, *Herrnhutismen*, 211.

5. Lundbye, *Herrnhutismen*, 211.

6. Koch, *Danmarks Kirke*, 120; Bredsdorff, *Den brogede oplysning*, 73.

7. Mulsow, *Enlightenment Underground*; Sorkin, *Religious Enlightenment*; Israel, *Revolution of the Mind*; Sheehan, *Enlightenment Bible*.

8. Peucker, "Pietism and the Archives," 399.

9. Habermas, *Strukturwandel der Öffentlichkeit*.

10. Peucker, "Textual History," 103.

11. Peucker, *Pietism*, 399; Atwood, *Community of the Cross*.

12. Peucker, "Textual History," 105.

13. Mettele, "Organizing Global Communication," 190.

14. Peucker, *Pietism*, 399; Anonymous author, *Diarium des Ledigen Brüder Chors in Copenhagen von Anno 1746 den 9ten Julii bis 1762 den 19. April* R.19.E.9f, Unitätsarchiv, Moravian Archives Herrnhut (hereafter cited as UA).

15. I owe many thanks to Christina Petterson, who identified the writer of the diary. Anonymous author, *Zeist Synode, Sessio XII. Freitag 20 May 1746 Nachmittags 4 Uhr*, R.2.A.19.1, UA; Michael Cröger, *Lebenslauf*, R.22.20.80, UA.

16. Neither the diary of the Moravian Society in Copenhagen nor its lists of members identify the writer. Cf. *Diarium 1746*, R.19.E.9f, UA; UA R.27.329.1-28, UA, Anonymous author, *Personkataloge aus Copenhagen 1742–69.*

17. Petterson, *Moravian Brethren*.

18. Mettele, "Constructions," 11.

19. See chapter 3 in the present volume; Mettele, "Constructions," 19, 21; Faull, *Moravian Women's Memoirs*; Vogt, "How Moravian," 85.

20. *Diarium 1746*, R.19.E.9f, UA: "Ich kriegte gleich mein Logie bey br. Brodersen Braadt u: Korn auf dem Rosengaard, die lieben herzen haben mich recht mit vieler liebe u: zärtlichheit empfangen, u: wir haben uns über einander gefreuet als Kinder." Translations of the diary of the Copenhagen Society are all by the author. I have endeavored in the translations to preserve the original wording in all its oddity.

21. Mettele, "Constructions," 22.

22. Mettele, 12–13.

23. Peucker, *Time of Sifting*, 22.

24. Mettele, "Constructions," 13; Peucker, *Time of Sifting*, 22.

25. *Diarium 1746*, R.19.E.9f, UA: "Ich wurde als in dem Chor introducirt, u: der led: brr: Arbeit mir aufgetragen, das geschah alles mit Gnade u: Legitimation von Lämleins Näheseyn, mein Herz war recht weich u: zershmolgen dabey. Hierauf sprachen wir neml: br: Præt: Brodersen u: ich einen jeden br. aparte kurtzl: in br: Lunds Stübgen. Der Br. Braadt wurde mir zur rechten hand u: als meinen Nächsten gehülfen in der led: brr: Sache gegeben."

26. See Tine Damsholt's chapter in the present volume; Mettele, "Constructions," 13. See also Faull, *Speaking*.

27. Also, the pastor, Henrik Gerner (1701–1786), confirms this in his reply to the king, Christian VI, regarding the Moravian Society in Copenhagen, signed 22 November 1742. See "Sagen mod Stiftsprovst Henrik Gerner," Royal Danish Library, Copenhagen (hereafter cited as RDL).

28. "Sagen mod Stiftsprovst Henrik Gerner"; Mettele, "Constructions," 13.

29. Peucker, *Time of Sifting*, 23.

30. *Diarium 1746*, R.19.E.9f, UA: "wir hatten beym br: Præt. eine sehr wichtige *Conferentz* des Lämleins Nähe seyn war mir dabey recht ein Drucklich u: *Respectabel* darin vorkam 1) das gute Lam erlaubte uns bald ein Abm: zu halten 2) das Lämlein erlaubte, das die ledige brr: ins künftige allein durch ihre eigne Chor-Arbeiter könten behandelt u:

bearbeitet werden. Ich nahm es als eine besondere Gnade an für uns, u: habe dem Heyl: gleich die Füße davor mit Scham u: Beugung geküßt."

31. *Diarium 1746*, R.19.E.9f, UA: "Hatten wir ein recht gesegnetes *Abm:*, das Lamm war mir ungemein nahr u: fühlbar in seinem *Mater* Bilde ia ich habe das Schlachtshaf J: X: gesehen, gekyßt u: mit Thränen gegeßen." That the Moravian Society in Copenhagen held communion was definitely a transgression of the limits for Moravian activities in Denmark-Norway in 1746. It is certain that the communion was exclusively for the Moravian Society, as they, according to the diary, did not hold communion on Sundays, when the absolutist state church conducted the sacrament. The diary of 1746 does not reveal whether the sacrament was conducted by the archdeacon, Henrik Gerner (1701–1786), or by a layman. In the diary's short descriptions of the communion, Cröger mentions no supervision by other clergy authorities, and the diary refers only occasionally to the attendance of Gerner. Instead, Cröger's descriptions of the communion underlines how the practice helped to establish a congregational community, through which the individual experienced the presence of Christ. See *Diarium 1746*, R.19.E.9f, UA.
32. The "Sifting Time" indicates a crisis in the Moravian Church. See Peucker, *Time of Sifting*.
33. The blood was seen as symbolic of passion and salvation, and the wounds of Christ as a place of comfort for the community. Peucker, *Time of Sifting*, 26–28. For more on the theological topoi, see the introduction in this volume.
34. Atwood, "Little Side Holes," 61.
35. Vogt, "Honor to the Side," 84, 94; Peucker, *Time of Sifting*, 72.
36. Peucker, *Time of Sifting*, 71.
37. Peucker, 72–73; Sheehan, *Enlightenment Bible*, 58.
38. Jensz, *German Moravian Missionaries*, 20; Schwarze, "History of the Text Book," 150.
39. Peucker, *Time of Sifting*, 72, 199; Jensz, *German Moravian Missionaries*, 20.
40. Mettele, "Moravian Brethren," 163.
41. Schwarze, "History of the Text Book," 150.
42. 9f. *Diarium 1746* R.19.E.9f UA.
43. Atwood, "Hallensians are Pietists," 52–57; Peucker, *Time of Sifting*, 18.
44. Francke, *Selvprøvelses fornødenhed*. See also the introduction and chapter 1 of this volume.
45. Peucker, *Time of Sifting*, 65.
46. See footnote 25.
47. Christensen, "Enevold Ewalds."
48. "Et Aandeligt Speyl," RDL; Brorson, *Nogle Psalmer*; Ewald, *Det gamle og nye Testamentes*; [Francke], *Selvprøvelses fornødenhed*; *Haand-Postill*.
49. Gerner, *Nogle Mærkværdigheder*, 96.
50. David, *Korte og Skritmeszige Betragtninger*.
51. Heiberg, "Fra Brydningstiden," 701; Lundbye, *Herrnhutismen*, 71.
52. [Francke], *Selvprøvelses fornødenhed*; "Et Aandeligt Speyl," RDL; Spener, *Christendoms Øvelse*.
53. "Kirkelige Stridigheder i København," RDL; [Francke], *Selvprøvelses fornødenhed*; "Et Aandeligt Speyl," RDL; Spener, *Christendoms Øvelse*.
54. David, *Korte og Skritmeszige Betragtninger*; Heiberg, *Fra Brydningstiden*.
55. Translation of Christian David's *Beschreibung und zuverlössige Nachricht von Herrnhut*. (Leipzig, 1735), 68, in Schwarze, *History of the Text Book*, 136.
56. Gerner, *Nogle Mærkværdigheder*, 15, 274; Lundbye, *Herrnhutismen i Danmark*, 74–80.
57. "Sagen mod Stiftsprovst Henrik Gerner," RDL: "Jeg giorde Aaret 1741: *Dominica Sexagesima* i mit Huus Begyndelse med Forsamlinger for dem, og siden dend tiid har vi fortfaret under vor Frelseres Bevarelse, og ofte sporet fra ham iblandt os en sand Velsignelse, ved det ikke alene de, der først indfandt dem, tiid efter anden ere blevne

meere styrkede og grundfæstede i Naaden, men endog ved det andre fleere efter deres egen indstændige Begiæring, og efter at de først ere blevne prøvede enten af mig, en *Catechet*, en *Student* eller anden, som har kundet være dertil i Stand." Translation by the author.

58. *Diarium 1746*, R.19.E.9f, UA: "da ich die Stadt sahe, shlung ich mir eine loß: auf in absicht meiner plans, die heiß: (d 9: Jul: 1745) dieser *wird sagen: ich bin des Herre; u: jener wird genemet werden mit dem Namen Jacob, u: dieser wird sich mit seiner hand den Herren zushriben, werden mit dem Namen Jsrael genemet werden* Jeh: 44,5." The translation of the watchword's Bible extract follows the King James Version.

59. *Diarium 1746*, R.19.E.9f, UA: "die loß: *Gott ist hingegangen* 2 Sam 7,2 daß *er sich ein Segens Volk in den zeiten möchte zu berichten.* Die Loß: ist auch hier in Copenh: von jahr zu jahr mehr erfüllet, das Segens Volck ist shon da, u: es geht immer weiter mit das zuberichten. Darum sind wir ledigen brüder auch von Lämlein in eine aparte Chor u: Classe gebracht u: mit einander auf seine erste Wunde gewiesen, daß wir mehr zubereitet werden mögten, u: so die aparte Chor-Gnade u: segen geniesen, die er uns verdient hat, bis wir mit Lammes Blut u: Lammes Sinn ausgesmückt u: zu seine wahre Jünglinge zubereitet worden sind."

60. Vogt, *Honor to the Side*, 94.

61. *Diarium 1746*, R.19.E.9f, UA: "die loß hieß: *wenn eure Sünder gleich blutroth ist, soll sie doch Schneeweiß werden, u: wenn sie gleich ist wie rosin-farbe, soll sie doch wir wolle werden* Es: 1,18. *Niemand ist heiliger als ein Sünder, der Gnade hat.*" The translation of the watchword's Bible extract follows the King James Version.

Bibliography

Published Sources

Atwood, Craig D. *Community of the Cross: Moravian Piety in Colonial Bethlehem.* University Park: Penn State University Press, 2004.

Atwood, Craig D. "Little Side Holes: Moravian Devotional Cards of the Mid-Eighteenth Century." *Journal of Moravian History*, no. 6 (2009): 61–75.

Atwood, Craig D. "'The Hallensians are Pietists; aren't you a Hallensian?' Mühlenberg's Conflict with the Moravians in America." *Journal of Moravian History* 12, no. 1 (2012): 47–92.

Baagø, Kaj. "Brødresocietetet" [The Moravian Society]. In *Vækkelsernes Frembrud i Danmark i første halvdel af det 19. Århundrede* [The outbreak of the revival movements in Denmark], edited by Anders Pontoppidan Thyssen, 18–28. Copenhagen: G. E. C. Gads Forlag, 1960.

Bredsdorff, Thomas. *Den brogede oplysning* [The multi-faceted Enlightenment]. Copenhagen: Gyldendal, 2003.

Brorson, Hans Adolf. *Nogle Psalmer om Troens Grund, Gud til Ære og Hans Kircke til opmuntring* [Some Psalms about the foundation of faith, in honor of God and to encourage His church]. Copenhagen: Vajsenhuset, 1732.

Christensen, Sigrid Nielsby. "Enevold Ewalds selvprøvelsesprogram" [Enevold Ewald's program for self-examination]. *Kirkehistoriske Samlinger* (2020): 7–30.

David, Christian. *Beschreibung und zuverlössige Nachricht von Herrnhut* [A description and reliable message from Herrnhut]. Leipzig: Samuel Benjamin Walter, 1735.

David, Christian. *Korte og Skritmeszige Betragtninger over de Otte Saligheder* [Brief and gradual meditations over the eight beatitudes]. Flensborg/Copenhagen: Vajsenhuset, 1733.

Ewald, Erevold. *Det gamle og nye Testamentes herlige Harmonie og fuldkomne Overeensstemmelse i den Lærdom om Christo* [The Old and New Testament's magnificent and perfect compliance in the doctrines on Christ]. Vols. 1–5. Copenhagen: Vajsenhuset, 1744–1750.

Gerner, Henrik. *Nogle Mærkværdigheder som angaaer Henric Gerner, hans Vita og Fata* [Noteworthy things regarding Henric Gerner, his life and destiny]. Copenhagen: M. Hallager, 1772.

Faull, Katherine M. *Moravian Women's Memoirs: Their Related Lives, 1750–1820.* Syracuse, NY: Syracuse University Press, 1997.

Faull, Katherine M., ed. *Speaking to Body and Soul: Instructions for the Moravian Choir Helpers, 1785–1786.* University Park: Penn State University Press, 2017.

Francke, August Hermann. *Haand-Postill, Eller Korte Prædikener paa Søndage og Hell: Dage* [Handbook with sermons for Sundays and holy days]. Copenhagen: Vajsenhuset, 1735.

[Francke, August Hermann]. *Selvprøvelses fornødenhed, førend man gaar til Guds Bord* [The necessity of self-examination before attending the Lord's Supper]. Copenhagen: Vajsenhuset, 1732.

Habermas, Jürgen. *Strukturwandel der Öffentlichkeit* [The structural transformation of the public sphere]. Frankfurt am Main: Suhrkamp Verlag, 1962.

Heiberg, Knud. "Fra Brydningstiden o. 1725–50" [From the time of upheaval, c.1725–50]. *Kirkehistoriske Samlinger* (1905): 1–40.

Israel, Jonathan. *A Revolution of the Mind: Radical Enlightenment and the Intellectual Origins of Modern Democracy.* Princeton: Princeton University Press, 2010.

Jensz, Felicity. *German Moravian Missionaries in the British Colony of Victoria, Australia, 1848–1908: Influential Strangers.* Leiden: Brill, 2010.

Koch, Hal. *Danmarks Kirke gennem Tiderne* [The church in Denmark through the ages]. Copenhagen: Gyldendal, 1949.

Lausten, Martin S. *Danmarks kirkehistorie* [Church history of Denmark]. Copenhagen: Gyldendal, 2004.

Lindhardt, P. G. *Den Danske Kirkes Historie* [The history of the Danish church]. Vol. 7. Copenhagen: Gyldendal, 1958.

Lindhardt, P. G. *Vækkelser og kirkelige Retninger i Danmark* [Revival movements and religious parties in Denmark]. Copenhagen: Det Danske Forlag, 1951.

Lundbye, J. *Herrnhutismen i Danmark* [Herrnhutism in Denmark: The Home Mission of the eighteenth century]. Copenhagen: Karl Schønbergs Forlag, 1903.

Mettele, Gisela. "Constructions of the Religious Self: Moravian Conversion and Transatlantic Communication." *Journal of Moravian History*, no. 2 (2007): 7–36.

Mettele, Gisela. "The Moravian Brethren as a Global Community." In *Pietism and Community in Europe and North America, 1650–1850*, edited by Jonathan Strom, 7–35. Leiden: Brill, 2010.

Mettele, Gisela. "Organizing Global Communication among Moravians during the Eighteenth and Nineteenth Centuries." In *Global Protestant Missions: Politics, Reform, and Communication, 1730s–1930s*, edited by Jenna M. Gibbs, 185–208. London: Routledge, 2020.

Mulsow, Martin. *Enlightenment Underground: Radical Germany, 1680–1720.* Charlottesville: University of Virginia Press, 2015.

Petterson, Christina. *The Moravian Brethren in a Time of Transition: A Socio-Economic Analysis of a Religious Community in Eighteenth-Century Saxony.* Leiden: Brill, 2021.

Peucker, Paul. "Pietism and the Archives." In *A Companion to German Pietism, 1660–1800,* edited by Douglas H. Shanz, 393–420. Leiden: Brill, 2014.

Peucker, Paul. "The Textual History of the 1742 Bethlehem Diary." *Journal of Moravian History* 18, no. 1 (2018): 102–12.

Peucker, Paul. *A Time of Sifting: Mystical Marriage and the Crisis of Moravian Piety in the Eighteenth Century.* University Park: Penn State University Press, 2015.

Schrøder, Ludvig. *Om Brødremenighedens Betydning for Kirkelivet i Danmark* [On the significance of the Moravians for religious life in Denmark]. Kolding: Lehman og Stange, 1902.

Sheehan, Jonathan. *The Enlightenment Bible: Translation, Scholarship, Culture.* Princeton: Princeton University Press, 2005.

Spener, Philipp Jacob. *Christendoms Øvelse, Eller Anviisning hvordan man skal blive en sand Christen* [Exercises in Christianity, or instructions for becoming a true Christian]. 1675; Copenhagen: Vajsenhuset, 1732.

Schwarze, W. N. "History of the Text Book of the Moravian Church." *Transactions of the Moravian Historical Society* 13, no. 3–4 (1944): 133–62.

Sorkin, David. *The Religious Enlightenment: Protestants, Jews, and Catholics from London to Vienna.* Princeton: Princeton University Press, 2008.

Thyssen, Anders Pontoppidan, ed. *Herrnhuter-samfundet i Christiansfeld* [The Moravian community of Christiansfeld]. Vols. 1–2. Aabenraa: Historisk Samfund for Sønderjylland, 1984.

Thyssen, Anders Pontoppidan. *Vækkelsernes Frembrud i Danmark* [The outbreak of the revival movements in Denmark]. Vol. 7. Copenhagen: G. E. C. Gads Forlag, 1977.

Vogt, Peter. "'Honor to the Side': The Adoration of the Side Wound of Jesus in Eighteenth-Century Moravian Piety." *Journal of Moravian History,* no. 7 (2009): 83–106.

Vogt, Peter. "How Moravian Are the Moravians? The Paradox of Moravian Identity." *Journal of Moravian History* 18, no. 1 (2018): 77–101.

Archival Sources

"Et Aandeligt Speyl" [A spiritual mirror]. In *Thottske Samlinger 1591,4°.* Copenhagen, 1732. Royal Danish Library, Copenhagen.

"Kirkelige Stridigheder i København 1733–1735" [Conflicts of the church in Copenhagen, 1733–1735]. *Den Ledreborgske Håndskriftsamling,* fol. 398. Royal Danish Library, Copenhagen.

"Sagen mod Stiftsprovst Henrik Gerner" [The case against archdeacon Henrik Gerner]. *Den Ledreborgske Håndskriftsamling,* fol. 405. Royal Danish Library, Copenhagen.

Anonymous author, *Diarium des Ledigen Brüder Chors in Copenhagen von Anno 1746 den 9ten Julii bis 1762 den 19. April,* Unitätsarchiv, Moravian Archives Herrnhut (UA). R.19.E.9f.

Anonymous author, *Personkataloge aus Copenhagen 1742–69*, Unitätsarchiv, Moravian Archives Herrnhut (UA). R.27.329.1-28.

Anonymous author, *Zeist Synode, Sessio XII. Freitag 20 May 1746 Nachmittags 4 Uhr*, Unitätsarchiv, Moravian Archives Herrnhut (UA). R.2.A.19.1.

Michael Cröger, *Lebenslauf*, Unitätsarchiv, Moravian Archives Herrnhut (UA). R.22.20.80.

Chapter 3

"The First Sparks of Self-Knowledge"
Moravian Everyday Practices and the Shaping of
Emotional and Civic Selves

Tine Damsholt

This chapter analyzes how we may understand the entanglements of religious practices in Moravian Christiansfeld and the secular discourse of emotions in late eighteenth-century Denmark-Norway. This discourse involved the idea of making good patriots: a new form of a civic self, based on the citizen's individual, heartfelt, and inward urge to do right—in regard to the community or the fatherland. From the perspective of cultural history and with an ethnological attention to everyday life, I suggest that forms and practices of the self within everyday life in the community of the Moravian Brethren (and in similar movements) make up a central field in the development of new kinds of emotional and civic selves, such as self-knowledge, self-improvement, and self-awareness.

The primary object of the Pietist enlightenment was the reformation of the heart, establishing a reborn, sin-conscious, and self-correcting person. This also implied confidence in the abilities of individuals to improve themselves. Likewise, reforming the heart was central in political philosophy of the time, for example, in Jean-Jacques Rousseau's ideas of the heart as pivotal in a civic, interior, and moral topography. Such new forms of subjectivity where moral imperatives were heartfelt (e.g., inward urges or emotions) were presupposed or entangled with a new form of governing in the emerging democratic nation-states. As Michel Foucault argued, this government of the self operated through the "souls of the citizens," the everyday life and life-conduct of the ethically free subjects.[1] Thus, as a contribution to this volume's discussions of the role of the Moravian Brethren in the broader process of modernization, I argue the emotional practices of the self of Moravian Christiansfeld can be seen as one of the conditions for the development of such a new civic self, with inward urges to do right in the Danish and Norwegian context.

Further, I will argue that the "heart" became central in the emotional topography of where this self-shaping should take place. Taking examples from *Instructions for the Moravian Choir Helpers* (1785–86) and the memoirs of Norwegian author Camilla Collett on her stay in Christiansfeld, I will address questions as to how a distinctive and emotional self was shaped in everyday practices. The overall objective is to demonstrate that religious and political discourses were not separate spheres. Instead, they were deeply entangled in the development of a new form of emotional and civic selfhood within the late eighteenth century's cacophony of ideologies and discourses, when Moravians, Methodists, and other radical Pietists rubbed shoulders with political radicals and scientists and when the most intense religious ardor might coexist in an individual along with a democratic spirit and patriotic sentiments.[2]

The Patriotic and Civic Self of Late Eighteenth-Century Denmark-Norway

The Danish-Norwegian double monarchy of the eighteenth century was a "multicultural state" tied together in a dynasty personified and ruled by the king of Denmark and Norway, who was also duke of Schleswig and Holstein. Within this unitary state a new interpretation of absolutism gradually emerged in the late eighteenth century, where the state was construed as a social contract between the ruler and the people. In the specific Danish-Norwegian version of contract theory, the king was supposed to listen to the general will of the people, as it was articulated in public debate or opinion.[3] It is thus possible to argue that Danish-Norwegian absolutism in the late eighteenth century was interpreted within a "republican" framework, with the people as the true sovereign and their patriotism the pivotal issue. Patriotism implied a particular perception of the citizen, where the ethical imperative consisted of putting aside his or her own self interests in favor of the common good. This utopian citizen-subjectivity—in eighteenth-century parlance, "the love of the fatherland"—was supposed to elevate the individual above his or her specific interests. Thus, morality and responsibility were expressed as an emotion: the feeling of love (of the fatherland), which became the central virtue in the complex of political ideas.

This specific eighteenth-century patriotic concept of love of the fatherland differed from the later national-romantic concept. A central message in patriotic rhetoric was that all the nations living side by side in the Danish-Norwegian state could be good citizens of the same father-land. Patriotism was thus a feeling that, in principle, all citizens could share because their origin, language, and culture were expected to be secondary to their patriotism; their inner urge to do right for the common good should exceed partial interests. Political attention was directed toward ways of establishing the desired patriotic selfhood: a civic self, permeated with love of the fatherland.[4] In keeping with the European culture of sensibility, the emphasis was on emotions, feelings, and a sensible heart as the seat of a person's proper moral responsibility for society.[5]

In his *Du contrat social* (1762), Rousseau developed ideas on how indi-viduals may be transformed toward this utopian subjectivity, of civic selves. He argued that civic selfhood had to be supported by what he called a civil religion. Traditional religion was unfit; Christianity implied servitude and dependence, and Rousseau considered these implications too favorable for tyranny.[6] He developed these didactic reflections fur-ther, especially the necessity of the inscription of the constitution in the hearts of citizens.[7] In Rousseau's philosophy, the heart was the central location in the interior, moral topography of the self.[8] Rousseau found education and the setting of a good example to be more successful than prohibition, coercion, and punishment. Thus, civic subjectivity should become an inward urge rather than an outer claim or external demand, as the idea was to shape a civic self, not an obedient slave. To reach or touch the heart was considered the central means for engaging the emotional self in the transformation toward the utopian subjectivity of the civic self.

This causal relationship between emotion and civic virtue made up the philosophical backbone of the contemporary "cult of sensibility."[9] The core concept was sensibility, defined as "the capacity for extremely refined emotion and quickness to display compassion for suffering," which was supposed to be expressed in spontaneous acts such as weep-ing or fainting.[10] Being emotional was not the same as living in the grip of passions, or giving oneself to amusements and sexual excess. Reason had to be enlisted to assist the soul, so that passions were transformed into "emotions" under the control of reason.[11] The correct balance had to be found between sense and sensibility, to use the title of Jane Austen's famous novel. The more recent perception of reason and emotion as two opposing categories is thus a problematic approach to an understanding of the later part of the eighteenth century. The concept of sensibility encapsulated everything to be pursued: self-knowledge and self-mastery in the perfect and balanced emotional self.

The Heart in the Religious Topography

The idea of the heart as the topography for morality also informed the contemporary Pietist versions of Christianity. With its emphasis on a personal and emotional relationship to God, Pietism also encouraged a heartfelt emotional language. A pivotal motif in both Pietism and patriotic political discourses seems to be the issue of self-shaping and self-improvement through (the monitoring of) emotions. This generated new forms of everyday practices, which Foucault would later call "technologies of the self."[12]

Following Foucault's genealogy, practices such as self-examination and confession partly developed within early Christian monasticism, establishing technologies that gradually constituted the idea of an inner, true core entity: the self. Foucault conducted his genealogy of "technologies of the self" in relation to the history of sexuality. This may be the reason he explored, in particular, the technologies later to be reinserted in the field of psychoanalysis. However, in exploring this issue he overlooked the field of other "technologies of the self" obtained in later versions of Christianity. He thereby missed Pietism and its fellow versions as an obvious case for a genealogy of technologies of an emotional and civic self.[13]

Several scholars have proposed that Pietism be pivotal in understanding enlightenment and the rise of a public sphere.[14] Pietism and its spiritual father, P. J. Spener, called for a "reformation in the reformation" or an "inner reformation." Moral and religious reform demanded genuine repentance and conversion, not through mere outward consent to doctrinal principles but only through an inwardly cultivated faith. True Christians carried out their obligations voluntarily and with conviction. One of the key Pietist terms, "*innerlichkeit*," stressed this inwardness, and the Pietists' spontaneous, conversational religious meetings—the conventicles—also emphasized feeling and emotion over intellect.[15] The primary object of Pietist enlightenment was the reformation of the heart, in establishing a reborn, sin-conscious, and self-correcting person. The similarities between key Pietist concepts and the patriotic ideas mentioned earlier are therefore striking, as are the structural similarities between Pietism, the Enlightenment, and the new political utopia.

Pietism and its radical versions, such as Methodism and the Moravian Brethren, also established educational institutions and practices for the improvement of the individual.[16] Self-discipline, a sense of obligations, and industriousness were core values in these education programs, and the pupils were provided with tools for their own improvement. Pietism was optimistic about creating disciplined, Christian citizens through instruction and reading. As for enlightenment, one of the key concepts of Pietism is light. Besides the dimension of reason, light has another emotional dimension, which was the prerequisite for the rebirth of a new individual possessing a moral sentiment.[17]

Several scholars have suggested that in these religious developments of new forms of subjectivity one catches a glimpse of the modern self-assured, social, and agential individual. Among these, Phyllis Mack argues that many historians of the eighteenth century tend to have a secular bias and thus fail to see how religious people also possessed agency, even if it was of another kind than the liberal model of individual autonomy. Investigating early Methodists, she explores a more complex version of agency, which also involved subduing some of one's own impulses and desires. This eighteenth-century Pietist individual agency implied self-negation as well as self-expression.[18] Thus, according to Mack, eighteenth-century religious movements were not marginal to the main history of modernization. Instead, they were central in convincing ordinary people of their capacity for self-transformation and self-improvement. Furthermore, in the radical Pietist "religions of the heart," new forms of monitoring and shaping of selves pivoted on emotions, since emotional self-mastery was the main precondition for individual agency.

To master and understand one's own emotions induced a lifelong emotional labor of self-analysis undertaken to improve oneself. Also, new genres of what Foucault called "self-writing" were developed, such as memoirs that conveyed a sense of emotional drama through their narrative form.[19] In the remainder of the present study, we will investigate the Moravian Brethren in particular as a relevant field in the development of new technologies of self-improvement within everyday practice and education.

As several scholars have argued, Moravian memoirs constituted a pivotal practice in shaping new genres and ideas about Moravian and individual selfhood.[20] Individuals were shaped by emotional vocabulary, narratives, and discourse—by what could be said and what could not. Conversion was existential and emotional rather than rational; it was bodily and often involved the shedding of many tears. Reading Zinzendorf was supposed to "melt the hard heart" and turn the "eyes into fountains of tears."[21] The outburst of tears marked the new beginning, the birth of a new self. Like Methodists, Moravians were participants in the cultural discourse of sensibility that preoccupied so many of their contemporaries and was practiced in the reading of epistolary novels.[22] The epistolary novel contained narratives about the emotional self, which was staged as a subject for intertwined emotion and morality.

The Moravian conversion narrative did not limit itself to contemplative introspection; it needed the description of everyday matters in order to prove God's presence in one's own life.[23] Thus, the Moravian self, configured in the memoirs, was not the autonomous self of the bourgeois nineteenth-century male autobiographies. The Moravian self was connected to the notion of the "related life" — related to their fellow travelers, their choir, and most of all to God.[24] This is remarkably parallel to the patriotic ideal of the civic self: not a self-absorbed human but a citizen engaged in the constant endeavor of improving oneself for the sake of the common good and one's fellow citizens.

Speaking the Heart

In Moravian communities, members were divided into social groups called choirs, which were distinguished according to age, gender, and family status. The groups lived together in their respective houses.[25] To ensure that the choir helpers took care of the *Seelenarbeit*—that is, the emotional work of the Brothers and Sisters in the proper way—instructions for each of the choirs were written so as to be distributed to the Moravian settlements all over the world, including Christiansfeld. These instructions were neither publicly known nor set rules but guidelines for understanding the workings of Christ in everyday life.[26] The instructions included advice on how to guide choir members in the most intimate of corporal concerns, such as pubescent girls' growth of pubic hair and breasts and the beginning of menstruation.[27] As Katherine Faull has argued, the tone pervading the instructions is one of love and compassion rather than stern supervision and punishment. Thus, the instructions were matters of care. In the manuals for how to guide men and women in their spiritual and physical growth, a central role was held by the *Sprechen*, or "speakings": at regular intervals each member was obliged to take part in an intimate one-on-one conversation with his or her choir helper about his or her inner development. The speakings involved introspection and articulation of the self, both of which have been argued to be crucial in the process of shaping the self.[28]

As such, the form of power to be practiced in the everyday was similar to the "pastoral power" or form of government that Foucault described in his later publications.[29] Pastoral power relies on the pastor's close attention to every single member of the flock and on the knowledge of "the inside of people's minds" and the revelation of their innermost secrets in order to guide and save them. Thus, "pastoral power" is linked with a production of truth—the truth of the individual.[30] The choir helpers should seek out the Sisters or Brothers in a friendly manner, as the "thorough acquaintance of the heart with her Sisters always remains her chief aim."[31] The monthly speakings can be seen as a pivotal practice not only in the exercise of pastoral power but also in shaping new conceptions of the self, as the speakings involved the introspection that would enable the choir member to speak frankly and openly about the concerns of his or her soul or heart.

We can investigate how the figure of the heart was a pivot in the emotional topography of the self that was enacted in the everyday practices of the choir houses through the *Instructions for the Choir Helpers of the Single Sisters*.[32] The most important task for the choir helper, this manual emphasized, was to "become as closely and thoroughly acquainted as possible with each of her Sisters, according to the conditions of their hearts."[33] Thus, the heart was the primary object of pastoral care. Furthermore, the heart is a recurrent figure in the detailed instructions, as illustrated in the following examples:

> "She will take into special considerations how things stand with the sister's *heart* [emphasis added], because if something is lacking here, then gifts and skills will not be sufficient."[34]

> "She may carry this matter around with her for a while, weeping in secret, until she trusts herself to speak to her choir helper about it, then dares finally to *pour out her heart* [emphasis added], perhaps with a few words but a flood of tears."[35]

These quotes are just a few of the numerous examples where the heart signifies the intertwined emotional and religious state of the choir members. Thus, a clearly emotional or affective topography of the choir was drawn up that the choir helpers had to navigate and within which the Single Sisters had to shape themselves. The heart not only was the central place in the inner topography but also seemed to be something filled and often bursting with tears.

Pouring out one's heart was not so much a vocal as a bodily practice, as it involved a "flood of tears." Thus, this religious figure of the heart was in keeping with the broader culture of sensibility, where art as the central medium often depicted people in terms of emotional affect. Novels on the hardships of heroes and heroines, and especially the detailed description of the emotional expressions they provoked, served as instructions for how to behave and express one's feelings. In these textualizations of emotions, tears were essential and were therefore described in detailed terminology: from sniffs to floods of tears.[36] In novels, the sharing of tears was often the culmination, the peak event, after which moral improvement through sensibility was bound to occur. The shared flood of tears seems to find a strong parallel in the Moravian emotional guidelines. Furthermore, the instructions for the Single Sisters' choir also entailed gendered ideas of the self: "The souls of sisters are of such a nature that they can easily be moved. A touching discourse or beautiful expression in a verse can make so deep an impression on their spirit that they are carried away by it and can imagine they have now discovered the foundation on which their heart can take repose, but in the end it is only a fleeting stirring of the spirit."[37]

The particular emotional nature of young girls as "easily moved" echoes the broader culture of sensibility and its gendered emotional topography, which involved a specific reading of the female body and its capacity for emotions.[38] Since the female body was considered more delicate than the male body, women's nerves were considered highly irritable and their emotions feeble and unstable. In turn, because of these frail and delicate nerves, women were thought to be more easily moved and less capable of enduring strong and deep emotions.[39] In the nineteenth century, emotions gradually became an exclusively female attribute, which again made the gendered and emotionalized body into a social destiny for women, eventually excluding them from public arenas, political as well as religious.[40]

The balanced ideal for the civic self, to be in command of excessively strong emotions through the gradual learning of self-mastery, was also found in the choir instructions, as the choir helpers were instructed to provide guidance to the young girls led astray by their "fleeting stirrings." They should not "destroy" the feelings the young girls had experienced, nor "talk them out of it," but instead were to lead the emotions in the right direction.[41] A firm foundation or repose for the heart was to be found only in Christ, which was achieved by learning to distinguish between fleeting emotions and a firm foundation. The earlier heightened sensibility and so-called blood and wound theology of the Moravians in the mid-eighteenth century had now been rejected.[42]

The ideal at the turn of the century seemed to be an emotionally balanced self, in keeping with developments within the culture of sensibility. This emotionally balanced selfhood appeared to be relying on self-knowledge. Persons "who proceed in indifference and lack of self-knowledge" should be met with sympathy rather than reproach, as the latter "could lead to a hardened and resentful heart" unapproachable for guidance or salvation.[43] The heart could also accommodate inappropriate feelings such as self-interest or self-love. Sisters with such a disposition should not be given too much attention; "she must not only reflect on those of sensitive and tender dispositions who have a self-loving nature and enjoy being cared for but rather those … who are gladly consumed by love for others."[44] The ideal was an individual absorbed in the love and care for others—in compassion—and not those too sensitive and tender who enjoyed being cared for, as they were characterized as having a "self-loving nature." The ideal emotional self should not be self-absorbed but first and foremost directed toward others, as the sense of compassion was regarded as the fundamental element in an individual's self-improvement. The speakings were considered important means for helping a Sister who became alarmed, distressed or lost, as a talk in "a straightforward manner" could help her "out of dangerous ignorance."[45] However, for the speakings to have an effect, "self-knowledge" was essential, because it was a prerequisite for self-transformation as well as the ongoing "work of the heart"—which also, in the Moravian Church, appeared to be permeating everyday practices.

Everyday Practices

This ongoing "emotional work"[46] also surfaced as a collective enterprise, as the instructions mention the "heart of the choir" several times. The (collective) heart of the choir may be interpreted as a figure for the shared mood in the Sisters' House.[47] The pursuit of shepherding the association of hearts "onto the right path" appears in several of the guidelines.[48] The collective mood of hearts seems to be comparable to a "flock" to be guided to the best pastures or places by its "shepherd": "Most important, the hearts of the choir live daily in the pastures of the gospel."[49] The right mood for the choir heart was to be an evangelic one of love and compassion, and the choir helper was—in keeping with the Foucauldian concept of pastoral power—to guide them in the right direction on the basis of her knowledge of each individual and the choir house as an entity. In the everyday life of the choir house, it was crucial to guide the individual as well as the collective heart in the right direction in order to create the appropriate and balanced mood:

> §44. There are many things that give a choir helper and her assistants enough to think about daily and weep over, and to pray about to the Savior, asking for His assistance in their inadequacy and for the guidance of his good spirit. They are concerned that: daily life in the choir be pleasing, blessed and cheerful, yet sedate and grounded; love and sincerity prevail in all the rooms; everything appears as simple and straightforward as it is, removed from all pretense and hypocrisy; nothing yield to idiosyncrasies such as willfullness, egotism, self-ishness, nor to unnecessary comforts from outside; further, no spirit of ridicule or condemnation, no slander or such things be tolerated, nor unfortunate reasoning that does not lead to improvement.[50]

In these guidelines, the balanced ideal is explicit: daily life must be blessed and cheerful, yet sedate and grounded. It must be simple and without unnecessary comforts. The right and shared mood was permeated with love, sincerity, and straightforwardness. But just as important was to avoid all that would undermine the right mood: pretense, hypocrisy, selfishness, willfulness, ridicule, or slander. Those individual moods appeared to destabilize the collective heart. Reasoning was delimited: only the reasoning that was necessary in terms of (self-)improvement was welcomed. Self-love and self-interest were the major weaknesses to be avoided by any individual.

The emotional work that each Sister had to undertake seemed to be twofold: to attune to the collective mood of her room (or the entire choir house); and to engage only in reflections that led her in the right direction of self-shaping. This self was shaped in everyday practices: the tacit and bodily practices as well as the self-articulating practices (e.g., speakings) comprised a balanced emotional self, inhabited by a pure heart devoid of self-interest. Only when the self was dwelling in a sincere heart devoid of self-interest would it stay open to grace and experience "the blessedness of a pure heart."[51]

Thus, the technologies of the self generated within the Moravian Brethren can be seen as entangled with the contemporary new form of patriotic and civic but gendered self, which was articulated in terms of relying on the citizen's individual, heartfelt, inward urges to do right by others and to avoid self-interest.

Emotional Work and Personal Truth

If the choir instructions give insights into the prescribed and ideal version of everyday life in the choir houses, how then was life among unmarried Sisters experienced by the Sisters themselves? Besides the *Lebensläufe*, a genre with only few everyday details, we do not have many "ego documents" from the young Sisters attending the institutions in Christiansfeld; thus, we lack descriptions of everyday life and moods from a young girl's perspective. A rare example is the memoirs from one of the first and leading female writers of novels in Scandinavia, Norwegian Camilla Collett (1813–1895), who lived at the boarding school in Christiansfeld between the ages of fourteen and sixteen. In her 1863 memoirs *I de lange nætter* (During the long nights), Collett gave a lively description of everyday life at the school.

The Christiansfeld school for boys was opened in 1775 and a month later a school for girls, which moved to a separate building in 1784.

During the heyday of the schools in Christiansfeld, in the 1790s, there were more than one hundred pupils from all over Scandinavia.[52] The schools became so popular among civil servants in the Danish and Norwegian state, among whom patriotic ideals of civic selves prevailed, that pupils from this background exceeded those with religious backgrounds in Moravian or even Pietist versions of Christianity. An ideal of "homeliness" was pursued in the girls' boarding school, where ten to twelve girls lived in "families" permanently supervised in their schoolwork, housework and few hours of leisure time.[53] In 1790, a *pro memoria* described in detail the guidelines that the house parents of the two schools had to follow. Although briefer, they follow the instructions for choir helpers in their core values. The emotional development of the heart—or *des Herzens Gang*—of the children had to be followed closely by and in confidential dialogue with the choir helpers. The ideal form of self—the *Bildung* or shaping of the young individual's mind, thoughts, and heart—implied "sincerity, nobleness, unaffectedness" whereas "the dark, hidden, blocked, [and] defiant" as well as the "naughty, resonating, [and] satiric" had to be suppressed.[54] Thus, the ideal self to be pursued in the schools was in keeping with the emotional-yet-balanced self, devoid of self-interest, which we have met in the choir instructions as well as in the patriotic discourse.

Collett was not unambiguously happy about her stay at Christiansfeld. She found the school unsuited to "accommodate every individuality of fate," and she found herself among those so ill suited.[55] Yet, Collett advised the reader against failing to appreciate an institution that held so much that was "good and honest" as its foundation, referring to the many others she had heard praising the quiet life in Christiansfeld as the happiest time of their lives. Nevertheless, to her it was "isolation and loneliness only in another more monastic form" than that to which she had become accustomed.[56]

The institution was full of "all these small daily duties, which in an institute stand on the minute," noting that in some weeks she had to get up at 5:15 a.m. to clean two rooms.[57] Collett rejected the idea of convent life as the purpose of the school. Instead, she argued, "one should gain knowledge of oneself, one's aptitudes and strengths."[58] However, this idea of self-knowledge as a precondition to improve oneself and the undertaking of the emotional labor it involved, emphasized by the fifty-year old Collett in her memoirs, was not far from the Moravian ideas of the self that we encountered above.[59]

Collett described her pre-school self as a "young shoot of a willow tree in the field" who was "natural" but lacked knowledge of the world and no self-understanding.[60] She felt ill fitted to live in a group of ten to twelve girls from different parts of Europe and its colonies, all of them more "self-assured and skilled" than her. Furthermore, she described herself as small, weak of health, and spoiled, and she found it difficult to subordinate herself to the school's "disciplined and constrained way of life, the bare modesty, the institutional food." The severe way of life, with its early rising, caused her pain and turned her into an object of teasing.[61] She ended up at the bottom of the pecking order of the group of girls, which she described as a "little republic" and "a state within the state" ruled through despotism by two girls from Copenhagen.[62] Luckily, after some time she became friends with a girl, Christiane, whom she described—in keeping with the ideal of a heroine from the sensibility literature—as too sensitive for the world:

> But her sensibility was too significant and would justly be a cause for anxious-ness in everyone who observed her. Our teacher, the wise Margrethe N., said from time to time—in the institute German was the everyday language—: My dear child, how will you fare with this? Save these big, hot tears, oh, you will need them later [*Mein Liebes Kind, wie wirst Du damit hinausreisen? Spare diese grossen, heissen Thränen, ach, wirst sie immerhein gebrauchen*]. An uncertainty in the homework, a hint of censure could make her suddenly change color; as could the suffering of a person, or a moving phrase in a book read aloud, a beautiful melody, the arrival of an acquaintance put her in a quivering yet silent emotion; she cried soundlessly, but never did I see bigger, heavier tears fall from a human eye, I say fall, pour out, as they never just ran smoothly.[63]

Even if the Moravian Brethren were, along with other heart religions, part of the contemporary discourses on feeling and sensibility,[64] they felt that young girls were too easily moved and that their emotions should be guarded carefully (see above). However, Collett saw feminine emo-tions as a kind of positive energy more than mere "irrational female sensibility."

In her descriptions of Christiane as being too sensitive, too inconsist-ent in her moods, too melancholic, too gay and ready to laughter, too beautiful, significantly empathetic, but first and foremost with a won-derful ability not just to cry but to pour her heart out, she depicted the girl as the perfect role model in a double sense—in terms of both reli-gion and gender. Christiane was described as the perfect emotional and religious subject of the Moravian institution, with her strong emotions and a blessed and pure heart, all of which was evidenced by her bodily practice involving silent floods of tears. She was "goodness in the shape of an angel," and never was she more moved and enlivened than by the Sunday services, which "in their noble simplicity could not be more beautiful and heartening than with the Moravians!"[65]

Furthermore, if Christiane looked you in the eye, it was like "looking into a heaven of love and tenderness."[66] But Christiane was also described as the perfect heroine of any sensibility novel of the period. In these novels, we find archetypes such as "virtue in distress" or "the man of feeling," who, because of their sensitivity, were seized by the wretchedness of the world while trying to do good, or even died.[67]

When Collett went home to Eidsvoll, Norway, she brought with her the acquaintance of a "species of perfect people" and "a treasure of bright impressions."[68] Even if Collett was skeptical toward the modest and restricted life in Christiansfeld, in retrospect she reflected positively on its influence. In her memoirs she acknowledged that it was through the support of her teachers there that she developed in herself a new strength and individuality.[69] She wrote, "Where did you strike like flint of steel the first sparks of self-knowledge from the young and un-awakened soul, and with austerity and tenderness guarded it towards self-humiliation, but also the melting, fortifying warmth of self-esteem ..."[70] Self-esteem and self-humiliation were to Collett two sides of the same coin: to master and understand oneself induced a lifelong emotional labor of self-analysis in order to improve oneself. Collett's statement certainly was in keeping with the understanding of self-mastery and self-shaping within "religions of the heart," which also involved subduing one's own impulses and being guided toward self-humiliation. The emotional and civic self that Collett enacted in her publications implied self-negation as well as self-expression. Self-knowledge was the precondition to emotional self-mastery and thus the self-transformation toward the ideal civic and balanced self. To Collett, as well as in "religions of the heart," emotions were the touchstone of individual truth.[71]

In the end, Collett acknowledged the importance of the "technologies of the self" that she had learned in Christiansfeld. Here she localized the first sparks of the lifelong emotional work involved in her self-shaping. Collett became the first realist Norwegian author with her 1855 novel *Amtmannens Døtre* (The district governor's daughters), in which the Moravian idea of personal and emotional truth is carefully thematized. The novel even carries the telling and Moravian-inspired subtitle "The Story of a Woman's Heart."[72]

Conclusion

One single Norwegian female's memoirs do not make for a broader formation of a new subjectivity across Danish and Norwegian societies.

However, we would underestimate the significance of the new emotional and balanced self that evolved in Moravian institutions and within the broader contemporary discourses on patriotism and sensibility if we viewed this self as solely a Moravian phenomenon. Instead, what I hope to have demonstrated are the entanglements of religious practices in Moravian Christiansfeld and the contemporary and secular discourse of emotions involving the making of patriotic civic selves in late eighteenth-century Denmark-Norway. Here emerged a new form of civic and emotionally balanced self—or at least the ideal of it.

This emotional and civic self was guided by the individual, heartfelt, inward urges to do right by others and to neglect or, even better, be devoid of self-love and self-interest. Furthermore, forms and practices of the self in everyday life among the Moravian Brethren pivoted on the development of new ways of shaping the self, such as self-knowledge, self-improvement, and self-awareness—what Foucault has coined "technologies of the self." These self-practices implied self-negation as well as self-expression in the pursuit of self-improvement. These practices of shaping the self pivoted on emotions, as emotional self-mastery based on self-knowledge and emotional truth was considered the main precondition for individual self-transformation. To master and understand one's own emotions induced a lifelong emotional project of self-analysis in order to improve oneself.

In everyday Moravian life, people worked hard to shape their own subjectivity through emotions. Moreover, on a societal level, religion contributed to convincing individuals of their capacity for self-transformation.[73] Owing to their popularity among Danish and Norwegian civil servants, the boarding schools in Christiansfeld had a societal impact well beyond the group of Moravian confessors.

The figure of the civic self, absorbed in doing good for the community rather than driven by self-interest, was also crucial in the ideas of *Folkehøjskole* (the Danish folk high school) and *friskoler* (private schools for "life" rather than exams) that N. F. S. Grundtvig proposed in the nineteenth century.[74] The implied confidence in the ability of individuals to improve themselves and the development of everyday practices to realize this potential can be regarded as decisive. As this confidence was neither solely religious nor stemming from political philosophy or sensibility literature alone, it demonstrates that religious, cultural, and political discourses were not separate spheres. Instead, they were deeply entangled in the development of a new form of emotional and civic selfhood within discourses of the late eighteenth century. It was a new form of selfhood that would come to permeate political and cultural discourses in the centuries to come.

Tine Damsholt is professor of European ethnology at the University of Copenhagen. She has written extensively on national and patriotic discourses in eighteenth- and nineteenth-century Denmark and political rituals in contemporary Western countries based on cultural history and ethnographic fieldwork. Subjectivity, materiality, temporality, emotions, body, and gender are recurrent themes in her research. She is currently investigating the transformed everyday life during the COVID-19 pandemic and how it affects the ways we understand and practice pasts, present, and futures in daily life.

Notes

1. Foucault, "Afterword"; Gordon, "Governmental Rationality"; Rose, *Governing the Soul*.
2. See Mack, *Heart Religion*, 6.
3. Norwegian historian Jens Arup Seip coined the term "opinion guided absolutism" to describe this idea. Seip, "Teorien."
4. Damsholt, *Fædrelandskærlighed*.
5. Schama, *Citizens*; Damsholt, "Staging Emotions."
6. Rousseau, *Social Contract*, 150.
7. See, for example, Rousseau, "Considerations," 165–66.
8. See Damsholt, "'Hand of King.'"
9. See Schama, *Citizens*.
10. Todd, *Sensibility*, 7.
11. Mai, "Efterskrift."
12. In his later courses of lectures, Foucault explored the genealogy of encounters between technologies for the domination of others and those of the self; see, for example, Foucault, "Technologies."
13. Faull has employed the Foucauldian genealogy on technologies of the self—and among them, parrhesia in particular—in analyzing Moravian everyday practices; see Faull, "Speaking and Truth-Telling." For notions of the self in Protestantism from a Foucauldian perspective, see, for example, McCutcheon, *Discipline of Religion*; Petterson, *Missionary*.
14. These include Fulbrook, *Piety and Politics*; Gawthorp, *Pietism*; Melton, "Pietism."
15. Melton, "Pietism," 314.
16. Melton, 314. Classifying the Moravian Brethren and other similar movements as "radical Pietism" may be debatable; however, in doing so I follow Mack, *Heart Religion*, and Faull, among others.
17. Horstbøll, "Læsning til salighed," 93.
18. Mack, *Heart Religion*, 8–9.
19. Mack, 24.
20. Faull, *Moravian Women's Memoirs*; Mai, "Potential"; Mettele, "Constructions." See also the introduction, chapter 8, and chapter 11 in this volume.
21. Mettele, "Constructions," 25.

22. Schama, *Citizens*; Todd, *Sensibility*.
23. Mettele, "Constructions," 29.
24. Faull, *Moravian Women's Memoirs*.
25. See also the introduction to this volume.
26. These instructions have recently been transcribed, translated to English, and analyzed in Faull, *Speaking to Body and Soul*.
27. Faull, "Girl Talk," 79.
28. Faull, 82–84; Faull, "Speaking and Truth-Telling," 157.
29. The use of the Foucauldian notion of pastoral care in analyzing Moravian speaking practices is more elaborated in Faull, "Speaking and Truth-Telling"; "Girl Talk."
30. Foucault, "Afterword," 214.
31. From §50. The translated version is in Faull, *Speaking to Body and Soul*, 58. All quotes are taken from this translation.
32. Faull, 23–58.
33. From §10, in Faull, 35.
34. From §6, Ibid., 33
35. From §26, Ibid., 45
36. Vincent-Buffault, *History of Tears*, 16–18.
37. From §11, in Faull, *Speaking to Body and Soul*, 36.
38. Barker-Benfield, *Culture of Sensibility*; Frevert, *Emotions in History*.
39. Frevert, *Emotions in History*, 105.
40. See Outram, *Body*. Mack argues this also to be the case for the female preachers and their role in Methodism; Mack, *Heart Religion*, 292–93, 298.
41. From §11, in Faull, *Speaking to Body and Soul*, 36.
42. Faull, *Girl Talk*, 88.
43. See §11, in Faull, *Speaking to Body and Soul*, 36.
44. From §37, in Faull, 51.
45. From §26, in Faull, 45.
46. See Mack, *Heart Religion*.
47. As Sara Ahmed has argued, moods are shared but involve what she coins "mood work" to get attuned. Ahmed, "Not in the Mood."
48. In example §39, in Faull, *Speaking to Body and Soul*, 51.
49. From §46, in Faull, 56.
50. From §44, in Faull, 54–55.
51. From §45, in Faull, 56.
52. Holdt, "Kostskolerne", 2. Holdt's account was based primarily on the school archives in Christiansfeld. For a discussion of Holdt's position in the historiography of Christiansfeld, see chapter 1 in this volume.
53. Holdt, "Kostskolerne," 17.
54. Holdt, 18–19. Original Danish: "et klart, oprigtigt, ædelt, uaffekteret Væsen ved Guds Naade maa indpodes i deres Hjerter, og det mørke, dulgte, indeklemte, trodsige, saa vel som det frække, raisonerende, satiriske maa holdes nede."
55. Collet, *I de lange nætter*, 301: "den magter ikke … at yde enhver Individualitet, enhver Skjæbne sin særskilte Forplejning."
56. Collet, 301: "For mig var det Afsondring, Ensomheden kun i en anden klosterligere Form end den, jeg havde været vant til."
57. Collet, 305: "alle disse daglige Smaapligter, der i et institut hænger i Minuttet."
58. Collett, 307: "Man skal lære at kjende sig selv og sine Anlæg og Krefter."
59. A letter from the young Collett written during her stay in Christiansfeld was recently found and published. In the short text in German, Collett is fairly optimistic; in spite of her weak health she is looking forward to her reunion with her family and fatherland: "Wenn Ich an das Wiedersehen meiner Eltern und meines Vaterland

denke, so vergeht mir Alles, Sorgen, Grillen, Krankheit." Cited in Moland, "Et brev," 328.

60. Collett, *I de lange nætter*, 301.
61. Collett, 302, 306: "Det regelmæssige og tvangfulde Liv, den nøgne Tarvelighed, Institutkosten vilde dertil lidet smage et Barn, der er opvokset i Frihed og en vis daglig Overflødighed." And: "at jeg ... havde ondt for at finde mig i Instituttets drøie Levemaade og tidlige Opstaaen, gav [hende især] Stof til Drillerier."
62. Collett, 302. It is noteworthy that Collett used political vocabulary to describe the distribution of power among the girls.
63. Collett, 304: "Men hendes Sensibilitet var for stor og maatte med Grund vække Ængstelse hos enhver, der iagttog hende. Vor Lærerinde, den kloge Margarethe N., sagde undertiden—i Instituttet taltes bestandig Tysk –: Mein Liebes Kind, wie wirst Du damit hinausreisen? Spare diese grossen, heissen Thränen, ach, wirst sie immerhein gebrauchen. En Uvisshed i Leksen, Skyggen af en Daddel, kunde bringe hende til voldsomt at skifte Farve; ligesaa kunde en andens Lidelse, et gribende Sted i en Bog, der forelæstes, en smuk Melodi, en Bekjendts pludselige Ankomst sætte hende i sitrende Bevægelse; dog var hun stille dermed, hun græd ikke hørlig, men aldrig har jeg set større, tungere Taarer falde fra menneskelige Øine, jeg siger falde, styrte; thi de gled aldrig."
64. Mack, *Heart Religion*, 5.
65. Collett, *I de lange nætter*, 304: "bevæget, oplivet af Gudstjenesten, der i sin ædle Simpelhed ikke kan være smukkere og mere opløftende end hos Herrnhuterne!"
66. Collett, 319, 304: "Godhed i en Engels Skikkelse" and "men fæstnede hun Blikket på En, da saa man ligesom ind i en Himmel af Kjærlighed og Blidhed."
67. Rousseau's *Julie ou la Nouvelle Héloïse* (1761) and Goethe's *Die Leiden des jungen Werthers* (1774) are classics in this genre. Collett mentioned that because of a lack of books to read, she told Christiane stories based on "more sentimental-romantic sources," implying she was familiar with this genre. Collett, *I de lange nætter*, 309. Also, the event of Christiane's death narratively was anticipated by Collett's remarks about her being too good and sensitive for this world—fully in keeping with the genre of sensibility.
68. Collett, *I de lange nætter*, 319: "i sin Art fuldkomne Mennesker" and "en Skat af lyse Indtryk."
69. Collett, 314.
70. Collett, 319: "Hvor har du som Flint af Staal slaaet den første Selverkendelsens Gnist af den unge uvakte Sjæl og med Strenghed og Ømhed fredet den til Selvydmygelsens, men ogsaa Selvfølelsens smeltende, styrkende Varme."
71. See Mack, *Heart Religion*, 15; Faull, *Speaking and Truth-Telling*, 161; Holdt, *Kostskolerne*, 30.
72. Mai, "Heart-Stories," 22–23.
73. See Mack, *Heart Religion*, 28.
74. See Damsholt, "'Hand of King'"; Korsgaard, "Grundtvig's Idea." Holdt also argued this Moravian legacy in the Grundtvigian school tradition; see Holdt, *Kostskolerne*, 26.

Bibliography

Ahmed, Sara. "Not in the Mood." *New Formations*, no. 82 (2014): 13–28.

Collett, Camilla. *Amtsmannens døtre og I de lange nætter* [The district governor's daughters and during the long nights]. Oslo: Gyldendal Norsk Forlag, 1974.

Barker-Benfield, G. J. *The Culture of Sensibility: Sex and Society in Eighteenth-Century Britain.* Chicago: University of Chicago Press, 1992.

Damsholt, Tine. *Fædrelandskærlighed og borgerdyd* [Love of the fatherland and civic virtue]. Copenhagen: Museum Tusculanum Press, 2000.

Damsholt, Tine. "'Hand of King and Voice of People': On Grundtvig's Ideas of Democracy and the Responsibility of the Self." In *Building the Nation: Grundtvig and Danish National Identity*, edited by J. Hall, O. Korsgaard, and O. K. Petersen, 151–68. Montreal and Kingston: McGill-Queen's University Press, 2015.

Damsholt, Tine. "Staging Emotions: On Configurations of Emotional Selfhood, Gendered Bodies, and Politics in Late Eighteenth Century." In *Structures of Feeling: Affectivity and the Study of Culture*, edited by Devika Sharma and Frederik Tygstrup, 98–115. Berlin: De Gruyters, 2015.

Faull, Katherine M. "Girl Talk: The Role of the 'Speakings' in the Pastoral Care of the Older Girls' Choir." *Journal of Moravian History*, no. 6 (2009): 77–99.

Faull, Katherine M. *Moravian Women's Memoirs: Their Related Lives, 1750–1820.* Syracuse, NY: Syracuse University Press, 1997.

Faull, Katherine M., "Speaking and Truth-Telling: *Parrhesia* in the Eighteenth-Century Moravian Church." In *Self, Community, World: Moravian Education in a Transatlantic World*, edited by Heikki Lempa and Paul Peucker, 147–67. Bethlehem, PA: Lehigh University Press, 2010.

Faull, Katherine M., ed. *Speaking to Body and Soul: Instructions for the Choir Helpers of the Single Sisters Choir (1785–86).* Penn State University Press, 2017.

Foucault, Michel. "Afterword: The Subject and Power." In *Michel Foucault: Beyond Structuralism and Hermeneutics,* 2nd edn., edited by Hubert L. Dreyfus and Paul Rabinow, 208–26. Chicago: University of Chicago Press, 1983.

Foucault, Michel. "Technologies of the Self." In *Ethics. Subjectivities and Truth: Essential Works of Foucault, 1954–1984.* Vol. 1. Edited by Paul Rabinow, 223–51. London: Penguin Books, 2000.

Frevert, Ute. *Emotions in History: Lost and Found.* Budapest: Central European University Press, 2011.

Fulbrook, Mary. *Piety and Politics: Religion and the Rise of Absolutism in England, Württemberg and Prussia.* Cambridge: Cambridge University Press, 1983.

Gawthorp, Richard. *Pietism and the Making of Eighteenth Century Prussia.* Cambridge: Cambridge University Press, 1993.

Gordon, Collin. "Governmental Rationality: An Introduction." In *The Foucault Effect: Studies in Governmentality*, edited by Graham Burchell, Colin Gordon, and Peter Miller, 1–52. Chicago: University of Chicago Press, 1991.

Holdt, Jens. "Kostskolerne i Christiansfeld" [The boarding schools in Christiansfeld]. *Sønderjydske Aarbøger* (1943): 1–48.

Horstbøll, Henrik. "Læsning til salighed, oplysning og velfærd. Om Pontoppidan, pietisme og lærebøger i Danmark og Norge i 17- og 1800-tallet" [Reading for salvation: On Pontoppidan, Pietism, and catechisms in seventeenth- and eighteenth-century Denmark and Norway]. *Fortid og Nutid* (June 2003): 83–108.

Korsgaard, Ove. "Grundtvig's Idea of a People's High School and Its Historical Influence." In *Building the Nation: Grundtvig and Danish National Identity*, edited by J. Hall, O. Korsgaard, and O. K. Petersen, 315–30. Montreal and Kingston: McGill-Queen's University Press, 2015.

Mack, Phyllis. *Heart Religion in the British Enlightenment: Gender and Emotion in Early Methodism*. New York: Cambridge University Press, 2008.

Mai, Anne-Marie. "Efterskrift" [Afterword]. In *Moralske fortællinger 1761–1805* [Moral tales, 1761–1805], 231–57. Copenhagen: Det danske Sprog- og Litteraturselskab, 1994.

Mai, Anne-Marie Mai. "Heart-Stories: Christiansfeld—an International German-Danish City of the Eighteenth Century." In *German-Danish Cultural Relations in the Eighteenth Century*, edited by Søren Peter Hansen and Stefanie Stockhorst, 11–24. Gottingen: Vandenhoeck and Ruprecht, 2018.

Mai, Anne-Marie Mai. "The Potential of the Eighteenth Century in Terms of Literary History." In *Nordic Light*, edited by Thomas Bredsdorff, Søren Peter Hansen, and Anne-Marie Mai, 65–78. University of Southern Denmark Studies in Scandinavian Languages and Literatures, vol. 81. Odense: University Press of Southern Denmark, 2007.

McCutcheon, Russell T. *The Discipline of Religion: Structure, Meaning, Rhetoric*. London: Taylor and Francis, 2003.

Melton, James Van Horn. "Pietism, Politics and the Public Sphere in Germany." In *Religion and Politics in Enlightenment Europe*, edited by James E. Bradley and Dale K. Van Kley, 294–333. Notre Dame, IN: University of Notre Dame Press, 2001.

Mettele, Gisela. "Constructions of the Religious Self: Moravian Conversion and Transatlantic Communication." *Journal of Moravian History*, no. 2 (2007): 7–35.

Moland, Torjus. "Et Brev fra den unge Camilla Wergeland" [A letter from the young Camilla Wergeland]. *Edda* 4, vol. 115 (2015): 326–33.

Outram, Dorinda. *The Body and the French Revolution: Sex, Class and Political Culture*. New Haven: Yale University Press, 1989.

Petterson, Christina. *The Missionary, the Catechist and the Hunter: Foucault, Protestantism and Colonialism*. Leiden: Brill, 2014.

Rose, Nicolas. *Governing the Soul: The Shaping of the Private Self*. London: Routledge, 1999.

Rousseau, Jean-Jacques, "Considerations on the Government of Poland." In *Rousseau on International Relations*, edited by Stanley Hoffmann and David P. Fidler, 162–96. Oxford: Oxford University Press, 1991.

Rousseau, Jean-Jacques, *The Social Contract and Other Later Political Writings*. Edited by Victor Gourevitch. Cambridge: Cambridge University Press, 1997.

Schama, Simon. *Citizens: A Chronicle of the French Revolution*. London: Penguin Books, 1989.

Seip, J. A. "Teorien om det opinionsstyrte enevælde" [The theory of opinion-guided absolutism]. *Norsk historisk Tidsskrift* 38 (1958): 397–463.

Todd, Janet, *Sensibility: An Introduction*. London: Methuen, 1986.

Vincent-Buffault, Anne. *The History of Tears: Sensibility and Sentimentality in France*. London: Macmillan, 1999.

Chapter 4

An Extended Weekend Excursion to Christiansfeld in 1796

Musical Practice and Aesthetics in a Late Eighteenth-Century Moravian Community

Peter Hauge

In late August 1796, Anna Sybille Reventlow, her husband Count Johan Ludvig, her sister Charlotte Schimmelmann, and head teacher J. F. Oest decided to go on an extended weekend visit to a small, newly built village bordering the Kingdom of Denmark-Norway in the northern part of the Duchy of Schleswig.[1] They had heard that it was worth visiting and wished to see with their own eyes a differently structured community with distinct aesthetic values. Setting out from their country estate, Brahetrolleborg, on the island of Funen, around five o'clock on a Friday morning, they left with "two decent horses harnessed to the carriage."[2] On the way they all joined Anna Sybille's and Charlotte's brother for breakfast before taking the boat across the narrow strait at Assens.[3] The party arrived at the village only five hours later and immediately began sightseeing; like all the other tourists, they called on attractions such as the church, the houses, and later a distillery and the striking cemetery. The only thing that disappointed Anna Sybille was that they could not go on a spending spree: the shops had already been emptied by the large number of guests flocking to the village that summer. It was especially during the summers—but also on other occasions, such as at Easter and Whitsuntide—that the village's population nearly doubled. The vast hordes of all kinds of tourists, including farmers as well as scholars and opinion leaders, started to create problems, and the following year the village decided to employ three guides to show tourists around in groups on Sundays.[4] In that way they could more easily manage the inquisitive guests gawping at the villagers, wishing to enter the private houses, watching the daily goings-on of the villagers, or even joining funeral services and processions although they were not acquainted with the deceased. Like the other visitors, the Reventlows were truly fascinated by the community's accomplishments, particularly the aesthetics in terms of their simplicity, purity, fervor, and harmony (in the overall sense of the word), as seen in the town planning, the architecture, the education of boys and girls, and not least the talent for trade, industry, and craft so evident in the village. Three days later, following the group's return to their estate on Funen, Anna Sybille wrote a lengthy letter in rather un-idiomatic French to her sister-in-law Louise Stolberg, telling her about the stimulating experience.[5] The charming village they had visited over that extended weekend was, of course, Christiansfeld.

Reading her letter, it is evident that Anna Sybille was not only impressed by the above-mentioned accomplishments of Christiansfeld. Throughout the document she portrays other important aspects of the closely knit community—aspects that were fundamental to the Moravian understanding of life as a liturgy and that played an enormous role in the residents' daily routines but that today tend to be overlooked in modern studies on the history of Christiansfeld. Music was indeed a fundamental part of communal life—as an all-important aspect of education and meditation—and was thus an integral part of Moravian aesthetic ideals. In the way that the town planning reflects simplicity and proportionality so does the music, even down to the minutest details. Anna Sybille's letter is especially permeated by the cultural qualities of music in everyday life, which the group observed on their tour around the village. That she bothers to mention Moravian music practices in Christiansfeld at all implies, first of all, that for outsiders the practices were distinct and stood out as something different from what they encountered in Danish society in general, including in the capital city; simply stated, the music practices of Christiansfeld were worth describing. Second, though her descriptions today may on the surface seem somewhat straightforward and unemotional, they are to the point and, most importantly, support other contemporary accounts both within and outside the Moravian community. Anna Sybille's narrative must be seen in a late eighteenth-century context. In particular, being an able keyboard player herself, she was interested in and knew intimately about cultural practices of music in society at large.[6]

The approach to life as well as the aesthetic values of the Christiansfeld community had wide-reaching consequences for their promotion of music. By employing Anna Sybille's description of the outing to Christiansfeld in 1796 as the red thread, the present chapter takes a closer look at the music in terms of the aesthetic discussions taking place at that time in Danish society in relation to hymn singing, music as a cultural practice within and outside the Moravian Church as represented through the music archives of Christiansfeld, and not least the daily routines and musical education of the community. The chapter will not deal specifically with the close relationship between music practices and theology, since numerous modern studies have already addressed this subject. In addition, both the music practices and the music repertoire were largely the same in all Moravian communities. The Moravian Church intentionally sought to ensure a common musical identity across all its communities, and the music collection of Christiansfeld reveals indeed that its practices are no different from those of other Moravian settlements.[7] The tight connection between theology and the music practices and repertoire in other Moravian communities are also evident in Christiansfeld.

Performing Hymns

The late eighteenth-century fascination with the Moravian village is evident in *Den danske Atlas*, a comprehensive description of the whole country (that is, comprising Denmark and the Duchy of Schleswig) begun in 1763 by the famous bishop, historian, and antiquarian Erik Pontoppidan. The seventh and final volume, which appeared in 1781, includes a description of Christiansfeld and a plate showing the outline of the village (see Figure 4.1).[8] Though the main emphasis is indeed on the Moravians' talent for trade and agriculture, the author mentions that each evening the congregation assembles to listen to readings from the Bible and to sing hymns accompanied by the organ, which for visitors in particular "is very engaging and touching."[9] Though the phrase is brief, it is nevertheless of great significance, for why does the author need to mention the community's chanting unless it was a remarkable feature of the Moravian settlement? The hymn singing of small communities in other parts of the country is mentioned nowhere else in the voluminous work at all, thus implying a distinction in quality to that which apparently was experienced in general in the Danish Lutheran Church.

Before Christiansfeld was founded in 1773, the Moravians — and how they used the chanting of hymns to attract new members to the community — were greatly mistrusted. The young priest Peder Olrog argues in his *Afhandling om Psalmernes Fornødenhed* of 1768 that it is well known that the singing of hymns leads directly into the hearts "and causes feelings in the heart which cannot be emphasized enough. The heart trembles with pious delight."[10] At the same time, he remarks that it may be misused and thus create more damage than benefit: "The heretics' abuse of singing has always made it necessary for those who have

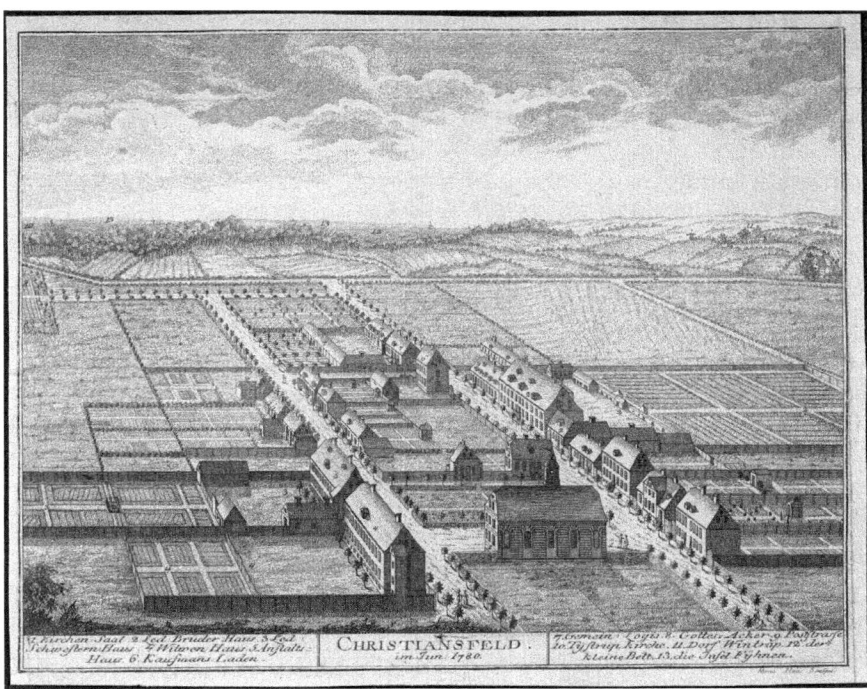

Figure 4.1. Christiansfeld as of June 1780. In the far background, it is possible to see the strait between Funen and Jutland. Source: Erik Pontoppidan and Hans de Hofman, *Den danske Atlas* (Copenhagen, 1763–83), vol. 7/1, foldout between pp. 208 and 209, Müllers Pinakotek 20, 25, III b, 40, Royal Library, Copenhagen.

a pure doctrine. It is not only in our time that harmful opinions, such as those of the Herrnhuters, are disseminated by hymns.... [T]his cunning, however, is ancient."[11]

When visitors began traveling to Christiansfeld and were allured by the community's beautiful, clean, and striking chanting, the fascination grew to such an extent that it led to serious discussions among intellectuals in Copenhagen regarding how to improve the singing of the congregations in the established Lutheran churches. An 1783 issue of the journal *Nyeste kiøbenhavnske Efterretninger om lærde Sager* includes a review of a collection of three new music publications by the court musician Niels Schiørring: a set of chorales; a collection of four-part chorales for voices, cornetts, and trombones; and a book of hymns or songs.[12] It is the second item that leads the reviewer to comment on Christiansfeld, hoping that Schiørring's publication "will be able to achieve its purpose, and with this work provide us with proper and edifying singing in the church instead of the inappropriate and disharmonic shrieking in which even those who are not lovers or connoisseurs of music will not find pleasure or edification."[13] The anonymous reviewer continues, explaining that the Latin-school boys in the provincial towns who serve the worship services in the Lutheran churches apparently believe that the loudest screamer is also the best singer. It is even worse in the small village churches and thus "in this way the wrong taste is bred from one generation to the next." Some might argue that the low quality of chanting is due to the large and inhomogeneous congregations, but, as the reviewer remarks,

> those, who have heard the congregation in Christiansfeld know from their own experience that it is possible to get three to four hundred people to sing properly when they are accustomed to it; and why not more? Their singing is slow and solemn, subdued and humble, harmonious and touching, everything that praying and praising singing should be. The reviewer hopes that no one is so intolerant that he should be offended by the example.[14]

Things had indeed changed since Olrog's remarks fifteen years earlier. It was not only theologians who noticed the great difference between the musical abilities of the Christiansfeld congregation and those of the Lutheran churches in general. When attending an evening service, Anna Sybille observes, among other things, that the congregation's "singing, their choir is of enchanting beauty and harmony; no one dares to join in singing who does not sing well."[15]

It might seem surprising that the congregation in Christiansfeld was able to maintain such a high standard in communal singing while congregations of the Lutheran denomination clearly struggled to produce a pleasant sound. It was the regular, daily practice in Christiansfeld that was the most important method for maintaining and nursing the musical sound of the whole congregation. That the Moravians continuously sought to heighten and maintain its quality is clearly emphasized as late as 1811 by Moravian musician and composer Christian Ignatius LaTrobe. In his published collection of anthems, which also includes a detailed introduction, he provides an insight into the musical practices that must also have been employed in Christiansfeld. LaTrobe argues that the Moravians seek to make the singing of hymns "uniform" and harmonious

> by encouraging all to join, but checking any disposition to vociferation in individuals, and have thereby, in some of their settlements, acquired a degree of perfection in congregational singing, which is not attainable where there is no attention to general effect, but where everyone is left to suit the strength of his voice, however grating, to the ardour of his feelings, or the vanity of his mind.[16]

Daily practice was important for another reason, too: the number of hymns performed in the Moravian congregations was overwhelming. The most authoritative and organized hymnal of the late eighteenth century, which remained in use in Christiansfeld well into the following century, was Christian Gregor's *Gesangbuch zum Gebrauch der evangelischen Brüder-Gemeine* (1778), with more than 1,700 hymns. The standard *Choralbuch* (also by Gregor), which includes more than 500 tunes, appeared in 1784.[17] It was therefore of paramount importance that members of the congregation attended the daily gatherings to sing, rehearse, and learn by heart those tunes that were part of their repertoire. It seems implausible that the congregation utilized the entire repertoire of hymns and tunes; nevertheless, the number of Moravian hymns available was amazing in comparison with that of the Danish Lutheran Church: Hans Thomissøn's hymnal (1569, used until 1699) includes 268; Pontoppidan's hymnal (1740) contains 76; Breitendich's book of chorales (1764) includes 191; and Schiørring's two books of chorales (1781 and 1783) have 103 in all.[18]

A third reason for rehearsing every day was that the performance practice was quite out of the ordinary. The liturgist did not plan in advance which hymns were to be sung, and thus the congregation had to be able to grasp the liturgist's intentions at a moment's notice. Count Zinzendorf explains, in the first hymnal appearing in 1734,

> One does not sing entire hymns of ten or twenty stanzas, but half and whole stanzas from as many songs as the context of the matter requires. Most members of the congregation are accustomed to this because, for the sake of simpler use, one sings on and on without the [hymn] number, singing such a "Liederpredigt" immediately and without a book. Thus, the hymns are changed in countless ways, depending on the nature of the circumstances.[19]

This practice of memorizing a large number of hymns (both text and music) did create some difficulties for congregations, leading to different recommendations as to how to select them beforehand instead of entirely at random.[20] Nevertheless, the overall idea described by Zinzendorf seems to have been followed in Christiansfeld even as late as at the end of the eighteenth century. This practice, too, is mentioned in Anna Sybille's letter. She recounts that when they attended the evening service, a *Singstunde*, "the liturgist read part of the letter to the Romans with a couple of explanations here and there; a few stanzas were sung. The liturgist arranges it as he wishes and creates interest by varying it a great deal."[21]

Educational Approaches

Anna Sybille and Johan Ludvig Reventlow were keen promoters of the school reforms as well as tenacious advocates for the abolition of the adscription laws, for agricultural reforms, and for the founding of industrial enterprises. Education had become a topic of major interest among intellectuals. It was around the time when Christiansfeld received its concession in 1772 that Johan Bernhard Basedow, once a renowned and rather provocative professor at Sorø Academy, published his book on education, *Elementarwerk* (1770–74). He was particularly inspired by Jean-Jacques Rousseau's *Emile* (1762). The restructuring of the educational system was therefore front of mind for many Danish reformers, which of course drew attention to the educational ideas practised in Christiansfeld and most likely the reason for the Reventlows' visit—and for their inviting the head teacher J. F. Oest to join the outing. Anna Sybille explains that they called on the two boarding schools, one for boys and another for girls, which comprised more than 120 pupils in all, from Norway, Sweden, and the "Indies," for example.[22] The schools in Christiansfeld not only provided music lessons for the boys; also, the girls received tuition, which was not customary in the schools associated with the many churches of Copenhagen.[23] Thus, when goldsmith and organist Friedrich Türstig settled down in Christiansfeld in 1778, his obligation—besides taking care of the instruments in the congregation hall and making sure that the singers rehearsed their parts in the cantatas—was to teach six to eight boys to play the violin and *Klavier* (organ, clavichord or harpsichord—an instrument with a keyboard). Later, when Türstig married Anna Kristiana Kastrup, her duty was to teach the girls music at the boarding school.[24] A couple of years prior to their visit to Christiansfeld, the Reventlows had already established a teacher's college, Bernstorfsminde, where Oest was employed. Finally, the year after their visit to the community and the boarding schools, they established one at their estate, a so-called Philanthropinum, which was inspired by Basedow's school in Dessau.[25]

The Moravian schools were based on Johann Amos Comenius's seventeenth-century pedagogical ideas. All children irrespective of gender, class, or ability should attend general schools to develop their skills as human beings, including languages, morals, and reflection; in addition, Comenius promoted that visual aids should be employed in teaching and that rules should be induced from examples and not the other way around.[26] It therefore seems quite natural that the Reventlows would visit the model village in the northern part of Schleswig to see with their own eyes how education and music were integrated in the small community as a natural part of everyday life. Slowly, reformers inspired by the ideas of the Enlightenment were convinced that it was possible to learn from the Moravians' regarding economic prosperity and production, as well as education, and to witness how well integrated music was—both in church and as an edifying recreational pursuit. Johann Abraham Peter Schulz, who had been employed as Court Kapellmeister in Copenhagen since 1787, also participated in the debates over how to raise the standard of singing in the Danish Lutheran Church. He explains that, especially among the rural population, knowledge of music was basically non-existent, and he characterizes their ordinary chanting as a "brutish scream with no intonation and harmony."[27] Schulz then suggests a way of educating the population in music and argues that the point of departure must be the schools and therefore also the teaching colleges that educate the future generation of music teachers. The students at the colleges should both be able to sing and know the basic elements of playing instruments, though the purpose was to foster not musical virtuosos but rather able and inspiring teachers.[28] LaTrobe argues that even using but a small part of their spare time, youngsters will be able to learn to play an instrument—a recreation that is preferred to that of "idle conversation":

> Under proper tuition, a moderate but sufficient degree of skill in the use of instruments may be more easily acquired than is generally imagined; nor need a young man misspend any of that time upon it, which ought to be devoted to those studies or pursuits, which are to occupy his future life. More or less, leisure will always be left for recreation, a small portion of which is sufficient for the purpose; and if his genius leads him to the acquirement of any useful art, that leisure will be more suitably employed in such a pursuit, than in sauntering, and idle conversation. By the latter, it becomes a source of mischief; but by the former, a real and rational recreation, both to mind and body.[29]

It seems highly likely that Schulz was inspired by the practices of the Moravian communities—certainly their views are similar. Schulz was clearly a popular composer among the many Moravian communities, as an overwhelming number of his musical works have survived in their archives (e.g., Herrnhut). Even Christiansfeld owns, for instance, a late eighteenth-century transcription of Schulz's incidental music to *Athalia*, a work that was performed at Charlotte Schimmelmann's residence in Copenhagen in 1787 before it was staged at the Royal Theatre two years later.[30]

In 1794 the journal *Maanedsskriftet Iris*, edited by Simon Poulsen, takes up the discussion regarding Schulz's proposition on how to educate the rural population. The editor or the anonymous writer recommends that instead of recreational activities such as playing cards, dancing, and visiting the inns, the youth should learn to play musical instruments as well as to read music rather than relying exclusively on the ears. However, those who do not have a talent for playing an instrument might practice singing. The writer asks rhetorically,

> but could the youth of country peasants get used to playing instruments? Wouldn't their fingers immediately become stiff from hard labor? Experience teaches us that there is hardly a village of peasants where there is indeed one or more whose fingers may move as fast … as if they were town musicians.[31]

Apparently, the peasants' hard manual labor—and thus stiff fingers—was often used as an excuse. However, as the writer argues, referring to Christiansfeld, which he had been visiting,

> We have an entire community as an example that this delightful pastime may be introduced. In Christiansfeld, I have heard pleasant concerts performed by the unmarried Brothers in their so-called Brethren House; but they are craftsmen whose daily work doesn't make the fingers suppler than the peasant's.[32]

The Music Archive

The music archive of the Moravian community in Christiansfeld comprises roughly 1,600 works in manuscript.[33] Most of them date to around the establishment of the community in 1772 or a decade or so after. In addition to the manuscripts, the archive also contains printed music mainly from the beginning of the nineteenth century by famous composers such as Mendelssohn, Haydn, and Mozart. For the education of musicians, especially keyboard players, the archive includes treatises on music performance practice such as basso continuo playing and realization, books on music theory and organ playing of the late eighteenth century, and finally, the chorale books and hymnals that were employed daily by the community. Basically, the extensive archive—in terms of not only the number of works but also the repertoire and genres it represents—may be divided into three categories, or special collections: (1) recreational music and music for intimate prayers performed, for instance, in the choir houses, especially the choir house of the Single Sisters, and gathered by individual members of the congregation; (2) music for liturgical services in the church, most often acquired by the organist or the Board of Elders; and (3) music for trombone ensemble, a distinct Moravian repertoire that is not found in the Lutheran Church and that is still played today. The earlier trombone repertoire consists mainly of chorales, while the more recent is arrangements of works for brass ensembles. This division of the music archive into three distinct sections reflects that it must have originally consisted of smaller collections and later, presumably during the nineteenth century, merged into one single archive and was placed in the church.[34]

Regarding the recreational music, it mainly comprises works for small ensembles (voice[s] and/or instrument[s] in various combinations), though there are also large orchestral works such as concertos and sinfonias. Thus, we have, for example, violin sonatas, string quartets, pieces for harpsichord or clavichord, arias for solo voice and accompaniment, and sonatas for harp, of which some belonged to Gertraut Christina Müller. An interesting item is her private music book into which she copied a wide variety of works such as rearrangements of operas by Mozart and Gluck, songs by Schulz, and original solo keyboard music by Türk, Naumann, and Couperin. Most of the composers were popular, contemporary late eighteenth-century composers. Müller's music book reveals that she must have had access to an extensive library of printed music or, perhaps more likely, another manuscript music book from which she copied.[35] Another interesting item is Müller's manuscript copy of the Czech composer Johann Baptist Vanhal's sonatas for violin and harpsichord, which most likely is a transcript of a printed edition to which she must have had access at some point—unless, of course, it was sent to her from abroad (see Figure 4.2). It is evident that music for recreational purposes was gathered from outside the community through private connections, or brought in by new members arriving in Christiansfeld. There is no difference in the congregation's musical taste and that of society in general when it comes to recreational music. It is more difficult to distinguish the music repertoire in the choir house of the Single Brethren from that in the Sisters' repertoire: the Brothers do not add their signatures on the music manuscripts to the same extent as the Sisters do. It seems likely, however, that they must have played the same genres and works as the Sisters, though their choice of instruments might have been different. Normally the Brothers would play on woodwind and brass instruments, the large string instruments like basses (but also violins), and the organ; the Sisters, on the other hand, most often played on chordal instruments such as harps, citterns, the harpsichord, and especially the clavichord, which was a highly popular instrument among the Moravians, as well as violins.[36]

The repertoire for the church services comprises a wide array of both anthems and cantatas for large as well as small orchestras, including vocal soloists and a choir, or in some cases even two choirs singing in antiphony. The earliest music catalog dates to the beginning of the 1770s.

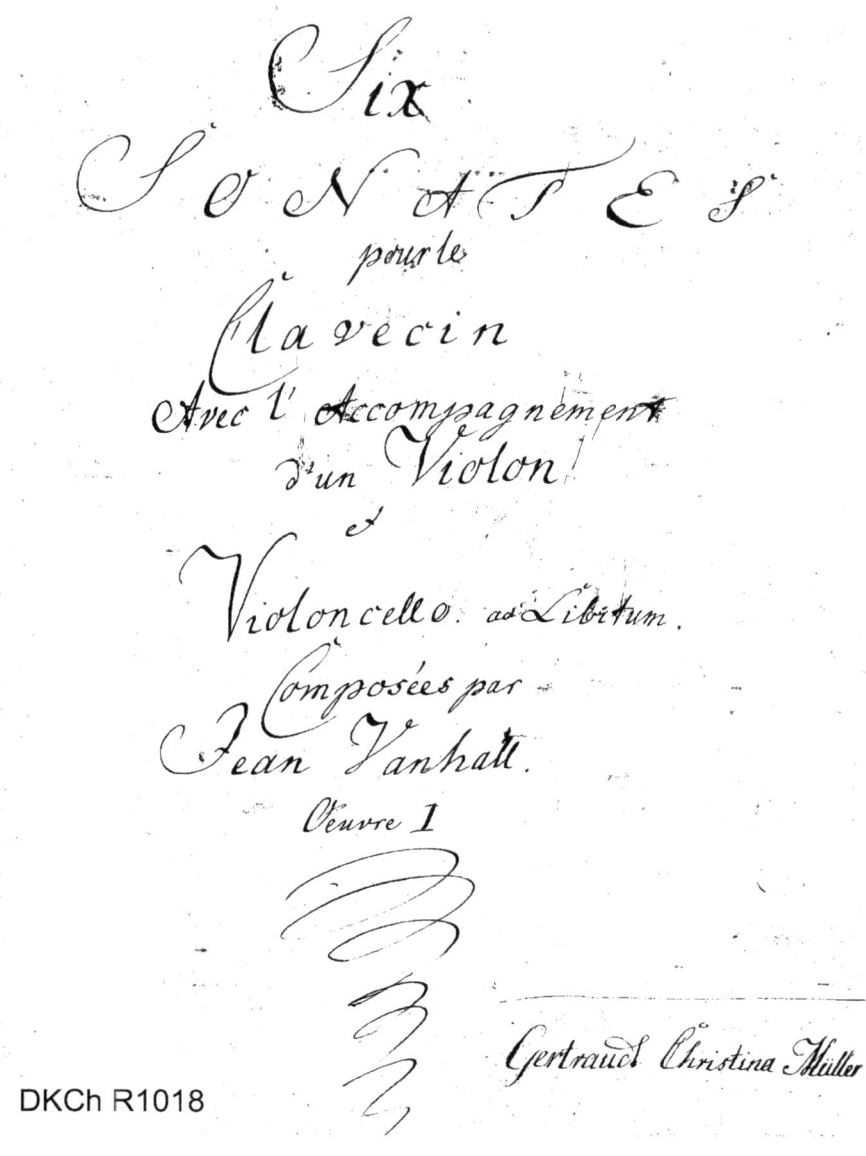

DKCh R1018

Figure 4.2. Johann Baptist Vanhal, *Six Sonates pour le Clavecin avec l'Accompagnement d'un Violon & Violoncello ad Libitum. Composées par Jean Vanhall Ouevre I,* is a transcript of his set of violin sonatas published around 1774 (RISM A/I V 398); Gertraut Christine Müller has added her signature on the title page. Reproduced with kind permission by Christiansfeld, DK-Ch, R1018.

Each work in the catalog, which is arranged alphabetically, includes a text incipit, the name of the composer, and the nature of the work (that is, whether it consists of recitatives, duets, solos, and choir music, for example)—thus easing the process of choosing the appropriate anthem or cantata to be performed for a particular liturgical event. Each entry has been assigned a number that at first glance seems to be a shelf mark; however, the numbering does not agree with that of the collection and, most importantly, many of the works never seem to have been in Christiansfeld at all. This suggests that the oldest catalog was a list of items sent from the Unity Board in Saxony and that, already during the early years, music for congregational use was selected in collaboration with the Unity Board in Herrnhut and possibly with the help of Christian Gregor, a prominent member of the board dealing with musical matters (see Figure 4.3).[37] The purpose was twofold: to facilitate the task of establishing a musical repertoire relevant for new Moravian settlements, so they did not have to start an extensive search for music; and most importantly, to ensure the Unity Board was able to retain control over the repertoire, thus creating unity across the Moravian settlements and avoiding the possibility that each congregation would develop independent and distinct musical tastes and traditions. It was a means of ensuring a common musical identity within the Moravian Church.

It also meant that the church promoted a set of common educational principles throughout its communities. This was not an original way of thinking: the development of a universal repertoire of Gregorian chant was based on the same outlook. In order to keep the Catholic Church together with a common identity in the early Middle Ages, the church found it necessary to create a musical repertoire that was to be performed in all congregations throughout Europe. The same may be said of the musical practice of the Reformation. The observation is important, for the common and very clear Moravian identity during the final decades of the eighteenth century implies that musical practices known in other Moravian communities most likely were also employed in Christiansfeld.[38] The liturgical music repertoire in Christiansfeld reflects the distinct musical taste—in terms of aesthetics, for instance—of the Moravian communities in general; essentially, it is the same repertoire that we find in the music archives of the Moravian towns in Saxony.

The third and smallest section of the music archive, which contains the repertoire for the trombone ensemble, was used until at least the beginning of the twentieth century. The ensemble was a regular feature of funeral services in the church as well as part of the procession to God's Acre, in addition to providing music and accompaniment for the hymns sung at interments. In her letter Anna Sybille explains that after

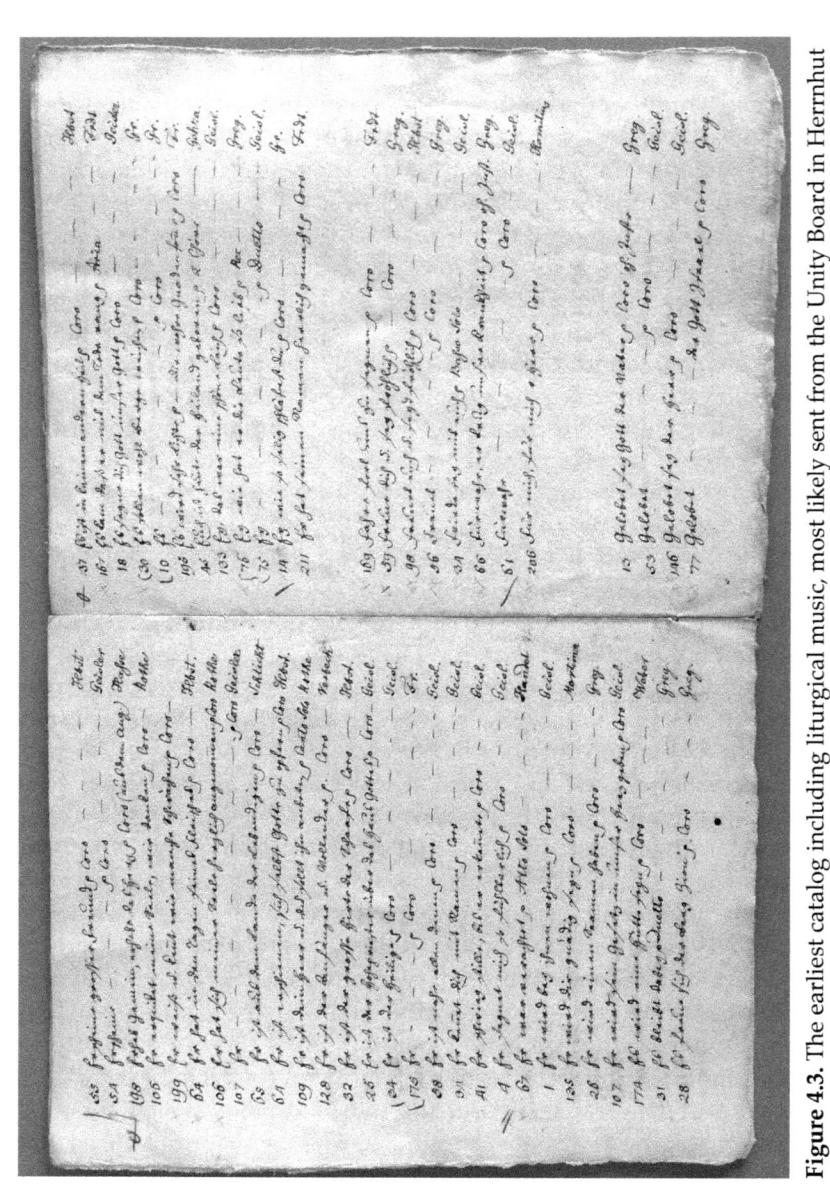

Figure 4.3. The earliest catalog including liturgical music, most likely sent from the Unity Board in Herrnhut to Christiansfeld in the 1770s. Works were ordered using the catalog, and transcripts were then sent to Christiansfeld. Reproduced by kind permission by Christiansfeld, DK-Ch, håndskrevne kataloger, 8.

lunch at the distillery on Sunday afternoon, they happened to bump into a funeral service taking place in the church; they decided to attend the service, and Anna Sybille remarks that witnessing the event was indeed worth the whole trip to Christiansfeld.[39] Hymns were sung and the pastor held a sermon after which the congregation left the church while the "wind ensemble" played solemn music. The procession to the cemetery began, and her husband and Oest placed themselves among the boys while she and her sister lined up with the "charming little girls." When they arrived at the entrance to the cemetery, the men went to the right and the women to the left; hymns were sung accompanied by the ensemble, the coffin was lowered into the grave, and then more hymns were sung—all "avec une solemnité, une tranquilité, une dévotion touchante."[40]

Instruments

As a whole, the music archive is thus an important source for understanding the wide range of musical activities taking place in Christiansfeld. Not only does it reveal detailed information on the performances in the choir houses and the church; it also tells us about the instruments that comprised the collegium musicum as well as the musical abilities of the performers. It would seem rather pointless if the music did not reflect the musicians' abilities: Why play or sing music that was too difficult and hence produce a poor performance? The basic section of the collegium musicum was the string section, consisting of around twelve musicians; in addition, among the members of the orchestra were at least two flute players, who might also be the performers playing the oboes. Most surprisingly, perhaps, the collegium musicum included an able bassoon player, since in the archive one finds works specifically scored for that instrument.[41] Indeed, there might even have been more than one bassoon player, for, when Anna Sybille is shown around the choir house of the Single Sisters on the late Friday morning, she notices that

> especially the cleanliness of the Sisters is striking: everywhere and in every corner, the house looks like yesterday. The hall where all these people sleep, bed by bed, is as clean, comfortable and as nice as possible. We are led from one small room to another, where five or six young girls sit at a table with an older one at another table as supervisor, engaged in various kinds of work: broidery and other knitwear, cotton weaving, ribbon weaving and other things. Their prayer room is beautiful and comfortable. There you can see a harpsichord, harps, violins, bassoons, etc. They are all musicians and add beautiful concerts to their morning and evening prayers, but no one is admitted.[42]

The description reveals that among the Single Sisters there was at least one who was able to play the bassoon, the largest and heaviest woodwind instrument, on which women rarely would perform in the eighteenth century—and certainly not in public. The general view among educators, Protestant theologians, and intellectuals was that blowing on large wind instruments such as the bassoon neither fitted the character of the female sex nor conveyed proper female decorum; then again, neither was the violin a fitting instrument, but it was indeed taught to young girls of the Moravian communities and there were certainly able women violinists in Christiansfeld.[43] Some of the works performed by the collegium musicum also include a harp, proving that it was not only considered a domestic instrument employed in private contexts. Among other instruments used for sacred anthems and cantatas, one finds trumpets and natural horns; at least one work required three gifted horn players.[44] Brass instruments were not part of the ensemble during the earliest years after the settlement's foundation but rather were incorporated gradually when Türsting arrived. In that way the community was able to maintain a separate trombone ensemble that participated in outdoor services such as funerals but also on more festive occasions in the church together with the collegium musicum. The orchestra, whose leader was the organist, could be extended with vocal soloists, most often women, as well as up to two separate choirs. Thus, women were vocal soloists—also in the church.[45]

As Anna Sybille mentions, the concerts or musical performances in the house of the Single Sisters were, unlike those at the Single Brethren, not public—that is, visitors from outside the congregation were not permitted to attend. Still, we have only very little information on the musical instruments that the Brothers had at their disposal. Through correspondence between Christiansfeld and Herrnhut we know that already before 1778 a one-manual organ with five stops had been installed in the choir house of Single Brethren, apparently built by one of the Brothers. In a letter addressed to Gregor in Herrnhut, pastor Johann Prätorius describes the organ as being "quite an ordinary instrument," that is, an instrument of average quality.[46] When a new organ by Johann Daniel Busch was installed in the church in 1778, the Single Sisters received the old one, which is still in use today.[47] Compared with the diary kept by the Brothers, the diary kept by the Single Sisters is much more informative when it comes to the performance of recreational music as well as music for private prayers. It is evident that musical life during the early years was somewhat meager; in particular, the Single Sisters seem to have missed singing and playing. However, in late July 1774 two Sisters of the congregation in Herrnhut, Anna Schuliußen and Marliesel Neumann, arrived in Christiansfeld. The choir house's diary entry provides us with the following information:

> 21 [July 1774]: the two Sisters, Anna Schuliußen and Marliesel Neumann, arrived at our place from Herrnhut; the former to serve at the guest house which is to be established here and the latter to start at the tailor's shop, which also did happen in the days following. We were very happy that our choir [choir house] was extended with two Sisters, as we had no music until then. So the joy was all the greater when Annerl brought out her cittern, with which she gave us much pleasure during our morning and evening prayers, as well as during other choir opportunities.[48]

The cittern (also known as an "English guitar") was a handy and light chordal instrument very popular among the Sisters of Moravian congregations (see Figure 4.4).[49] During the final week of Lent in April 1775, they note in their diary that they held the first *Gemeinstunde* in the newly built choir house, which included music making ("zum Ersten Mal in der gemein stunde schöne musiciert"). On that occasion, Sister Maria Christina Langgaard, who was also an able singer, played the harp accompanying some Sister singers.[50] The instrument was presumably the

Figure 4.4. Benigna von Zinzendorf (1725–1789) playing on a cittern, or "English guitar." Oil painting by Johann Valentin Haidt, c.1760. From the collection of the Moravian Archives, Herrnhut, GS.053.

so-called *Spitzharfe* (arpanetta) that, placed on a table or on the player's lap, was mainly used for accompanying singers; one of these is still in Christiansfeld.[51] At the beginning of January 1779, the diary mentions that "we had our first Sabbath *Liebesmahl* this year; it was charmingly entertained by our Sister singer [*Chor Sängerin*]. Our wish was that the dear Savior may further His present little choir, that He let it grow and increase and with His grace and through its graceful singing of praise make us His entire joy."[52]

It was not only hymn singing for which the Moravians were famous. The concerts—including those performed in the choir house of the Single Brethren and the public performances in the village such as when banquet music was played on festive occasions—became very popular, attracting audiences from among the community itself and, not least, crowds of enthusiastic foreign visitors. It seems that the focus on music became greater than ever, which in the end unfortunately created serious disputes within the congregation and sometimes led to disturbances among the audience. Musicians were given gratuities for playing at banquets and festive occasions that had nothing to do with community's liturgical life. In 1814 the Board of Elders felt forced to dismiss organist Johann Hermann Mankell, who was responsible for the performances and the ensembles.[53] During the nineteenth century, musical activities more or less came to a standstill. Very few works were added to the existing repertoire, and the sociable musical activities outside the control of the church had quietened significantly. However, it should be emphasized that the economic recession and the wars at that time also took their toll on Christiansfeld.[54]

Music and Aesthetics

Liturgical music, such as anthems and cantatas for the church services in the Moravian communities, was very different from that to which congregations in the Lutheran Church were accustomed. Aesthetics in terms of simplicity, intimacy, and purity played an enormous role for their selection of appropriate music for liturgical purposes. Music of the contemporary late eighteenth-century "galant" style or the concept of *Empfindsamkeit* was popular, as it, more than music of previous times, seemed to meet their demands. First and foremost, however, music should not draw the congregation's attention away from the text and its meaning—an idea that was certainly not foreign during the Counter-Reformation.[55] It was of paramount importance for the Moravians that music was not highly virtuosic or dramatic when performed as part of the service and liturgy. Consequently, choir music was primarily homo-phonic in structure—sometimes to such a degree that it sounded like recitation—avoiding polyphony with imitations between the different choir parts as much as possible. When music was practised in private as a leisure-time activity, playing a repertoire of a more virtuosic kind was not a problem; this is indeed evident in the secular repertoire of the Christiansfeld music collection. LaTrobe, who published a collection of liturgical anthems by composers such as Freydt, Gregor, and Naumann, explains in his introduction that

> by the following specimens of Anthems [in this edition], sung in the Church of the Brethren, it will be easily perceived, that neither in the vocal, nor instru-mental parts, any attempt is made to exhibit the skill of the performers by a display of extraordinary powers of execution, which might lead to the atten-tion of the congregation into an improper channel. More elaborate composi-tions are reserved for exercise at home. Vocal fugues also, are not used in the Church, as being unintelligible to the congregation, who wish to understand the words of the Anthem.[56]

LaTrobe's view explains why the music of the *Empfindsamer* and "galant" style was so much more popular than works of the high baroque. The simplicity of the anthems needed to reflect the musical practice according to which the congregation replied by singing a hymn expressing the same sentiments as the text of the anthem. The slow, exalted, and harmoni-ous hymn singing so much praised by visitors would be in complete contrast to the anthems if these were of a virtuosic character. According to LaTrobe,

> Correctness and *Simplicity*, the two grand sources of beauty in the performance of Music, producing a sweet confluence of harmony, by the combination of plain unadorned notes, ought chiefly to be attended to. Graces, so called, are much oftener the excrescences of ignorance and conceit, than the fruits of good taste; and where experience and skill are wanting to direct the performer in the use of them, they are sure to disgrace both the composer and himself.[57]

The statement explains the special character of the music performed in the Moravian congregations. It is evident that the Moravian composers of anthems and short cantatas went to great lengths to maintain the idea of simplicity, a harmonious sound without ornamentation, and a clear text that often sounds like a harmonized declamation.[58] In some instances, they went to extremes by removing sections of a piece if it compromised the aspiration to simplicity. When they wished to play music by non-Moravian composers, they frequently were forced to carry out heavy revisions by removing "unacceptable" sections, which in turn often caused very sudden and audible modulations. In addition, they would habitually replace the original secular or even sacred (Lutheran) texts with one more appropriate for Moravian liturgical purposes. One might argue that the close connection between text and music—that is, that music's purpose is to illustrate and emphasize the emotions and rhetoric of the text—is lost. Numerous examples in the collection of liturgical music in Christiansfeld reveal that the replacement of the original text with an appropriate Moravian one created a spiral of new problems. However, it was not a problem for the Moravian congregation or even contemporary outsiders; rather, it is an issue on which we today tend to focus. The Moravian understanding of the work concept—the musical Artifact—was that it was an open-ended and dynamic concept. They might have argued that it was not an artifact but rather a practical means to communicate directly with the heart. Thus, musical compositions were changeable and malleable according to their special purposes. It should be noted that this pasticcio practice was not unusual in the late baroque: many an opera was composed in this way—that is, by selecting movements or arias from different works and combining them into new works, as well as replacing a text with a new one.[59] Today we tend to force a modern definition of the work concept onto a repertoire and a period when it certainly had not yet been formulated.[60]

Conclusion

Within the first decade of the foundation of Christiansfeld, rumors about the accomplishments of the village—as a community with successful industries, a very different way of living with a clear emphasis on communal life, and a cultural life in which music played a significant role—generated an interest among the middle classes, intellectuals, clergy, civil servants, and aristocracy. It became fashionable to make an excursion to Christiansfeld, especially during the summer months, to spend a night and experience the clean, light, and calm village, buy items at the shops, and attend some of the liturgical services. This is what the Reventlows did in 1796. Their fascination with Christiansfeld should been seen in the context of contemporary Danish society and reveals, perhaps implicitly, more about the conditions of life (socially, educationally, and culturally) in other parts of the country and in the capital city than about conditions in Christiansfeld itself. Intellectuals like Kapellmeister Schulz in Copenhagen were inspired by the accomplishments of Christiansfeld when it came to music and music education of the general public. Though the intellectuals might not have been convinced that Comenius's ideas were optimal for eighteenth-century boys and girls, the model village at least forced them to rethink outdated pedagogical approaches and enhance the pupils' learning in new ways.

During long periods, particularly in the first half of the eighteenth century, Danish music was highly influenced by the regents' strong leanings toward Halle Pietism and the views of the influential Lutheran clergy. Sacred music and congregational singing were neglected in the Danish Lutheran Church, so much so that discussions began to appear on how to educate the congregations and improve hymn singing. Very often the public arguments took as their point of departure reports by visitors who had witnessed events and services in Christiansfeld. The community's music collections were part of a practical archive, in that its items were not determined by a specific collector's predilections but rather based on servicing a whole community in all its needs, both liturgical and secular. However, the archive is more than an important documentary record of the community's history; when seen in a broader context, it also reveals aspects of late eighteenth-century Danish music history. It is not surprising that the approximately 90,000 citizens of the capital city looked in awe at the small village in Jutland with its highly active cultural life, both within and outside the auspices of the church and, significantly, in which the whole community participated. At the same time, it should be remembered that the music performances in Christiansfeld—and the community's advancement of music aesthetics, music education, and the love of music as a recreational activity—was in line with other Moravian communities of the time; in that sense, it was not an innovative or a particularly dynamic musical village. When seen in the context of Danish society in general at the end of the eighteenth century, however, it is clear that Moravian music culture was distinct and became a model for proponents of better education, using optimal pedagogical means of realizing Basedow's idea that the ultimate goal of education was the well-being and prosperity of the nation.

Peter Hauge has a degree from the Academy of Music and an MA and PhD (music) from City, University of London. His fields of interest are Renaissance and Baroque music and he has published extensively on music theory, music aesthetics, and history of music. He has worked on the cultural heritage and collections of music in Christiansfeld and has received several prizes including the Louise Dyer Award (Musica Britannica), the Worshipful Company of Cordwainers' Prize, the Sir Jack and Lady Lyon's Performance Scholarship, and a Major State Studentship (British Academy).

Notes

1. Count Johan Ludvig Reventlow married Anna Sybille Schubart in 1778. They were both highly interested in social reforms and the ideas of the Enlightenment, and together they transformed their manor into a cultural and educational center; Johann Friedrich Oest was employed at the school on the estate. Anna's sister, Charlotte, married Ernst Schimmelmann in 1782 and together they were among the most influential patrons of the arts in Denmark. Count Reventlow had close connections with Christiansfeld (according to Briant, the community's pastor in 1784, he was a friend of the Moravians), supplying Christiansfeld with wool from his estates in Schleswig; see Holdt, "Brødrekolonien Christiansfeld," 103. Various aspects of the present chapter have been dealt with in earlier articles on the music of Christiansfeld, including Hauge, *Works*; "Music Collection," 28–36; "Honningkager og motetter," 65–74. Important for the present study are Reventlow, *Musikken*; "Musik og sang," 633–708.
2. Letter, 23 August 1796, in Bobé, *Efterladte Papirer*, 103–7.
3. See numbers 12 and 13 in Figure 4.1.
4. See Holdt, "Brødrekolonien Christiansfeld," 84–85.
5. Louise Stolberg was married to Count Christian Stolberg; living in Holstein, a few miles from Hamburg, they were keen participants in discussions on literature, politics, and reforms.
6. In her letters, Anna Sybille recounts events at the opera in Copenhagen and mentions playing the keyboard instrument; see Bobé, *Efterladte Papirer*, 38, 50, 133, among others. Another interesting account is by the farmer Eskel Sørensen, who visited Christiansfeld around Easter of 1798. He describes similar music performances and performance practices distinct from what he encountered in the Lutheran Church; see Sørensen, "En fynsk bondes besøg," 193–205.
7. For further references and discussions on the topic, see, in particular, Knouse, "Moravians," bibliography; Wehrend, *Musikanschauung*; Knouse and Crews, *Moravian Music*; Caldwell, "Moravian Passion Liturgies."
8. Pontoppidan and Hofman, *Den danske Atlas*, 7:208–10.
9. Pontoppidan and Hofman, 7:210.
10. Olrog, *Afhandling*, 18–19.
11. Olrog, 18–19: "Sangens Misbrug af Kiettere har stedse giort den fornøden for dem, som har en reen Lære. Det er ey først i vor Tid, at skadelige Meeninger, saasom Herrenhuthernes, ere udspredte ved Hielp af Psalmer … men denne List er gammel."
12. Review in *Nyeste kiøbenhavnske Efterretninger*, 541.
13. Ibid.: "kunde naae sin Hensigt, og ved dette Arbeide skaffe os en ordentlig og opbyggelig sang i Kirken, i Steden for den utidige og uharmonerende Skraalen, hvori endogsaa den, der ikke er Elsker eller Kiender af Musik, ikke maae kunde finde Behag eller Opbyggelse."
14. Ibid., 542: "hvo som har hørt den Christiansfeldske Menighed, veed af egen Erfaring, at det kan gaae an, at bringe 3 til 400 Mennesker til at synge ordentligt, naar de vænnes dertil; og hvorfor ikke flere? Deres sang er langsom og høitidelig, sagte og ydmyg, harmonerende og rørende, alt hvad den bedende og lovsyngende Sang bør være. Recensenten haaber ikke, at nogen er saa intollerant, at han skulde stødes over dette Exempel."
15. Bobé, *Efterladte Papirer*, 104–5: "Nous assistames à la prière du samedi au soir. Leur chant, leur chœur est d'une beauté, d'une harmonie charmante; personne n'ose entonner que qui chante bien."
16. LaTrobe, *Anthems for One*, 2.
17. Gregor, *Choral-Buch*. Gregor was a highly influential member of the Unity Board in Herrnhut and an important figure in terms of Moravian music.

18. Thomissøn, *Den danske Psalmebog*; Pontoppidan, *Den Nye Psalmebog*; Breitendich, *Fuldstændig Choral-Bog*; Schiørring, *Kirkemelodierne*; *Choral-Bog*. Thanks are due to Bjarke Moe for enlightening me on the subject.
19. Quoted in Caldwell, "Moravian Passion Liturgies," 20; translation by present author.
20. Caldwell, 20–21.
21. Bobé, *Efterladte Papirer*, 105: "Le prêtre lut une partie de l'épitre aux Romains avec quelques mots d'explication par-ci par-là; quelques couplets furent chantés. Le prêtre arrange cela comme il veut et y met de l'intérêt en variant beaucoup."
22. Bobé, 104: "Il y a deux grands instituts d'éducation pour des pensionnaires, un de garçons, un de filles, chacun de plus de 60 enfants, divisés chacun en plusieurs classes. Vous y voyés des enfants de tous pais, beaucoup de Suédois et de Norvégiens, aussi des Indes."
23. On Moravian education in German congregations, which would have been similar to conditions in Christiansfeld, see Wehrend, *Musikanschauung*, 60–72. See also—and especially in regard to the churches in Copenhagen—Pontoppidan and Hofmann, *Den danske Atlas*, 2:93–163.
24. There are several documents concerning Türstig's duties in the archives: In Christiansfeld, for example, see P A II R 1 B, 8 September 1778, 125; 10 October 1778, 136; 9 November 1778, 149–50; 14 December 1778, 165–66.
25. See Siggaard Jensen, Korsgaard, and Kristensen, *Pædagogikkens idehistorie*, 150–53. Oest was an acquaintance of Basedow.
26. See Leek, "John Amos Comenius," 226–27.
27. Schulz, *Tanker*, 2–3. Schulz's tract also appeared in the journal *Minerva*, February 1790, 254–67.
28. Schulz, *Tanker*, 5–6.
29. LaTrobe, *Anthems*, 2.
30. See Herrnhut, Unitätsarchiv der Evangelischen Brüder-Unität; *Athalia*, DK-Ch, R397.
31. *Maanedsskriftet Iris*, 157–58: "men kan Landalmuens Ungdom vænnes til at traktere Instrumenter? Deres Fingre bliver strax stive ved det strænge Arbejde?—Erfaring lærer, at der er neppe en Bondebye, hvori der jo er Een og undertiden Flere hvis Fingre kan løbe ligesaa hurtige … som om de havde Stads-Musikanterne."
32. *Maanedsskriftet Iris*, 158: "At denne og fornøilige Tidsfordriv kan indføres, derpaa have vi et heelt Societæts Exempel. Paa Christiansfeldt har jeg selv hørt smukke Concerter opføre af de ledige Brødre i deres, saa kaldede, Brødrehuus; men disse ere Haandværkere, hvis daglige Arbeider giør Fingrene ikke smidigere end Bondens."
33. A list of all the music manuscripts of the eighteenth century in Christiansfeld is available in the RISM (Répertoire International des Sources Musicales) Catalog of Musical Sources online database (http://www.rism.info/home.html); use the search term "DK-Ch." Works after 1800 are not listed in RISM.
34. This interpretation is supported by the early catalogs, which only include liturgical music for the church services.
35. Shelf mark, DK-Ch, R986.
36. See Wehrend, *Musikanschauung*, 60–68. The cittern and harp are discussed below.
37. Gregor often assisted the Christiansfeld community with musical issues such as new organs, organ builders, and locating gifted organists. See, for example, Christiansfeld, "Akten betreffend Orgelbau," V A R 13; P A II R 5 (dated 4 October 1774); Christiansfeld, V A R 13 B; and Herrnhut, R 21 A no. 55c (letters from Prätorius to Gregor dated 15 February 1778, 4 October 1778, 5 November 1778, and 5 May 1779). Thus, in close collaboration with Gregor, the community in Christiansfeld decided to order a brand-new organ from Johan Daniel Busch ("Königlich Dänischer und Groß Fürstl, Schleswig-Holsteinischer privilegierter Orgelmacher über die Fürstentümer und Grafschaften"). It was installed in the church in 1777 and inaugurated with Gregor's anthem "Lasset

uns dem Herrn singen," which apparently was composed especially for the occasion. Christiansfeld, P A II R 5.

38. Wehrend's findings regarding the Moravian congregations in Saxony thus may be transferred to other locations, in particular Christiansfeld. See Wehrend, *Musikanschauung*.

39. Bobé, *Efterladte Papirer*, 105–6.

40. Bobé, 106.

41. See Hauge, *Works*, 155–64.

42. Bobé, *Efterladte Papirer*, 103–4: "Il y regne une propreté, un ordre, une diligence charmante; la propreté des soeurs est surtout frappante; la maison a l'air partout et dans chaque coin d'être neuve d'hier. La salle où dorment tous ces personnes lit à lit, est propre. aisée, jolie au possible. On nous mène d'une petite chambre à l'autre où 5 où 6 jeunes filles sont assises à une table et une plus agée à une autre table comme surveillante, occupées à toutes sortes d'ouvrage, broderies et autres tricotages, fileries en cotton, métiers à ruban et autres de toutes espèces. Leur salle de prière est belle et riante. Vous y voyés clavécin, harpes, violons, bassons etc. Elles sont toutes musiciennes et joignent de beaux concerts à leurs prières du matin où soir, mais personne n'y est admise."

43. On gender and musical instruments, see Steblin, "Gender Stereotyping," 128–44.

44. Antonio Rosetti's concerto for natural horn (no shelf mark, but RISM A/I RR 2599a), includes three natural horns.

45. The Moravians even developed a distinct voicing for the choir: they replaced the traditional four-part choir consisting of soprano, alto, tenor, and bass (SATB) with two sopranos, alto, and bass (SSAB)—that is, three female voices and a single male. The male tenor voice was rarely employed. LaTrobe includes detailed information the accompaniment of hymns; see LaTrobe, *Hymn-Tunes*. See also Caldwell, "Moravian Sacred Vocal Music," 98.

46. Christiansfeld, V A R 13 B, "Akten betreffend Orgelbau," 4 October 1774; P A II R 5, 4 October 1774; letters from Prätorius to Gregor, 15 February 1778, 5 November 1778, and 5 May 1779, Herrnhut, R 21 A no. 55c; see Reventlow, "Sang og musik," 657.

47. Christiansfeld still has instruments dating back to the final quarter of the eighteenth century: keyboard instruments such as a harpsichord, a clavichord, and organs; brass instruments including a natural horn dating to before 1842; and an arpanetta (*Spitzharfe*). Brouwer and Johansen, "Catalogue on the Exhibition," 62–65.

48. Christiansfeld, Schwesternhaus Diarier, S A I R 1 (21 July 1774): "D. 21. Kamen die 2 Schwestern Anna Schuliußen u Marliesel Neumann von Herrnhuth bei uns an. Erstre zum Dienst bei der Pensionsanstalt die alhier eingerichtet werden solte u letztre solte die Schneidereÿ anfangen, welches in den folgenden Tagen auch geschah. Wir waren sehr froh das unser Chor um ein par Schwestern vermehrt wurde, weil wir bis daher gar keine Music gehabt hatten, so war die Freude um desto gröser, da die Annerl ihre Zitter mit brachte, womit sie uns mit derselben in unsern Morgen u Abendseegen und übrigen Chorgelegenheiten manches Vergnügen machte."

49. See Libin, "Musical Instruments," 39, 45; Holman, *Life after Death*, 144.

50. Christiansfeld, Schwesternhaus Diarier, S A I R 1 (9 April 1775).

51. See illustration in Brouwer and Johansen, "Catalogue on the Exhibition," 64.

52. Christiansfeld, Schwesternhaus Diarier, S A I R 1 (16 January 1779): "hatten wir unser erstes Sabbath Liebesmahl in diesem Jahr, es wurde von unsern Chor Sängerin lieblich unterhalten unser wunsch ging dahier das der liebe Hld sei Hiesiges Chörlein auch nach weiter bringen möge das Er es wachsen u. zunehmen laße, nach seiner gnade u. durch sein gnädiges benedeÿen uns zu seiner ganzen freude machen."

53. Reventlow, "Sang og musik," 676–78.

54. Thyssen, "Stilstand og Fornyelse," 60–77.

55. Thus, the Council of Trent (1545–65) worked on a new set of guidelines regarding music performed during mass. The recommendation on which they finally agreed is similar to that later proposed by the Moravian Society. See Grout and Palisca, *History of Western Music*, 234.
56. LaTrobe, *Anthems for One*, 3.
57. LaTrobe, 2–3.
58. For examples of liturgical anthems performed in Christiansfeld, see Hauge, *Works*, 1–214.
59. See Hauge, *Works*, xxiii–xxiv.
60. See, for example, Goehr, *Imaginary Museum*.

Bibliography

Manuscripts

Various sources located in the archives at Christiansfeld.

Printed Sources

Bobé, Louis, ed. *Efterladte Papirer fra den reventlowske Familiekreds* [The surviving Reventlow family papers]. Vol. 9. Copenhagen: Lehmann and Stage, 1895–1922.

Breitendich, Frederik Christian. *Fuldstændig Choral-Bog* [The complete choral book]. Copenhagen: Paul Herman Höcke, 1764.

Brouwer, Frans, ed. *The Impact of Music on Moravian Community Life*. Kolding: Christiansfeld Festival, 2015.

Brouwer, Frans, and Niels-Ole Bo Johansen. "Catalogue on the Exhibition: Pearls from Christiansfeld's Musical Life, 1 June–31 August 2015." In Brouwer, *Impact of Music*, 53–67.

Caldwell, Alice M. "The Moravian Passion Liturgies of 1791: An Echo of the Singstunde." In Brouwer, *Impact of Music*, 20–27.

Caldwell, Alice M. "Moravian Sacred Vocal Music." In Nola Reed Knouse, *The Music of the Moravian Church in America*. London: Boydell & Brewer, 2008, 88–132.

Goehr, Lydia. *The Imaginary Museum of Musical Works*. Oxford: Oxford University Press, 1992.

Gregor, Christian. *Choral-Buch, enthaltend alle zu dem Gesangbuche der evangelischen Brüder-Gemeinen vom Jahre 1778 gehören Melodien* [Choral book including all melodies for the 1778 hymn book of the Brethren]. Leipzig: Breitkopfischen Buchdruckery, 1784.

Grout, Donald J., and Claude V. Palisca. *A History of Western Music*. New York: W. W. Norton, 2001.

Hauge, Peter. "Honningkager og motetter: Musiklivet i Christiansfeld i slutningen af 1700-tallet" [Honey cakes and motets: Musical life in Christiansfeld in the late eighteenth century]. *Magasin* 29, no. 1 (2016): 65–74.

Hauge, Peter. "The Music Collection of the Moravian Society, Christiansfeld." In Brouwer, *Impact of Music*, 28–36.

Hauge, Peter. *Works from the Music Collection of the Moravian Society, Christiansfeld*. Copenhagen: Dansk Center for Musikudgivelse, 2015.

Holdt, Jens. "Brødrekolonien Christiansfeld indtil Aar 1800" [The Brethren settlement, Christiansfeld, until 1800]. *Sønderjyske Aarbøger* 3 (1940): 53–187.
Holman, Peter. *Life after Death: The Viola da Gamba in Britain from Purcell to Dolmetsch.* Woodbridge: Boydell Press, 2010.
Jensen, Hans Siggaard, Ove Korsgaard, and Jens Erik Kristensen. *Pædagogikkens idehistorie* [The Intellectual History of Pedagogy]. Aarhus: Aarhus Universitetsforlag, 2017.
Knouse, Nola Reed. "Moravians." In *Oxford Music Online*, accessed June 2021.
Knouse, Nola Reed, and C. Daniel Crews, eds. *Moravian Music: An Introduction.* Winston-Salem, NC: Moravian Music Foundation, 1996.
LaTrobe, Christian Ignatius. *Anthems for One, Two or More Voices.* London: printed for the editor, [1811].
LaTrobe, Christian Ignatius. *Hymn-Tunes, Sung in the Church of the United Brethren.* London: J. Bland, for the author, [1790?].
Leek, Joanna. "John Amos Comenius — The Initiator of Modern Language Teaching and World Understanding." *Studia Neofilologiczne* 7 (2011): 223–32.
Libin, Laurence. "Musical Instruments in Early Moravian Communities." In Brouwer, *Impact of Music*, 37–46.
Maanedsskriftet Iris [The monthly journal Iris], no. 3 (1794): 157–58.
Nyeste kiøbenhavnske Efterretninger om lærde Sager [Journal: Recent Copenhagen news on learned matters] 34, no. 2 (1783): 541–42.
Olrog, Peder. *Afhandling om Psalmernes Fornødenhed* [Dissertation on the necessity of hymns]. Copenhagen: August Friderich Stein, 1768.
Pontoppidan, Erik. *Den Nye Psalmebog* [The new hymn book]. Copenhagen, 1740.
Pontoppidan, Erik, and Hans de Hofman. *Den danske Atlas eller Konge-Riget Danmark* [The Danish atlas or the Kingdom of Denmark]. Copenhagen: Godiche, 1763–83.
Reventlow, Sybille. "Musikken I de herrnhutiske brødremenigheder i det 18. og 19. årh.: Det musikalske repertoire i Brødremenigheden i Christiansfeld fra 1772 til ca. 1860" [The music of the Moravian Brethren in the eighteenth and nineteenth centuries: The musical repertoire of Moravian Christiansfeld, 1772–c.1860]. Mag.art. diss., University of Copenhagen, 1973.
Reventlow, Sybille. "Musik og sang" [Music and song]. In *Herrnhuter-samfundet i Christiansfeld II* [The Moravian community of Christiansfeld Vol.2], edited by Anders Pontoppidan Thyssen, 633–708. Aabenraa: Historisk Samfund for Sønderjylland, 1984.
Schiørring, Niels. *Choral-Bog* [Choral book]. Copenhagen: Gyldendal, 1783.
Schiørring, Niels. *Kirkemelodierne.* [The church melodies]. Copenhagen: M. Hallager, 1781.
Schulz, Johann Abraham Peter. *Tanker om Musikkens Indflydelse paa et Folks Dannelse* [Thoughts on the impact of music on the education of a people]. Copenhagen: N. E. Lycke, 1790.
Sørensen, Eskel. "En fynsk bondes besøg i Christiansfelt 1798" [A Funen peasant's visit to Christiansfeld in 1798]. In *Skik og sæd hos bønderne sidst i det 18. og først i det 19. århundrede: De kendte manuskripter af Eskel Sørensen (1771–1835)* [Customs and habits of the peasantry in the late eighteenth and early nineteenth century: The known manuscripts of Eskel Sørensen (1771–1835)],

edited by Laust Christensen, 193–205. Copenhagen: Landbohistorisk Selskab 1989.

Steblin, Rita. "The Gender Stereotyping of Musical Instruments in the Western Tradition." *Canadian University Music Review* 16, no. 1 (1995): 128–44.

Thomissøn, Hans. *Den danske Psalmebog* [The Danish hymn book]. Copenhagen: Laurentz Benedicht, 1569.

Thyssen, Anders Pontoppidan. "Stilstand og Fornyelse 1800–1848" [Stagnation and renewal, 1800–1848]. In *Herrnhuter-samfundet i Christiansfeld I* [The Moravian community of Christiansfeld Vol. 1], edited by Anders Pontoppidan Thyssen, 11–101. Aabenraa: Historisk Samfund for Sønderjylland, 1984.

Wehrend, Anja. *Musikanschauung, Musikpraxis, Kantatenkompositionen in der Herrnhuter Brüdergemeine* [Ideas on music, musical practice, cantata compositions in the Moravian congregation]. Frankfurt am Main: Peter Lang, 1995.

Chapter 5

The Moravian Church in Christiansfeld Past and Present from the Perspective of the Sociology of Religion

Margit Warburg

The application for the nomination of Christiansfeld to become a UNESCO World Heritage site was supported by an exquisite, two-volume compilation of scholarly discussions and documentary material. The authors introduced the proposal for inscription according to UNESCO's criteria as follows: "Christiansfeld bears exceptional testimony to the culture of the Moravian Church, which has existed since the 18th Century. The denomination's culture is expressed in the town's layout, architecture, and craftsmanship as well the continuance of Moravian activities and traditions."[1]

I shall here draw attention to the last part of the quotation, "the continuance of Moravian activities and traditions." While it is true that material cultural heritage does not need to be part of a still living culture and tradition to fulfill UNESCO's criteria, it is also clear from reading the inscription proposal that it was an important asset that the Moravian congregation is a prominent and active part of the town of Christiansfeld. It means that the town is still a living expression and prime model of the ideals of a Christian life as set forth by the Moravians in the eighteenth century.[2] Thus, while the title of the present book raises the issue of the sustainability of Moravian Christiansfeld, this sustainability concerns both the material heritage and the living cultural heritage represented by the existing Christiansfeld congregation.

The Christiansfeld congregation—or, as they are called in Danish, *Brødremenigheden*—is a religious minority community in a country dominated by a majority church, the Evangelical Lutheran Church in Denmark (*Folkekirken*). The congregation shares the same confessional foundation as the majority church, including *Confessio Augustana* from 1530, and it has always been important for the congregation to demonstrate that it is not a sect cut off from the national church.[3] Today, the congregation has a status as a free congregation with a special relationship to the church.[4] This status means that the Christiansfeld congregation is not part of the Danish Evangelical Lutheran Church organization, a bishop in *Folkekirken* does not supervise the pastor, and the members of the free congregation do not pay the common church tax. However, unlike all other free congregations in Denmark, the Moravians are not offspring of religious currents within the Danish Evangelical Lutheran Church; instead, they settled as immigrants and belonged to an already established transnational minority religion.

Theories of the Foundation and Spreading of a New Religion

For a quarter of a century I have studied another transnational minority religion, the Baha'is. The Baha'i religion was founded in the 1860s by the Iranian prophet Baha'u'llah (1817–1892), following a schism in Shi'i Islam. Baha'i soon distanced itself significantly from Islam, and as a result of highly organized proselytizing from early 1900 onwards, it established a presence in nearly all countries of the world. Today, the religion counts about six million adherents with nearly four hundred members in Denmark.[5]

The Baha'is believe that with Baha'u'llah's prophecy God decided to unify all humankind into one religion and one world civilization. In line with this central doctrine of world unity, the Baha'is condemn racial prejudices and praise ethnic and cultural pluralism. They also insist upon equal rights and opportunities for men and women. Because the Baha'is believe in a prophet after Muhammad they are considered heretics by most Muslims, and the Baha'is of Iran have regularly been severely persecuted.

From the perspective of sociology of religion, there are striking similarities between the Baha'is and the Moravians with regard to their establishment, spreading, and consolidation as a transnational minority religion with a global outlook. I will therefore draw upon the theoretical insight gained from my studies of the Baha'is to analyze the sustainability of the Moravian congregation, particularly in Christiansfeld. This is not a trivial issue; sociologists of religion have studied a large number of religious minority groups past and present and the great majority of these religious groups shared the common fate that they did not survive beyond the first few generations.

The term "founding" may suggest a more ordered and deliberate process than is often the case. Many religions originate from a schism occurring after a long period of significant religious tensions that cannot be resolved within the frame of the mother creed. Other religions emerge as independent creeds right from the beginning, but then they generally draw heavily on past religious traditions. In the often turbulent initial phase, a charismatic leader is frequently an essential figure in promoting the religious innovations needed to attract people to form a new religious movement.

Sociologist Max Weber (1864–1920) discussed the central position of a charismatic leader in his analyses of leadership and authority.[6] Weber borrowed the term "charisma" (from Greek: gift of grace) from Lutheran jurist Rudolf Sohm (1841–1917) as a form of authority among the early Christians.[7] However, unlike Sohm, Weber saw charisma not as an expression of a leader's irresistible personal quality but rather as the result of the interaction between the leader and his or her followers.[8] The leader is bestowed with charismatic authority by the followers. Of course, the leader's personal appeal is still important, but charismatic rule refers to something beyond the personal qualities of the leader. This "something" is the combination of the followers' inclination to treat the leader as extraordinary and the leader's extraordinary exercise of power.[9]

The period following a community's founding is critical. New religious movements are fueled by the enthusiasm and energy among the first followers; these are ephemeral assets, however, which soon must be channeled into activities that benefit further development and sustainability of the new religious movement. A charismatic leader is an extraordinary figure, and the movement cannot continue for a long time unless the leadership is routinized, as Weber put it.[10] This routinization and succession of leadership is particularly critical after the death of the founder.

I will now briefly discuss the founding phase and subsequent transformation of the Moravian movement into a more stable transnational religion in a globalized setting, from the perspective of the sociology of religion. Of the factors that influence the course of a religious movement during routinization and its transformation into a more sustainable new religion, the following three are particularly important: relations to the surrounding majority society, organizational stability, and demographic development of the group.

The Moravian Church as a New Religious Movement

The Moravian Church originated as a pre-Reformation Protestant movement, Unitas Fratrum, inspired by Czech church reformer Jan Hus (1369–1415). During the Counter-Reformation, members of Unitas Fratrum and other Hussite movements were heavily persecuted, and they fled from their Czech and Moravian homelands.[11] In 1722, about a hundred refugees from this group were given asylum at the estate of Berthelsdorf in Saxony by permission from the local count, Nicolaus von Zinzendorf (1700–1760). He instructed the estate manager to find a place for the refugees, who were mostly artisans, and the far-sighted manager selected a site at a road running at the foot of the mountain Hutberg. The plot was of little use to agriculture but gave good access to towns where the settlers could sell their products.[12] Here the Moravians established their new village, Herrnhut.

Zinzendorf was preoccupied with the ideas of religious brotherhood that prevailed among the more radical pietists of the time. He gradually engaged himself in the fate of the Moravians at his estate, organized the congregation, and soon became their leader. A leader was certainly needed: the community at Herrnhut was split into factions. During the summer of 1727, Zinzendorf personally reorganized the community and their work.[13] His efforts in uniting the Moravians culminated in a communion service in the church of Berthelsdorf on 13 August 1727. According to Zinzendorf's own narrative in his diary, a great wave of revival engulfed the congregation during this service.[14]

Elizabeth Zorb, an early scholar of the Herrnhut Moravians, presents in a few succinct words Zinzendorf as a typical example of a charismatic religious leader: "Zinzendorf proved to be one of those rare religions geniuses whose confident faith was highly contagious, who seemed to spread assurance of God's love and grace by his very presence, and whose influence on the spiritual life of succeeding generations was immeasurable."[15]

In his sermons Zinzendorf taught the Moravians to look upon all aspects of daily life, including work, as worship.[16] These sermons later served as one of the role models for Max Weber's famous linking of Protestant ethics with the spirit of capitalism. As Weber phrased it, Zinzendorf "glorified the loyal worker who did not seek acquisition, but lived according to the apostolic model, and was thus endowed with the charisma of the disciple."[17]

From the 1730s the Moravians were so well established in Herrnhut that they could turn their energy to active proselytizing; again, this was organized by Zinzendorf, who later traveled to establish new

Figure 5.1. *Zinzendorf as Teacher of the Peoples,* Johann Valentin Haidt, c.1747.
Note the artist's comprehension of the interaction between leader and audience.
From the collection of the Moravian Archives, Herrnhut (Unitätsarchiv, GS.583).

congregations.[18] This expansion of the Moravian network was guided by
a "strategic global vision and accompanied by the conscious attempt to
preserve."[19]

The Relations to the Surrounding Majority Society

A new religion is typically in a state of tension in relation to the surrounding society. Among the followers, there is usually a strong feeling
of division between "them" and "us," and this is reflected in both attitudes and behavior. The reactions from the surrounding majority are also
expressed in typical patterns of attitudes and behavior. I have illustrated
the mutual attitudes and behavior in the fourfold combination scheme
shown in Table 5.1. This combination scheme is useful for structuring
empirical material on minority-majority relations in Christiansfeld, both
historically and today.

Table 5.1. A scheme of minority-majority attitudes and behavior.

	Minority-intern	**Minority-majority relations**
Attitudes	Group identification	Prejudices
Behavior	Self-segregation	Discrimination

Group identification means a general feeling of belonging. However, it is more than that; it is also a *wish* to belong to the group and a joy of belonging. Group identification does not evolve automatically; it must be built up among the followers by socializing them into the thinking and habits of the religion and by showing them what distinguishes the members of the movement from the surrounding society, including how to dress properly. An example of this can be found in Andreas Øster's memoirs from his childhood in Christiansfeld around 1900, where he describes the particular bonnets worn by the Moravian women. The bonnet was tied under the cheek by a ribbon and showed the civil status of the wearer: red for girls and young women, pink for unmarried women, light blue for married women, and white for widows.[20] Insiders knew the significance of these colors, but probably most of the non-Moravians in Christiansfeld did not. These color codes, which were universal among the Moravians, are still in use today at certain occasions, such as at the Lovefeast.[21]

The Moravians' group identification with emphasis on worship and work was distinctly expressed in the materiality of their culture. Their idea of an ideal Christian society is consistently reflected at all levels at Christiansfeld: from the town plan itself, with order and symmetry, through the design of the buildings for a communal life to the high degree of craftsmanship invested in the architectural elements of the buildings, such as the doors, gateways, windows, stairs, handrails, and hinges.[22] Today, Moravian identity is also represented by many artifacts for sale. A famous example is the Moravian Advent Star, made by intricate folding of paper or plastic sheets and sold worldwide online.[23]

The behavior associated with group identification is self-segregation. Some religious minority groups, like ultra-orthodox Jews in Israel, practice a high degree of self-segregation. The Baha'is, who are very open to outsiders, also have regular meetings only for members.[24] For followers of any minority religion it is probably necessary from time to time to keep to themselves and be together without the presence of non-followers in order to maintain group identification. However, in the case of proselytizing religions it is also necessary to be inclusive toward potential converts and encourage them to participate in meetings, services, and other

Figure 5.2. *Moravian Single Sister*, unknown artist, c.1810–20. The ribbon tying the bonnet is pink in the painting, which shows the unmarried status of the woman. From the collection of the Moravian Historical Society, Nazareth, Pennsylvania.

common activities. Striking the right balance between exclusiveness and inclusiveness is thus important for a movement that wishes to have a sustainable growth.[25]

The majority-minority attitudes are often expressed in the form of prejudices. It is well known that the majority may express different and usually negative prejudices about minorities. Prejudices are generalized statements about members of the minority, and the justification for such prejudices is based on nothing more than the fact that they belong to the minority. Prejudices can rarely comply with a reality check, but they are surprisingly fact resistant. Prejudices serve primarily to confirm feelings among the majority that they are different from, and usually also better than, the minority.

Minorities also express prejudices. These prejudices are often negations of virtues praised in the minority group. In Home Mission circles in Denmark in the late 1800s it was said that before the mission came to this or that place, the people there had lived a sinful life with many children born out of wedlock.[26] This claim usually lacked demographic proof, but that did not matter, because it served the higher purpose of confirming the moral superiority of Home Mission members.[27] In his memoirs, mentioned earlier, Andreas Øster likewise noted that the Moravians felt they were a little more distinguished and pious than people from outside the congregation.[28]

Discrimination means to treat people differently only because they belong to a particular group. Discrimination has negative connotations, and most cases of discrimination of minorities have negative consequences ranging from unequal treatment on the labor market to downright persecution. Positive discrimination exists, however; one example is the introduction of quota systems in higher education, as in the United States, to achieve a more balanced gender or ethnic composition of students.

Historically, the Moravians were subject to discrimination, most severely, of course, in the Habsburg Empire, but also quite a few of the Protestant kings and princes were uneasy with the missionary activities of the Moravians and put restrictions on them. In some cases, they had to leave the country altogether. As a notable example, Zinzendorf himself was expelled from his homeland, Saxony, in 1736.[29]

The Danish Moravian Society in Copenhagen was established in 1739 and in the beginning it was tolerated by the pietist King Christian VI (reigned 1730–46).[30] However, the king was also worried about losing control of the religious movements outside the state church, and in 1741 he issued a decree, *Konventikelplakaten*, that forbade all religious gatherings not approved by a pastor in the Danish Evangelical Lutheran state church.[31] In principle, this made the Danish Moravian Society in Copenhagen illegal; in practice, however, it was tolerated.[32]

In the case of Christiansfeld, the Moravians met with positive discrimination in the form of economic privileges when in 1771 the Danish government invited them to build the town.[33] This is well known, and I shall not expound on it further as it is treated in detail elsewhere.[34] Later, in the 1800s and early 1900s, national tensions between citizens of Danish and German identity in Christiansfeld sometimes led to mutual discrimination.[35]

Organizational Stability

It is obvious that expansion and consolidation of a new religion with more than a few scores of followers requires some internal organization and management structure. This task is rarely what preoccupies the founders of new religions, who often rely on charismatic leadership with all its advantages for attracting new followers. However, it is common for charismatic leadership to develop an authoritarian and unpredictable management culture.[36] The subordinate leaders often find that their executive powers are insecure, being at the whim of the leader, and that disgrace may strike at any moment. An illustrative example is Robert Balch's study of the economic and organizational dissolution of a religious hippie commune, the Love Family.[37]

It is typical of charismatic leadership that Zinzendorf made several radical decisions that shook the Moravians.[38] For example, in 1744 he ordered a strict separation of the sexes among unmarried members of the Moravian congregations, which meant that many young people in Herrnhut had to move from their family homes to the communal choir houses. This created widespread resistance and led to numerous exclusions.[39] Interestingly, Zinzendorf combined his charismatic capabilities with a strong sense of administration through written regulations, and the Moravians have continued this tradition.[40]

During the last ten years before his death in 1760, Zinzendorf interfered less and less with the practical affairs of the Moravian movement.[41] The governance of the movement was organized along uniform principles; however, it is characteristic of charismatic leadership that this transition toward a routinized leadership was only accomplished in the years after Zinzendorf's death. Leadership was now collective and strongly centralized in Herrnhut, where the Unitäts-Ältesten-Conferenz (UAC) had to approve nearly all decisions made by the local communities.[42]

The Moravian Church was at that time organizationally geared to engage further in proselytizing and worldwide expansion. However, the economy was a critical issue in this context. Debt crises in the mid-1700s and early 1800s had a pronounced negative impact on the stabilization and expansion of the Moravian movement.[43] There are striking parallels to some of the challenges that have faced other new religions, such as the Baha'is.[44]

The Demography of a Religious Minority Group

Successful proselytizing is essential for a religious movement that aims at growth or at least sustainability. This conclusion is based on the demography of religious groups, which I shall briefly introduce below.[45] Well-organized religious groups keep track of their members, and often there exists sufficient data to perform a demographic analysis, including projections of future development. This is also the case with the Moravian Church in Christiansfeld, which possesses a wealth of archival material.[46] This chapter, however, relies on published demographic data.[47]

Conventional population demography is based on keeping track of all the population movements that affect the total number of a given population over a certain period. These movements (variables) include births of new citizens and the settlement of new immigrants, both of which increase the population during the period under study. Conversely, deaths and emigration decrease the population in the same period. These variables are linked together in this basic democratic equation:[48]

Growth = births – deaths + immigration – emigration

In the demography of religious groups, numbers increase through recruitment of new members and immigration. In principle, nobody is born into a religious group; children are recruited as members by their parents, usually through a ceremony such as infant baptism. There are two different sources of recruitment to a religious group: conversion of new members from outside, which I designate "exo-conversion," and recruitment of members born into families that are already members. This type of recruitment, I call "endo-conversion," is the parallel to births in a conventional demographic analysis of a population.

The decrease in numbers comes from deaths, resignations, and emigration. Both new and consolidated religious groups experience high rates of demographic loss through people leaving the group. All of these variables are linked together in the demographic equation for religious groups which I formulated in my study of the Baha'is:[49]

Growth = endo-enrollments + exo-enrollments + immigration
– emigration – resignations – deaths

In a new religion, exo-conversions dominate in the first few generations; however, it is typically observed that endo-conversions become relatively more significant as the movement matures. One explanation is that the consolidation of the community and bringing up of the next generations, and their socialization into community life, consume human resources that otherwise might be used for external proselytizing.

The Moravians are known for their mission activities all around the world and can boast of success in some countries outside Europe—for example, in Tanzania, where it undoubtedly helped that the territory came under German colonial rule in 1891.[50] In Europe, however, the traditional organization of the Moravians in communal houses and with crafts and industrial production in-house meant that there were limits to the number of new converts that could be accommodated. Anders Pontoppidan Thyssen even writes that in the early years of the 1800s, potential new members to the congregation in Christiansfeld were not always welcome.[51]

Religious groups that are not actively proselytizing will depend on endo-conversions for recruitment of new members. Reliance on endo-conversions was perhaps a viable strategy a century ago and is still practiced in some tradition-laden religious minorities, such as the Old Order Amish. However, with the average fertility rates observed in most industrialized countries today, it is rare that a religious minority group can reproduce itself. As a rule of thumb, this would require that, on average, a woman gives birth to 2.1 children, and this number is not reached today in many parts of the world, neither in Europe and North America nor in China. The number of births in a religious group sets an upper limit on the number of endo-conversions, and among the children brought up in the group, resignations are also common. The consequence is that unless an appreciable input of new members comes from stable exo-conversions, the religious group will gradually become smaller and smaller.

In the case of Christiansfeld, the traditions of communal living in sex-segregated choir houses combined with few opportunities for establishing a living outside the choir house industries meant in practice that there were restrictions on getting married, and many members remained single for their whole lives.[52] These customs resulted in a comparatively low fertility rate. The number of *Ortskinder*—that is, children born into the congregation—was quite low from around 1800 and remained so.[53] The low fertility rate in the Christiansfeld congregation stands in contrast to the situation in the majority society in the 1800s, where the fertility rates were generally high. During that century, the population in Denmark grew from a little over 900,000 to about 2.5 million.[54] In North Schleswig, the population growth was relatively lower but still positive.[55]

Regarding the two migration terms in the equation, immigration and emigration, Thyssen reports that from the late 1700s and some decades on, there was a significant immigration of Moravians especially from Germany.[56] With regard to emigration, a possible factor could be mission abroad, but the strong early Herrnhut mission on the Danish West Indies apparently did not involve missionaries from Denmark.[57] From the 1830s, both immigration from abroad and emigration from Christiansfeld to other countries were not quantitatively significant, and these population movements furthermore largely balanced each other.[58]

Figure 5.3 shows the development in membership in the Christiansfeld congregation. It is noteworthy that the number of members decreased quite rapidly during the 1800s, contrary to what would be expected if the size of the congregation had kept pace with the general population growth. I ascribe this primarily to the low birth rate in the community.[59] The membership seems to have stabilized around the year 2000, and

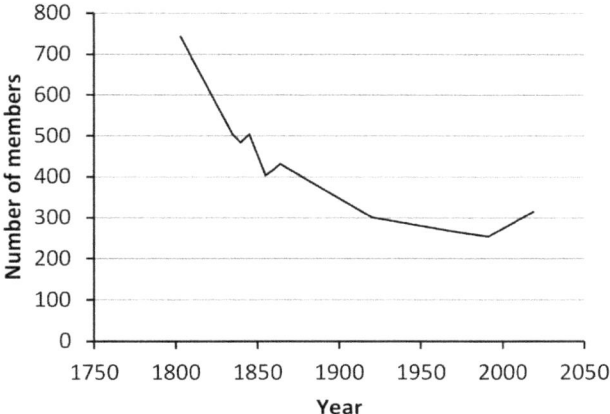

Figure 5.3. Number of adult members of the Christiansfeld congregation. Sources: Elklit, "Befolkning og fattigforsorg," 106; Thyssen, "Det store og det lille herrnhutersamfund," 92, 95; Bøytler, personal communication, email, 23 April 2020. Figure by Margit Warburg.

by 2019 the congregation had grown slightly to 315 adult members and 32 children.[60]

The Moravians in a Globalization Perspective

The Moravians of Christiansfeld may be a small religious group in Denmark, but they are also part of the larger community of Moravians around the world and have been so since the 1730s, when Moravian international proselytizing gained momentum.[61] In the course of this expansion, they earned a positive reputation of what an observer in 1787, in the age of Enlightenment, called *Weltbürgerschaft* (world citizenship).[62] Historian Gisela Mettele asks how the Moravians, who were "scattered across the globe in settlements and missionary outposts," were able to maintain such a communal identity at a time when international communications were irregular and uncertain. She answers this question by emphasizing the close institutionalized links between the worldwide settlements and the central leadership in Herrnhut, in addition to the knowledge of shared rituals and festivities, commonly read magazines or other devotional literature, the circulation of reports about different activities around the world, and German as the common language. Later in the nineteenth century, English gradually displaced German as the everyday language in the American and British Moravian congregations, and the strong influence of the Herrnhut leadership weakened.[63]

In 1857, the Moravian Church was reorganized according to a new constitution, whereby "unity provinces" became more independent organizations according to geographical and linguistic criteria.[64] From the mid-1900s, with the increasing success of Moravian proselytizing, new unity provinces were formed outside Europe and the United States. This development is particularly pronounced in Tanzania, which alone harbors four unity provinces and is clearly a continental hub for the expansion of the Moravian Church in East and Central Africa.[65] Today, the approximately thirty unity provinces worldwide form the organizational backbone of the international Moravian Church, which counts about 1.3 million members in total.[66] The Unity Synod with delegates representing all the provinces gathers every seventh year and is the supreme body of the Moravian Church. The Unity Board is the standing council of the international church from one Unity Synod to the next. It consists of one member from the Provincial Board of each of the provinces.[67]

The characterization of the Moravians in the 1700s is strikingly similar to the Baha'is in the 1900s, when the religion expanded and its followers strived to obey the command of their founding prophet to work for the unification of humankind. The Baha'is also see themselves as "citizens of the world."[68] I therefore find it relevant here to share some of my approaches to the study of the Baha'is and their position in a world undergoing globalization. I will concentrate on what I call the dual global field model.

The Dual Global Field Model

My dual global field model is based on studies on globalization in particular by the sociologist of religion Roland Robertson and his colleague JoAnn Chirico.[69] In their analysis of globalization and the role of religion, they propose a model they call the "global field" (Figure 5.4).

In compliance with a classical sociological view, Robertson and Chirico consider *individuals* and *national societies* as the two primary social actors on the national level. They further include two additional, global constituents: the world system of societies and humankind. The world system of societies is the system of international diplomacy and its institutions, such as the United Nations system. Humankind is all seven thousand million human inhabitants of the earth. From a globalization perspective, these two global entities—world system of societies and humankind—have become increasingly significant in how both individuals and national societies conceive of the world and, in particular, how they conceive of

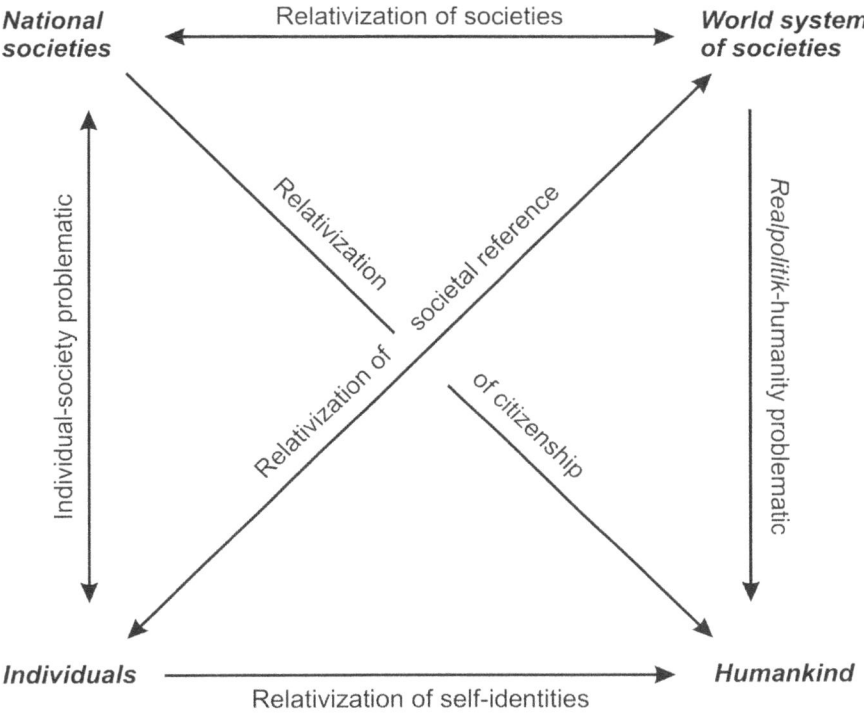

Figure 5.4. The global field model. Source: Warburg, *Citizens of the World*, 88–91. Figure by Margit Warburg.

it in religious terms. Robertson and Chirico refer to these processes as relativization.

The global field model, however, is majority oriented and therefore does not take into account that many religious organizations, even the larger ones, represent transnational *minority* groups.[70] Their members are residents of many different countries, but they have a feeling of commonness, of sharing a history and a destiny with other members worldwide, despite the fact that they do not share a common national background. Such groups are transnational imagined communities. This expression is an extension of Benedict Anderson's concept of the "imagined community," which he used in his analysis of nation-states and nationalism to explain why people of the same nation may feel a commonness and solidarity even though they do not know one another personally.[71]

Religious groups like the Mormons, the Seventh-day Adventists, and the Baha'is are typical examples of minority religions that are represented in many countries around the world—and so are the Moravians.

Members of transnational imagined communities through their nationality are also members of that imagined community that is the nation-state
(or national society in Robertson's terms). This means that they think
and act in some situations as national citizens, and in other situations
as members of the transnational imagined community. This situation of
thinking and acting in two *complementary* modes is characteristic of many
minorities and other social subgroups with distinct identities. It is the
main feature of the dual global field model (Figure 5.5).

In this model, the transnational imagined community of a religious
group is placed inside the general global field as a smaller replica of this
field. In the case of the Moravian Church, the three reference points of the
inner square in the model would be the "national Moravian community,"
which could be Christiansfeld; the "Moravian international organization," which would be the Unity Board; and the "world of believers,"
which would be the approximately 1.3 million Moravians worldwide.

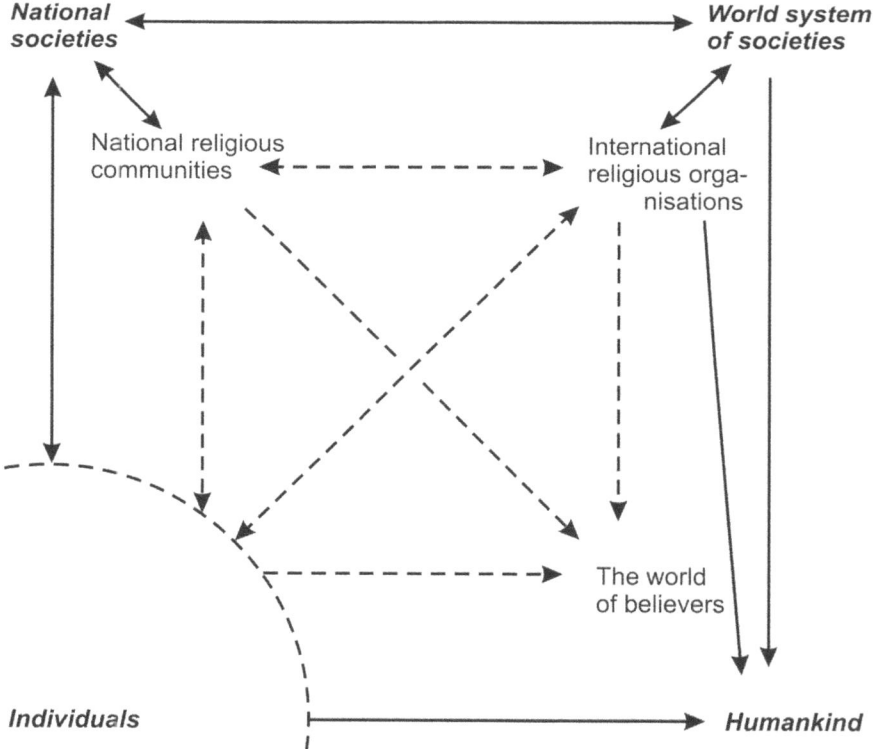

Figure 5.5. The dual global field model. Source: Warburg, *Citizens of the World*,
107. Figure by Margit Warburg.

The two global fields—the general field and the inner field of the religious minority—share the individual who has the ability, through his or her "relativizations," to move between the general mode and the mode of the religious minority. The arrow that points from the international religious institutions to humankind could indicate international mission activities on behalf of the Moravian Church worldwide. An example is the Star Mountain Rehabilitation Center in Ramallah for mentally disabled Palestinian children and youth. This project is run by the European Continental Province by delegation from the Unity Board.[72]

If we look at the top of the dual global field model, we find the actors engaged in the nomination of Christiansfeld to become a UNESCO World Heritage site. The actors here are UNESCO (the United Nations system is part of world system of societies), the Danish national society (represented by the Danish state assisted by Kolding municipality), and the Christiansfeld congregation (the national religious community).

Summary and Conclusion

Moravian Christiansfeld has its roots in a charismatically led new religious movement, which successfully accomplished a routinization of leadership. This meant that systematic proselytizing could be undertaken. By the mid-1700s, the Moravian Church had already developed into a truly transnational religious community, which was undoubtedly a strength. On the local level—that is, in Christiansfeld itself—relations to the surrounding majority society seemed to have achieved a fruitful balance between openness and restrictions so that the congregation could uphold its special religious-cultural characteristics. However, its growth during the 1800s and for some time after was hampered by an unfavorable religious demography.

Christiansfeld represents a national religious community in the dual global field model, and the town is an element in the Danish national cultural heritage.[73] Since 2015, Christiansfeld has represented not only national but international cultural heritage, approved by the world system of societies—in this case, UNESCO. This places a responsibility on the shoulders of both the Christiansfeld congregation and Danish society as such to ensure the sustainability of Christiansfeld as a site of living cultural heritage. The sustainability of the Christiansfeld congregation hinges on a strategy for upholding and developing the cultural characteristics while facing the challenges of assimilation and religious demography.

Margit Warburg is dr. phil. and professor of sociology of religion, University of Copenhagen. Her research interests include the relationship between religion and migration, religion and globalization, religion and demography, religious minorities, no religion, and civil religion. She has published in the *Journal of Ritual Studies*, *Nordic Journal of Religion and Society*, *Social Compass*, *Journal of Church and State*, *Journal of Contemporary Religion*, *Journal of Religion in Europe*, and *Implicit Religion*.

Notes

1. Berg, Marcussen, and Stoklund, *Danish World Heritage Nomination*, 154.
2. Berg, Marcussen, and Stoklund, 154–55.
3. Berg, Marcussen, and Stoklund, 127.
4. Espersen, *Kirkeret*, 179–83; Ramsdal-Thomsen, "Frie menigheder"; see also *Brødremenigheden i Christiansfeld*, the website of the Moravian congregation in Denmark (http://brødremenigheden.dk/).
5. Warburg, "Baha'is of the North," 77–92.
6. Adair-Toteff, "Max Weber's Charisma," 189–204.
7. Smith, "Faith, Reason, and Charisma," 32–60.
8. Weber, *Readings and Commentary*, 217–20; Wallis and Bruce, *Sociological Theory*, 129–30; Smith, "Faith, Reason, and Charisma."
9. Smith, "Faith, Reason, and Charisma."
10. Weber, *Readings and Commentary*, 220; Adair-Toteff. "Max Weber's Charisma."
11. Zorb, "Reflections on Moravian Pietism," 115–21.
12. Lafrenz, "Moravian Church's Settlement Congregations," 189–212.
13. Vogt, "'Everywhere at Home,'" 7–29; Burkholder, "'As on the Day,'" 182–210.
14. Burkholder, "'As on the Day.'"
15. Zorb, "Reflections on Moravian Pietism."
16. Mettele, "Constructions of the Religious Self," 7–36.
17. Weber, *Protestant Ethic*, 176.
18. Mettele, "Constructions of the Religious Self"; Thyssen, "Det store og det lille herrnhutersamfund," 17–24.
19. Vogt, "'Everywhere at Home.'"
20. Øster, *Barn i herrnhuternes Christiansfeld*, 39.
21. Bøytler, *Gribe og begribe*, 119–20.
22. Berg, Marcussen, and Stoklund, *Danish World Heritage Nomination*, 156–59.
23. See Herrnhuter, https://shop.herrnhuter-sterne.de; see also chapter 7 in the present volume.
24. Warburg, *Citizens of the World*, 365–67.
25. Warburg, 397–423.
26. Balle-Petersen, "Guds folk i Danmark," 96.
27. Warburg, "Andre guder."
28. Øster, *Barn i herrnhuternes Christiansfeld*, 43.
29. Thyssen, "Det store og det lille herrnhutersamfund," 20.

30. Holst, "Den herrnhutiske Brødremenighed"; Berg, Marcussen, and Stoklund, *Danish World Heritage Nomination*, 87–88.
31. Holst, "Den herrnhutiske Brødremenighed."
32. Thyssen, "Det store og det lille herrnhutersamfund," 35–38. See also chapter 2 in this collection.
33. Mettele, "Identities across Borders," 155–77.
34. Berg, Marcussen, and Stoklund, *Danish World Heritage Nomination*, 87–95; Petterson, "From Communal Economy," 25–48.
35. Thyssen, "Det store og det lille herrnhutersamfund," 81–92; Øster, *Barn i herrnhuternes Christiansfeld*.
36. Weber, *Readings and Commentary*, 217–20.
37. Balch, "Money and Power," 185–221.
38. Thyssen, "Det store og det lille herrnhutersamfund," 24–28.
39. Thyssen, 25.
40. Thyssen, 45–49; Mettele, "Identities across Borders".
41. Thyssen, "Det store og det lille herrnhutersamfund," 29.
42. Mettele, "Identities across Borders."
43. Thyssen, "Det store og det lille herrnhutersamfund," 28–29, 60–66.
44. Concepts and approaches for analyzing resource mobilization in proselytizing movements can be found in Warburg, *Citizens of the World*, 374–423.
45. Warburg, 264–71.
46. See chapter 10 in this collection.
47. Thyssen, "Det store og det lille herrnhutersamfund"; Elklit, "Befolkning og fattigforsorg," 103–42.
48. Newell, *Methods and Models*, 8. There is nearly always some uncertainty when assessing the numbers of births, deaths, and so forth for the specified period. A correction term, "error of closure," is usually added to the basic demographic equation to make the numbers fit with the observed growth. Newell, *Methods and Models*, 8; Warburg, *Citizens of the World*, 265–66. For simplification, this correction term is neglected here because it is not needed to demonstrate the principles of religious demography.
49. Warburg, *Citizens of the World*, 266.
50. Gabbert, "Social and Cultural Conditions," 291–308.
51. Thyssen, "Det store og det lille herrnhutersamfund," 48.
52. Thyssen, 54–56; Elklit, "Befolkning og fattigforsorg," 110–11.
53. Thyssen, "Det store og det lille herrnhutersamfund," 56; Elklit, "Befolkning og fattigforsorg," 108–13.
54. Lassen, "Population of Denmark," 134–57.
55. For example, in the period between 1871 and 1920 the population of North Schleswig grew by only 8 percent, compared with 51 percent population growth in Denmark proper and 63 percent in Prussia. Rerup, "National Minorities," 263.
56. Thyssen, "Det store og det lille herrnhutersamfund," 58–59.
57. Thyssen, 18–20; Richards, "Distant Garden," 55–74. The Moravian Danish Mission was founded much later, in 1843.
58. Elklit, "Befolkning og fattigforsorg," 122.
59. Elklit, 109.
60. Bøytler, personal communication, email, 23 April 2020.
61. Mettele, "Identities across Borders."
62. Salzmann quoted in Mettele, 155. The concept of world citizenship dates back to Greek philosophers of antiquity. It was a popular term during the Enlightenment. Warburg, *Citizens of the World*, 517–18.
63. Mettele, "Identities across Borders," 155.
64. Mettele.

65. Bøytler, *Ecclesiology and Culture*, 86–94.
66. Bøytler, *Gribe og begribe*, 175.
67. Bøytler, 63–65.
68. Warburg, *Citizens of the World*, 516–21.
69. Robertson, *Globalization*, 25–31; Robertson and Chirico, "Humanity, Globalization," 219–42; Warburg, *Citizens of the World*, 88–108.
70. Warburg, *Citizens of the World*, 93–98.
71. Anderson, *Imagined Communities*. See also Casanova, "Religion," 415–41.
72. Bøytler, *Gribe og begribe*, 205.
73. Hartby, "Gingerbread and Brethren."

References

Adair-Toteff, Christopher. "Max Weber's Charisma." *Journal of Classical Sociology* 5, no. 2 (2005): 189–204.

Anderson, Benedict. *Imagined Communities: Reflections on the Origin and Spread of Nationalism*. Rev. edn. London: Verso, 1994.

Balch, Robert. "Money and Power in Utopia: An Economic History of the Love Family." In *Money and Power in the New Religions*, edited by James T. Richardson, 185–221. Lewiston: Edwin Mellen, 1988.

Balle-Petersen, Margaretha. "Guds folk i Danmark" [God's people in Denmark]. *Folk og kultur Årbog for Dansk Etnologi og Folkemindevidenskab* 6, no. 1 (1977): 78–126.

Berg, Annemette Løkke Borg, Lene Lindberg Marcussen, and Karen Stoklund, eds. *Danish World Heritage Nomination: Christiansfeld a Moravian Settlement*. Kolding: Kolding Municipality, 2014.

Burkholder, Jared S. "'As on the Day of Pentecost': Revivalism, John Greenfield, and the Memory of August 13, 1727." *Journal of Moravian History* 19, no. 2 (2019): 182–210.

Bøytler, Jørgen Helge. "Ecclesiology and Culture in the Moravian Church." PhD diss., University of Aarhus, 2009.

Bøytler, Jørgen. *Gribe og begribe. Liv og tradition i Brødremenigheden* [Grasp and comprehend: Life and tradition in the Moravian congregation]. Christiansfeld: ProRex Forlag, 2015.

Casanova, José. "Religion, the New Millennium, and Globalization." *Sociology of Religion* 62, no. 4 (2001): 415–41.

Elklit, Tove. "Befolkning og fattigforsorg" [Population and care for the poor]. In *Herrnhuter-samfundet i Christiansfeld* [The Moravian community of Christiansfeld], edited by Anders Pontoppidan Thyssen, 103–42. Aabenraa: Historiske Samfund for Sønderjylland, 1984.

Espersen, Preben. *Kirkeret. Almindelig del* [Church law: General]. Copenhagen: Jurist- og Økonomforbundets Forlag, 1993.

Gabbert, Wolfgang. "Social and Cultural Conditions of Religious Conversion in Colonial Southwest Tanzania, 1891–1939." *Ethnology* 40, no. 4 (2001): 291–308.

Hartby, Inger. "Gingerbread and Brethren." 1001 Stories of Denmark. Retrieved 8 March 2022 from http://www.kulturarv.dk/1001fortaellinger/en_GB/christ iansfeld.

Holst, Rikke. "Den Herrnhutiske Brødremenighed, 1727" [The Moravian Brethren, 1727]. danmarkshistorien.dk. 30 January 2019. https://danmarkshistorien.dk/vis/materiale/den-herrnhutiske-broedremenighed/.

Lafrenz, Jürgen. "The Moravian Church's Settlement Congregations as Independent Settlements of Typological Significance." In Berg, Marcussen, and Stoklund, *Danish World Heritage Nomination*, 189–212.

Lassen, Aksel. "The Population of Denmark, 1660–1960." *Scandinavian Economic History Review* 14, no. 2 (1966): 134–57.

Mettele, Gisela. "Constructions of the Religious Self: Moravian Conversion and Transatlantic Communication." *Journal of Moravian History* 7, no. 2 (2007): 7–36.

Mettele, Gisela. "Identities across Borders: The Moravian Brethren as a Global Community." In *Pietism and Community in Europe and North America, 1650–1850*, edited by Jonathan Strom, 155–77. Leiden: Brill, 2010.

Newell, Colin. *Methods and Models in Demography*. London: Belhaven Press, 1988.

Øster, Andreas. *Barn i herrnhuternes Christiansfeld* [Childhood in Moravian Christiansfeld]. Åbenrå: Historisk Samfund for Sønderjylland, 1965.

Petterson, Christina. "From Communal Economy to Economic Community: Changes in Moravian Entrepreneurial Activities in the Eighteenth Century." *Journal for the History of Reformed Pietism* 3, no. 1 (2018): 25–48.

Ramsdal-Thomsen, Marie. "Frie menigheder—Danske valg- og frimenigheder." [Free congregations: Danish voluntary and free congregations]. *Religion i Danmark* (2010). https://samtidsreligion.au.dk/religion-i-danmark/rel-aarbog 10/mrt/.

Rerup, Lorenz. "National Minorities in South Jutland/Schleswig." In *Ethnicity and Nation Building in the Nordic World*, edited by Sven Tägil, 247–81. Carbondale: Southern Illinois University Press, 1995.

Richards, Helen. "Distant Garden: Moravian Missions and the Culture of Slavery in the Danish West Indies, 1732–1848." *Journal of Moravian History* 7, no. 2 (2007): 55–74.

Robertson, Roland. *Globalization: Social Theory and Global Culture*. London: SAGE, 1992.

Robertson, Roland, and JoAnn Chirico. "Humanity, Globalization, and Worldwide Religious Resurgence: A Theoretical Exploration." *Sociological Analysis* 46, no. 3 (1985): 219–42.

Smith, David Norman. "Faith, Reason, and Charisma: Rudolf Sohm, Max Weber, and the Theology of Grace." *Sociological Inquiry* 68, no. 1 (1998): 32–60.

Thyssen, Anders Pontoppidan. "Det store og det lille herrnhutersamfund" [The universal and particular Moravian community]. In *Herrnhuter-samfundet i Christiansfeld* [The Moravian community of Christiansfeld], edited by Anders Pontoppidan Thyssen, 11–102. Aabenraa: Historiske Samfund for Sønderjylland, 1984.

Vogt, Peter. "'Everywhere at Home': The Eighteenth-Century Moravian Movement as a Transatlantic Religious Community." *Journal of Moravian History* 6, no. 1 (2006): 7–29.

Weber, Max. *The Protestant Ethics and the Spirit of Capitalism*. Translated by Talcott Parsons. Mineola: Dover, 2003.

Weber, Max. *Max Weber: Readings and Commentary on Modernity*. Edited by Stephen Kalberg. Oxford: Blackwell, 2005.

Wallis, Roy, and Steve Bruce. *Sociological Theory, Religion and Collective Action*. Belfast: Queen's University, 1986.

Warburg, Margit. "Andre guder. Et religionssociologisk perspektiv" [Other gods: A perspective from sociology of religion]. In *Minoriteter. En grundbog. Fjorten synsvinkler på Minoritetsstudier* [Minorities: A textbook; Fourteen angles on minority studies], edited by Helen Krag and Margit Warburg, 37–59. Copenhagen: Spektrum, 1992.

Warburg, Margit. "The Baha'is of the North." In *New Nordic Religions*, edited by James Lewis and Inga Tøllefsen, 77–92. Leiden: Brill, 2015.

Warburg, Margit. *Citizens of the World: A History and Sociology of the Baha'is from a Globalisation Perspective*. Leiden: Brill, 2006.

Zorb, Elizabeth. "Reflections on Moravian Pietism." *Pennsylvania History: A Journal of Mid-Atlantic Studies* 25, no. 2 (1958): 115–21.

Chapter 6

Living with World Heritage
Authority and Knowledge in Contemporary Moravian Christiansfeld

Rasmus Rask Poulsen

In the summer of 2015, Christiansfeld, a Moravian Church settlement in Southern Denmark was added to UNESCO's World Heritage list. The prestigious recognition was a harbinger of increasing outside interest in both the historic townscape of the Christiansfeld settlement and the life and values of its Moravian congregation. Both have become objects of interest and inquiry by state agencies, cultural experts, and tourists.

The recognition of Christiansfeld as a World Heritage site was the culmination of over two decades' worth of negotiation, planning, and extensive restoration of the eighteenth-century built environment that comprises the prestigious site today. The local political initiative in the 1990s to pursue the UNESCO listing was supported by the Moravian congregation and Danish government agencies. This process coincided with the largest privately funded urban restoration project in Danish history, which began in 2003 and covered most of the historic buildings and public spaces within the twenty-one hectares of Moravian Christiansfeld. Successive restorative projects continue to this day and, as of 2015, the cost of the projects amounted to about 33.5 million euros (250 million Danish krone).[1]

Apart from the thorough restoration, the emergence of modern mass tourism is perhaps one of the most tangible changes that heritagization has brought to the town. Since its World Heritage listing, the official number of annual visitors to Christiansfeld has increased fivefold from 8,000 visitors in 2014 to between 30,000 and 40,000 in the following years.[2] As part of Kolding Municipality's active engagement in the preservation of the town's cultural heritage and application for World Heritage,

Christiansfeld Centret, a local visitors' center tasked with handling tourism and heritage management, was founded in 2009. As the on-site government authority, the center was created in cooperation with the Danish Moravian Church and Realdania.[3] Furthermore, a council consisting of government agents, local politicians, members of the Moravian council of elders, and the manager of the visitors' center (who, incidentally, is also the "UNESCO site manager") supervises this management according to legislation and local partnership agreements on sustainable policies and practices. Crucial to this chapter, the visitors' center also employs a corps of part-time tour guides who show tourists around the World Heritage site. As such, formal and informal cooperation has existed for many years between local stakeholders in Christiansfeld: Kolding Municipality, local residents, and the Moravian Church.

Interpreting Christiansfeld

The purpose of this study is to understand how the contemporary Moravian Brethren of Christiansfeld engage with the recent growth in external interpretation of their collective identity and values in the context of heritagization. As such, the study explores the ways in which the negotiation and authorization of knowledge is a crucial element of World Heritage designation for the Moravian Brethren in Christiansfeld.

External interpretations of Moravian heritage proliferated in the years following Christiansfeld's inscription on the World Heritage list. However, not all interpretations are consistent with how Moravians understand their heritage, identity, and values. Erroneous stories bother local Moravians, as they argue that these misrepresent their heritage values and their customs. By all accounts, such stories existed well before 2015 and World Heritage prominence, but in the years that followed they gained a much larger audience. This phenomenon demonstrates how heritagization can accentuate differences or create new ones, as heritage-making brings dissonance to social contexts with various local actors beset on interpreting, disseminating, and arguing about what various heritage things do and mean to people in the present.[4]

I argue that the concern with these stories, expressed by some of my interlocutors in Christiansfeld, reflects a general concern among some Danish Moravians about control over the various representations and interpretations of Moravian heritage. To understand why the accuracy of these stories mattered to some Moravians, I examine how Moravian interlocutors categorized various forms of knowledge about heritage, and how the sources of knowledge and the stories they produced were distinguished by their proximity to Moravian life. This brings the chapter to an investigation of the continual negotiation of Moravian heritage as a subject for interpretation and mediation by local Moravian and non-Moravian "heritage actors." Below, I will demonstrate how Moravians responded to some of the stories that circulated in Christiansfeld. To clarify matters, I first discuss the various forms of knowledge that seemed to converge and collide in Christiansfeld. In response to these stories, I argue, some Moravians in Christiansfeld would employ a normative distinction between Moravian forms of endo-knowledge and non-Moravian forms of exo-knowledge. For this model of endo- and exo-knowledge I am indebted to David Berliner's work on exo- and endo-nostalgia in relation to heritage.[5] The model is proposed to understand how Moravians value and categorize different forms of knowledge according to the source of knowledge and the proximity of the "knowers" to the congregation, past and present.

The apparent tension between forms of knowledge demonstrates that religious and social experience ranks higher than academic texts and non-Moravian interpretations of heritage, according to Moravian interlocutors. An emphasis on the authority of Moravian knowledge, I further argue, is used by some Moravians to assert control over the narrative and perception of Moravian heritage, identity, and values in an increasingly unpredictable World Heritage context. By determining the legitimacy of various forms of knowledge, the Moravian congregants seek to align the predominant interpretation of themselves and their heritage with their contemporary self-image. Thus, the ongoing struggle to influence or control the legitimacy of what counts as accurate knowledge about them (and the subsequent interpretations) is essentially a struggle for the community's ability to control and recognize its identity and values. In the following, the distinction between forms of knowledge will first be categorized in terms of whether the knower is external or internal to the Moravian Church in Denmark. However, the line between what qualifies as either "endo-knowledge" or "exo-knowledge" is continuously blurred through everyday negotiation and use of sources.

The study is based on anthropological research informed by qualitative data collected during five months of ethnographic fieldwork in Christiansfeld, in the latter half of 2016 and early 2017 along with several shorter visits in the following years.[6] During my first longer stay in Christiansfeld, I tried to accustom myself to local life and the Moravian congregation in town.

In short, this analysis is not based on how *all* local Moravians saw the matter. The particular long-term fieldwork was done by observing and participating in everyday practices of the community. I did this to understand how World Heritage status and related processes affected the contemporary everyday life of the congregation, and how Moravians understand their town, themselves, and their past in relation to World Heritage as a transformative social and cultural process. As such, the following analysis is yet another contribution to the external (or exo-) knowledge about Moravian heritage described in this chapter. Ideally, this study joins the other sources of exo-knowledge that local Moravians in Christiansfeld take to be reputable accounts of their lives. Again, this explicitly positions my account and reflections along the endo-perspectives of these interlocutors.

Forms of Knowledge

It was the day of the Moravian Church hall's reopening—a day that many of my Moravian interlocutors had anticipated, as it was the first service in the grand church building in months following a thorough restoration. In the southern vestibule of the church building, a small group of Moravians, dressed in their best clothes, were passing time as they waited for the service to begin. Among them were members of the church's brass band, who were preparing their instruments before they would walk onto the church square to play a short hymn in lieu of the church bells, as is tradition before Moravian celebratory services. Shortly before the service, a man in the group, Søren, asked whether anyone had heard the new story of the sand-filled ashtrays by the entrance of the church room. Apparently, he went on, a local tour guide had told tourists that Moravians would step into the ashtray before they entered the church hall, as a religious gesture, as a symbolic footbath. This was the reason why there was sand on the wooden floors of the church. As Søren recounted the scenario, the other churchgoers laughed, and some shook their heads in disbelief. A few days after the reopening of the church, I asked Simon, a Moravian interlocutor, about the ashtray story. He explained, "People who ask us about those things, well, you could make them believe all the stuff about Jesus and the forty days in the desert. You've got all the power. There's not much else to say than it's practical. It's very practical, because it's easy to clean." The use of the sand was a custom many churchgoers remembered from their childhoods; the community had kept it because it was a simple, practical remedy that would slowly *sand* the floor (i.e., grind it) and absorb any residual downpour from the outside. What Simon also inferred was that local guides hold a certain authority in defining Moravian heritage and therefore their interpretations hold a greater audience than that of the individual Moravian.

When presented to you, these stories may seem trivial or innocent, as they are mostly inaccurate interpretations of Moravian history or religious practices. However, to many of the Moravians with whom I worked, these curious stories mattered. The reason, they argued, is that such stories mis*represent* and mis*interpret* who the Moravian Brethren believe they *are* and, just as importantly, who they believe they *were*. The stories, some locals suggested, were likely manufactured and spread by tourists or local tour guides. However, their origin was hard to locate, as they were transferred by word of mouth. One of the most dreaded public perceptions of Moravian heritage is the frequent comparison between the Moravian Brethren and the Amish people of North America, proposed solely as an evocative shorthand by outsiders. On the Amish comparison, Gerda, an elderly Moravian, said, "When [name of a guide] says that we are comparable to the Amish, that's the kind of thing we have to have removed. These are two widely different things. They are so widely different. They have nothing to do with each other." Here the role of the tour guide emerges. Tour guides have become the professional and, in Christiansfeld, official mediators of Moravian history, culture, and religion. Being the visible arbiters of information about Moravian life, they carry a certain authority in their communication and have considerable agency to develop their own narratives around the past and present of Moravian Christiansfeld. In this sense, guides inhabit a pivotal role in local tourist contexts, as authorities that inform the tourists' knowledge and feed them their narratives, their value judgments.[7]

Before we move on, I must stress that use of the plural "guides" does not include all guides all the time; rather, *some* guides are *sometimes* perceived to have a loose grip on what Moravians believe to be the right version of various matters of their church's past and present. In recent years, the Christiansfeld Center has sought to streamline guide scripts and knowledge to minimize misconceptions, and this takes place in accordance and coordination with senior members of the church. An important aspect has been the recruitment of a few members of the Moravian Church whose insight and experience other Moravians, with whom I spoke, would privilege over that of non-member guides. The central problem here was that sometimes tour guides would tell stories that were almost unrecognizable to members of the Moravian community, like the explanation of the sand's purpose. It seemed, one Moravian interlocutor said, that everything about Christiansfeld had to mean something. Again, the ashtray story may seem like an insignificant detail, a mere misunderstanding of Moravian customs, but to many Moravians such details were important. They expressed genuine concern about how others interpret and understand their cultural heritage.

To disentangle the various claims made about stories, their accuracy, and their legitimacy, I propose that we define two general forms of knowledge about Moravian heritage in light of my earlier distinction between exo- and endo-knowledge. The first is Moravian forms of knowledge (endo-knowledge), which is knowledge provided or mediated by Moravians from Moravian sources. The other is a form of non-Moravian knowledge (exo-knowledge), which is knowledge of Moravian heritage provided by non-Moravians. The primary difference between these two forms of knowledge appears to be the sources that inform them and consequently their authority in the eyes of church members with whom I worked. In the article "Multiple Nostalgias," anthropologist David Berliner explores nostalgia as a factor in the heritagization of Luang Prabang in Laos. In his analysis, Berliner shows how nostalgia takes on different shapes in the field and is a performative force with a transformative effect on people and objects in the heritage context. Social agents, although socially and geographically disconnected, share a nostalgic attachment to the past and the present of this heritage site. For the purposes of this study, I deploy Berliner's distinction between two forms of "nostalgic postures" in terms of endo- and exo-nostalgia as the two ends of a continuum. The main difference between these postures is the fact that a sense of endo-nostalgia is a longing for a personally experienced past that implies ownership over it, whereas exo-nostalgia is a vicarious longing for a past one has not personally experienced. The analytical advantage of this continuum is that it leaves room for the multiple meanings of nostalgia found in the ethnography of the "grey area of ambivalence" between each end of the spectrum. The distinction between them is not absolute because experiences are complex and as such can qualify as both.[8]

In the remainder of this chapter, I argue that some forms of knowledge about Moravian heritage might qualify as both "endo" and "exo" because they may share the same source material, be it a historical text or an experience. The advantage I see in Berliner's models is the notion of a "continuum" between the opposing "endo" and "exo" ends of the model, which makes it possible to account for the complexity found in the ethnographic material from Christiansfeld. As such, some claims of knowledge can be both "endo" and "exo" at different moments depending on who makes them and how the person has derived the knowledge. This is to maintain that knowledge is not an immutable phenomenon; thus, for the model to capture the nuances of the ethnography, it is important to note the field of ambivalence and convergence between the two ends of the continuum. An example of something that can be said to be both endo and exo forms of knowledge are the texts displayed on posters in the local visitor center. Information provided here about the church has been produced in cooperation with senior members of the church. Similarly, in the summer of 2019 the many travels of Reverend Jørgen Bøytler, first as a Moravian missionary and then as general secretary to the global Moravian Church, were exhibited with posters and pictures. Both examples of cooperation show us that forms of knowledge can be both endo and exo at the same time and that the categories are in flux rather than fixed. The point here is that while external interpretations and representations of Moravian life sometimes differ from how some Moravians perceive it, there are also instances of cooperation and align-ment in interpretation and representation. Next, we examine what the categories may nevertheless tell us about the heritagization of Moravian Christiansfeld following its UNESCO recognition.

Disentangling

The two categories of knowledge I propose are, first, forms of endo-knowledge, which is Moravian forms of knowledge about Moravian heritage, values, and identity and has a set of distinct features. Based on my ethnographic material I propose that such knowledge is derived from direct social and religious experience, cultural transmission, and personal as well as collective memory usually exclusive to Moravians. In general terms, this knowledge concerns individual and collective Moravian identity and the past and present experiences of Moravians with whom members identify in the present.[9] This category of knowledge often holds authority, according to a number of Moravian congregants, over the other category of knowledge—namely, forms of non-Moravian knowledge (i.e., exo-knowledge)—because Moravians attribute legiti-macy to firsthand social and religious experience as well as memory. This preference is over non-Moravian sources like historical texts, which interlocutors in turn would argue are the basis for external interpretation of Moravian heritage. The analytical distinction is meant to illuminate our ethnographic and analytical interest at hand, namely the knowl-edge of Moravian heritage and its part in the local heritage discourse. The negotiation of heritage as knowledge about the past is a continual process, and as a cultural, social, and political resource, heritage is a medium for communication and the transmission of values and ideas. To understand what this knowledge means and how it is used, we must identify who negotiates knowledge and what their sources are.[10] What the heritage actors negotiate is the ability to speak authoritatively about Moravian culture as heritage to others.

In a setting like Christiansfeld, a World Heritage site with a living religious heritage community, where members of the Moravian community can be understood as "original observers" to heritage, the authority of external interpreters like tour guides or experts does not stand alone as it may do in heritage places without host communities.[11] Possessing endo-knowledge about Moravian life, contemporary Moravians reduce the given distance between source, interpretation, interpreter, and audience. They are, in other words, directly and subjectively invested in the interpretation of Moravian heritage, whereas a setting without a living community is left solely in the hands of outside actors. In this way, the distance between interpreter and the matter interpreted is much wider. This means that such interpretation of heritage is vicarious and distanced over time. Nevertheless, external actors are part of the interpretation of numerous communities all over the world, just as they are in Christiansfeld, where the number of non-Moravian heritage actors is growing and changing.[12] This category of heritage actors also contributes to the circulation and interpretation of Moravian heritage just as the Moravian community does. However, interpretations of Moravian Christiansfeld as heritage can diverge and cause dissonance from time to time, as Frederik Barth writes on the inevitability of external intervention in local forms of knowledge: "An environment of non-local others and their knowledge systems, practices, and strengths will always impinge on local worlds from the outside."[13]

This brings us to the questions of who the interpreters are, whence they derive their knowledge, and how Moravians classify these forms of knowledge.

Books, Memory, and Experience

Moravians differentiate between the quality of various sources that support interpretations and knowledge about the Moravian past and present. Such sources, I found, were not always equally available to everyone. Some were accessible only to those who were (active) members of the church or had grown up inside it (endo-knowledge)—the primary source here is social and religious experience. Other sources, such as books or posters in an exhibition, were public and thus available to everyone. The crux of the matter was, some Moravians told me, that the latter lacked the experiential and sensual qualities of lived and socialized practice that are inescapably linked with considerable authority in terms of knowing what Moravian life is and was. This was illustrated by a disagreement between Niels, a Moravian, and a local tour guide. Niels believed that this type of disagreement had emerged after the World Heritage recognition in the summer of 2015, which expanded the field of interested heritage actors who felt they were entitled to be interpreters and intermediaries of Moravian heritage.[14] In other words, the perceived (i.e., by local Moravians) authority over what the past means and who holds such authority is transformed as part of the heritagization of Moravian culture. Here we see authority not as something stable or final but as an ongoing process of negotiating and distributing authority. This affected the need for accuracy in representations of Moravian history and heritage. Niels noted,

> Now while this has become UNESCO you really have to be precise and try to be as correct as possible. There might be things, that somebody like me has been raised with, that are the wrong information. I've always been used to this kind of information, so I get goddamned angry when some schoolteacher comes and tells me something that isn't true. Because that's what I'm raised with.

Here he alludes to a general distinction made by Moravians between the different interpreters and their access to knowledge—specifically, between non-Moravians and Moravians and the availability of forms of endo-knowledge about Moravian heritage. While the guide claimed to know that he was right by basing his knowledge on books, Niels was not convinced: "He said, 'It says so in this and that book,' and then I said, 'Yes, yes, it's just people who wrote that book, then it doesn't have to be true just because it's in a book.'" Seeing as both parties were engaged in negotiating aspects of Moravian heritage, their individual positions in the social landscape of Christiansfeld seemed to determine their access to the legitimate source and essentially the authority of their claim. The first reason may be that the guide was a non-Moravian local. The guide's interest in Moravian heritage had only recently surfaced, Niels argued— an example of the rising level of attention that Moravian Christiansfeld has seen in recent years. The argument was that this group's investment in Moravian matters was a new thing and thus socially and experientially vicarious. This was why it did not compare to Niels's own inherited sense of Moravian heritage as part of his identity. This brings about another reason for Niels's frustration, namely the difference in their individual proximity to endo-knowledge and collective memory.

Maurice Halbwachs's concept of "collective memory" shares many features with the argument made by several of my Moravian interlocutors.[15] Halbwachs argues that every community constructs its identity based on collective memories, and memory, like heritage, is a cultural process that engages the past subjectively in the present through interpretation and negotiation by communities and individuals. This is relevant because Moravian heritage becomes part of Moravian identity through memory work, and because ideas regarding identity are inevitably supported by a sense of the past. Who we are now is related to how we remember who we *were*. While this sort of shared social memory does not hold the accuracy of history, it can provide a strong sense of belonging and communion with a past one has not personally experienced. In this sense, collective memory is entirely subjective, as opposed to history, which Halbwachs sees as an attempt to objectively differentiate and categorize the past in chronological order to make the past universally available. At the same time, collective memory is intimate and exclusive to the community that remembers, because such memories can belong only to a specific community through which they are socially and culturally transmitted. Collective memory becomes a way to socialize individuals into a community who share a coherent and meaningful vision of the past.[16]

The arguments made by Moravians rests upon a notion that Moravian memory and identity is exclusive to church members as a somewhat coherent religious and social unit that transcends time. As Simon reflected during an interview, "When I walk up the stairs of the Sisters' House, I miss my old dented steps.... You think, 'These stairs are bumpy because someone has walked on them throughout two hundred years,' and that means something to me, because those people [who] walked there did so for a reason and that was the church life." What this act of remembrance shows us is an example of how Moravian interlocutors related to other Moravians of the past in Christiansfeld. That the stairs of the Sisters' House inspired an emotional response shows that Simon saw and felt a relation between his own life in the present and the genealogical group of Moravians past. Such sensations or notions of fellowship with those who went before are not necessarily meaningful for everyone. Another experience in Christiansfeld illustrates this.

Working in the church hall one day, I helped a group of volunteers moving pews back to the church hall after having been repainted during the church's restoration in the summer and autumn of 2016. There, I talked to Joan, whose family had been Moravians for generations. "Earlier, I stood here working and I didn't really feel like it, but then I thought of my family who had lived in this town and worked," she said as she was cleaning a pew. A littler later during a break in her work, Joan looked knowingly at me as she was standing under one of the green and gold-colored chandeliers hanging from the high ceiling of the church. "Do you know how it works?" she asked and reached for a hardly noticeable handle on the chandelier's underside. Smoothly, she pulled the handle and the chandelier came down in a slow motion while a counterweight rose to the ceiling. "I remember this from when I was a child," Joan said. "That you knew this, it was sort of funny, then you were home." She smiled as she let on that knowledge about this sort of thing was akin to a secret, a privilege known to a few.

These mundane notions of the past that give meaning and value to the present are part of how Moravians construct their identity through memory work. In many ways, these different engagements with the stairs and chandeliers reflect Paul Connerton's definition of "locus of memory" as a configuration of space that evokes memory, in the sense that objects have agency but in relation to lived experience or habitual activity. "To 'live' an artefact is to appropriate it, to make it one's own,"[17] which means that familiar things through continual use and engagement in daily life become subjective phenomena that situate one in the world spatially and temporally in meaningful ways. These things are *known* and not *known about*, Connerton writes, pointing to the direct and experiential "matter-of-factness" that places and things can hold in the memory work they do. They are mundane but integral to one's identity and sense of place, because they are sensuous and have permeance, although not spectacularly so.[18] Rather, they serve many needs and are not just objects of memory (like memorials); as such, they engender memory but not only memory. I would argue that the objects in the church hall or the stairs of the Sisters' House are loci of memory, because they are mundanely engaged as things among other things but they come to evoke memory through continued experience. As loci ("effective carriers of cultural memory"), they are "lived" with as subjective carriers of memory, which makes the present valuable and meaningful because of their reach into a collective past. However, their meaning as Moravian memories or loci are exclusive to those who share said identity. In Connerton's words, the stairs and chandeliers are *known* to Moravians and merely *known about* by others.

This distinction speaks to the qualities of what I term "endo" and "exo" forms of knowledge. The "lived-with" character of the presented loci of memory shows us their fundamental experiential and habitual status to those in whose lives they exist and to which they give special meaning. The things here are simply more than their function, because they hold the capacity to engender emotional responses in those who know through their use and sight, which is what makes them "known" in Connerton's terminology. In this way, they order and reaffirm a sense of belonging through time and space that lies at the heart of what I take endo-knowledge to represent. This is, among other things, what remains exclusive to local members of the church. In the next section, I pursue this notion of exclusivity through experience and membership, namely religious or ceremonial experience.

Exclusive Access

To negotiate authority over the past by way of either history or memory speaks to the qualities of each concept as a form of knowledge about the past. Where history distances the past and puts it at arm's length, it also exempts the past from the subjective qualities of memory, which dissolve one's distance to the past.[19] In this way, memory holds more (emotional) weight and fosters a sense of immediate relation not found in history. The subjective nature of memory renders it easily contestable, David Lowenthal argues, but this does not prevent memory from being a flexible and paradoxical force. Its lack of verifiable sources frees memory from the subtlety and constraints that make history scientific and reliable, as memory instead awards a wider, more profound and sensitive insight into the past than historical knowledge.[20] Niels's perspective rested on various forms of endo-knowledge, which had been given to him throughout his life, through social and cultural transmission and collective memory as a member of an old Moravian family. This privileged him with access to an exclusive reservoir of sources of endo-knowledge. By contrast, he argued that the guide's opinion was based on the information found in publicly available books on Moravian history, which provided vicarious historical knowledge. As such, the guide's exo-knowledge did (according to Niels) not necessarily carry the same authority in a discussion about Moravian affairs as Niels's own endo-knowledge did.

The notion of exclusive access to social memory was evoked by another Moravian interlocutor, June, who felt that members whose family had been part of the congregation for generations would inherently know more than others about Moravian culture. June said, "I've got stories about some of the houses here and the people who've lived here, even before I came to town, because I am part of an old Moravian family." She continued by stating that regular membership was essential to knowledge, since it provided privileged access to religious experiences; for instance, "The basic things that happen in church, you can't read that, you have to experience it." This point implicitly reminds us that the Moravian faith is rooted in German Pietism, a form of Protestantism that emphasizes the individual believer's personal relation to and experience *with* and *of* the divine. Thus, religious experience is also an important source of knowledge about Moravian identity and values.

Here June invoked collective memory resulting from her family ties. Signifying that she had stories that exceeded her years, June situated herself as someone in touch with Moravians as a genealogical community. This position resonates with what Niels said, above, when he expressed anger at being corrected by a tour guide who in his eyes had only recently become invested in Moravian heritage. To Niels and to June, Moravian heritage would seem not as much a matter of historical interest and curiosity as a matter of being subjectively part of a religious and social community whose values inform one's personal identity in the present by way of the past. Consequently, to be a Moravian interpreter of Moravian heritage entails access to exclusive forms of knowledge that are essentially not attainable by non-Moravians.

Thus, in the presented reflections by Moravian interlocutors concerning knowledge about Moravian heritage, a crucial distinction emerged between being and not being Moravian. Being a member of the Moravian community grants Moravians an acute understanding and sense of belonging to the Moravian community and its heritage values. This sort of knowledge of the past, along with its transmission, nurtures a sense of belonging to a coherent and lasting community whose values transcend time and space.[21]

The importance of attendance at and involvement in Moravian services was a recurrent theme in interlocutors' arguments regarding valid knowledge about Moravian life and customs. Without ritual participation, they argued, any person would lack essential experiential knowledge. Interlocutors normatively differentiated between forms of knowledge that were "sourced from" ceremonial experience in church and forms of knowledge that were not. Such experiences kept what Moravians saw as their non-exotic Moravian practices from being mis*interpreted* and mis*represented*. As June pointed out, "everyone can read about all that, but you can't feel what it is to sit in church and participate in communion, for example, not if you haven't tried it. Then you don't know what you're talking about. In my opinion, there's a big difference." The difference June identified was a distinction between the actual quality of sources of knowledge, which held that historical texts as a source of knowledge about Moravian heritage did not necessarily provide the insight provided by sensuous and empirical experiences. She also argued that such an experiential necessity would privilege endo-knowledge, because Moravians are more invested in Moravian heritage by default owing to their sense of belonging to the community.

These statements so far support the distinction between endo and exo forms of knowledge; however, as we will see, several sources inhabit what Berliner termed "the grey area of ambivalence," where sources can be said to be both authoritative according to some Moravians *and* written by authors external to the Moravian Church. This ethnographic nuance complicates the potential either-or categorization of forms of knowledge and again shows us that we are looking at a process of continual negotiation of authority. Such entanglement reveals that authority over heritage is neither a given nor inherent. Rather, what heritage means can mutate and take on new meanings unknown to those who claim to own it or identify with it, which, I would argue, only accentuates the need for control and alignment of heritage phenomena.

The privileging of experience over verbal or written sources of knowledge, admitted Erik, a Moravian tour guide, was an inherent challenge for all heritage actors—and also for tourists, whom he always encouraged to attend services. As for non-Moravian tour guides and other locals, he doubled down on his claim and proposed, "You must familiarize yourself with it, in the manner that you're not a bystander, but through participation. Only in that way can you get to the core of what this is." This distinction between passive bystander and active participant reproduces other Moravian claims about the significance of active agency regarding World Heritage. Along with historian of religion Robert Orsi, we could say that the central point here is that "by telling their stories, the writers blur the line between the past and present and transform themselves from the objects of history into its subjects and narrators."[22] In this sense, storytelling about the Moravian past and present becomes a way of attaining agency. However, as this chapter shows, Moravians do not hold sole authorship of these stories. Their authority has been challenged and they have responded by means of authorizing what they know through their experience, memory, and membership.

In summary, this would also stipulate that an essential difference exists between being Moravian and not, which pertains to an almost immanent sense of identification and belonging to the community, and to Christiansfeld as a decidedly Moravian place in the world. Exo-knowledge, as opposed to endo-knowledge, primarily stems from various sources employed and written by non-Moravians, like historical texts, which become the basis for exo-mediation and interpretation of Moravian heritage. Thus, a key difference between forms of knowledge is the access to collective and personal experience and memories as a subjective investment in Moravian past and present.

Between these two ends of the continuum, within the "grey area of ambivalence," are more inclusive and, according to Moravians, qualitatively more reliable sources of both endo- and exo-knowledge. These sources of knowledge are all publicly available and inclusive by design, such as non-Moravian participation in Moravian religious rituals or specific written sources authored by both Moravian and non-Moravian experts. One of these sources is the widely respected two-volume anthology *Herrnhuter-samfundet i Christiansfeld* (The Moravian community of Christiansfeld), of nearly eight hundred pages, edited by church historian Anders Pontoppidan Thyssen; on several occasions I saw this work on Moravian bookshelves or heard it referenced in discussions about Moravian heritage. This anthology on Moravian Christiansfeld stands out from the array of available textual sources that support knowledge about Moravian Christiansfeld.[23]

Occasionally called "the yellow Bibles" by Moravians, the anthology contains twelve detailed research articles on Moravian Christiansfeld's history, its architecture, and the congregation's (historical) socioeconomic and religious life. The authority of this publication as a source of knowledge about Moravian identity and history seems undisputed by Moravian interlocutors. This was illustrated to me one day when a staff member of the Christiansfeld Center turned to Marie, a senior figure in the church, with a question. Admitting that she did not know the answer, Marie suggested that the staffer read Thyssen's anthology. "It's him we follow, if we're in doubt," she said, noting the meticulousness of its archival work as proof of quality.[24]

Privileged as a well-researched source of knowledge on Moravian Christiansfeld of the past, this source complicates the distinction between Moravian and non-Moravian knowledge. In a sense, its contents represent the range of source material authored by various interpreters whom Moravian interlocutors would privilege as reliable and nuanced sources of knowledge. Additionally, within the inclusive category of publicly available sources are two publications authored by Reverend Jørgen Bøytler on Christiansfeld's material heritage and Moravian theology and history.[25] The "yellow Bibles" especially illustrate the fact that there are legitimate and authoritative sources of exo-knowledge that sustain what some Moravians in Christiansfeld think is the correct version of shared past and present identity.

Conclusion

One of the reasons why the described affirmations of authority are important in negotiating what Moravian heritage means, I believe, is the question of control. In this case, control is about defining the parameters of when heritage is meaningful and legitimate and when it is not. The issue of control over heritage comes up particularly in times of cultural change, like a World Heritage recognition, that results in outside interest.[26]

This study has sought to describe how the Moravians with whom I worked took part in the designation of authority to sources and forms of knowledge. In trying to capture this process of authorizing postures and insight according to membership, experience, and social memory, I presented two forms of knowledge about Moravian life intended to occupy opposite ends of a continuum. The distinction between endo-knowledge and exo-knowledge allows us to categorize what some Moravians mean when they argue that they in fact are more invested in or knowledgeable about Moravian pasts and values than others. Far from exhaustive, most of the presented ethnographic data that I place within this classificatory model does not necessarily fit exclusively into one or the other form of knowledge. Instead, some of the examples provided here are located in between, in "the grey area of ambivalence," where sources (such as an academic anthology on the history of Moravian Christiansfeld) can be both authoritative and not authored by Moravians—even though interlocutors would argue that non-Moravian sources do not provide the same insight as the experience of regular church services. Both claims can exist at the same time, which points toward some conclusive (but again, not exhaustive) points about how the World Heritage designation has affected conceptions of knowledge among the Moravians in Christiansfeld with whom I had the chance to work. In a metatextual way, this study is an addition to existing sources of exo-knowledge about Moravian Christiansfeld. As such, these reflections can perhaps best be judged by their ability to reflect or illuminate local Moravian experiences.

Without control over this process of heritage formation, local communities that identify with given heritage values may be subjected to external, authorized understandings of themselves. Therefore, the ability to assume control over definitions of heritage, and to retain active agency, is crucial for communities who *practice, inhabit,* or *identify with* cultural heritage phenomena. In emphasizing the importance of Moravian agency, the community may grant itself a decisive part to play in the heritage-making of Christiansfeld and of themselves. The rhetorical distinction between what I call endo-knowledge and exo-knowledge can thus be seen as an effort to control or influence the local discourse and knowledge about the Moravian community's identity, its values, and its past. Details matter in this regard.

In the end, I argue that Moravian efforts to set a normative scale for what counts as valuable or reliable knowledge is part of how some members of congregation have become aware of their vulnerability and agency in a World Heritage context. I see the privileging of exclusive Moravian sources of knowledge, such as collective memory, as a means to assert some kind of control in the continual negotiations over who the

Moravians *were*, who they *are*, and what others *know* about them. As such, the normative classification by interlocutors about forms of knowledge is a response to outside contestations to local Moravian knowledge about their shared religious and cultural heritage.

Rasmus Rask Poulsen is a PhD fellow at the Danish Folklore Archives, Royal Danish Library, and the section of Ethnology, University of Copenhagen. He has previously worked at the cross-European HERILIGION project at the Department of Anthropology, University of Copenhagen, on the heritagization of religious practice, objects, and places at the three Danish World Heritage sites (Jelling, Roskilde, and Christiansfeld). His current project is a study of heritagization of the Moravian communities in Christiansfeld, Bethlehem, and Herrnhut with a particular focus on the effects of UNESCO's World Heritage program on daily life as well as the use and understanding of history in the settlements.

Notes

1. Frandsen and Troense, *Christiansfeld*, 60–62; Realdania, *Værdiskabende udvikling af kulturmiljøer*.
2. Locals suggest that the actual number of visitors to Christiansfeld is much higher, as these numbers only account for people who enter the visitor center.
3. For more information about the center and its responsibilities, see the Christiansfeld Museum website (https://www.christiansfeldcentret.dk/en).
4. Tunbridge and Ashworth, *Dissonant Heritage*.
5. Berliner, "Multiple Nostalgias."
6. The data collected during this initial fieldwork was the basis for my master's thesis in anthropology at the University of Copenhagen (Poulsen, "Like Living Stones.").
7. Feldman and Skinner, "Tour Guides," 5–7.
8. Berliner, "Multiple Nostalgias," 782.
9. On this relation between individual and collective identity among Moravians, see chapter 2 in this volume.
10. Graham, "Heritage as Knowledge," 1007.
11. Lowenthal, *The Past*, 338.
12. Smith, *Hosts and Guests*; Waterton and Smith, "Recognition and Misrecognition"; Stasch, "Primitivist Tourism"; Khanom et al., "Host–Guest Authentication."
13. Barth, "Anthropology of Knowledge," 4.
14. Niels said, "I feel there is tendency among the Tyrstrup-core (non-Moravian locals), or what you want to call them, who are not Moravians and never have been, who've just been on the side-lines and now have a sense of ownership, because now Christiansfeld has become the whole town."

15. Halbwachs and Coser, *On Collective Memory*; Wertsch, *Voices*, 60–66.
16. Wertsch, *Voices*.
17. Connexton, *How Modernity Forgets*, 32.
18. Connexton, 21.
19. Lowenthal, *The Past*, 381.
20. For a nuanced discussion on the entanglement memory and history, as well as the use of both, see Assmann "Transformations."
21. Assmann "Transformations."
22. Orsi, *Madonna*, xi.
23. Among these textual sources were a series of books written by Moravians including Øster, *Barn i herrnhuternes Christiansfeld*, and Rønnow, *Brødremenigheden*, and non-Moravians including Petersen, *Christiansfeld*; Nissen, *Hjerternes By*; and Frandsen and Troense, *Christiansfeld*.
24. The chapters concern Moravian Christiansfeld's demographic and social development, its professional and economic structure, its boarding school system, its townscape and buildings, Moravian music, and theological traditions. Thyssen, *Herrnhuter-samfundet*. See also chapter 1 in this book.
25. Bøytler, *Gribe og begribe*; Bøytler and Jessen, *Christiansfeld*.
26. In this, I follow archaeologist Laurajane Smith. Her point is here that the ability of local groups to control their heritage is a fundamental aspect of the creation of cohesive meaning, knowledge, and identity, or, in short, the community's "place in the world." The capacity to have control over heritage arises when cultural conflict and change occurs, like when outside experts subject heritage communities to imposed standards or definitions. The possibility of losing active agency in the face of imposed policies or attributes threatens to destabilize the presumed cohesion of heritage identity and causes friction and dissonance. Without control, communities become exposed to foreign objectives and ideas about their identity. Smith, *Uses of Heritage*, 288–90.

Bibliography

Assmann, Aleida. "Transformations between History and Memory." *Social Research* 75, no. 1 (2008): 49–72.
Barth, Fredrik. "An Anthropology of Knowledge." *Current Anthropology* 43, no. 1 (2002): 1–18.
Berliner, David. "Multiple Nostalgias: The Fabric of Heritage in Luang Prabang (Lao PDR)." *Journal of the Royal Anthropological Institute* 18, no. 4 (2012): 769–86.
Bundsgaard, Inge. "Skolevæsenet 1864–1920" [The school system, 1864–1920]. In Thyssen, *Herrnhuter-samfundet i Christiansfeld*, 579–632.
Bøytler, Jørgen. *Gribe og begribe, liv og tradition i Brødremenigheden* [Grasp and comprehend: Life and tradition in the Moravian congregation]. Christiansfeld: ProRex, 2015.
Bøytler, Jørgen, and Jørgen Toft Jessen. *Christiansfeld, livet og husene* [Christiansfeld: Life and the houses]. Søborg: Det Danske Idéselskab, 2015.
Connertor, Paul. *How Modernity Forgets*. Cambridge: Cambridge University Press, 2009.
Elklit, Tove. "Befolkning og fattigforsorg" [Population and care for the poor]. In Thyssen, *Herrnhuter-samfundet i Christiansfeld*, 103–42.

Engqvist, Hans Henrik. "Byplan og bygninger" [Town plan and buildings]. In Thyssen, *Herrnhuter-samfundet i Christiansfeld*, 417–90.

Feldman, Jackie, and Jonathan Skinner. "Tour Guides as Cultural Mediators: Performance and Positioning." *Ethnologia Europaea—Journal of European Ethnology* 48, no. 2 (2018): 5–14.

Frandsen, Søren, and Stine Troense. *Christiansfeld—En levende by* [Christiansfeld: A living town]. Odder: Narayna Press, 2014.

Graham, Brian. "Heritage as Knowledge: Capital or Culture?" *Urban Studies* 39, no. 5–6 (2002): 1003–17.

Halbwachs, Maurice, and Lewis A. Coser. *On Collective Memory*. The Heritage of Sociology. Chicago: University of Chicago Press, 1992.

Lowenthal, David. *The Past Is a Foreign Country—Revisited*. Cambridge: Cambridge University Press, 2015.

Khanom, Shahida, Brent Moyle, Noel Scott, and Millicent Kennelly. "Host–Guest Authentication of Intangible Cultural Heritage: A Literature Review and Conceptual Model." *Journal of Heritage Tourism* 14, no. 5–6 (2019): 396–408.

Nissen, Henri. *Hjerternes By—Christiansfeld—Verdensarv—Vores arv* [Town of hearts—Christiansfeld—World heritage—Our heritage]. Christiansfeld: Udfordringens Forlag, 2015.

Orsi, Robert A. *The Madonna of 115th Street: Faith and Community in Italian Harlem, 1880–1950*. 1985; New Haven: Yale University Press, 2010.

Øster, Andreas. *Barn i herrnhuternes Christiansfeld* [Childhood in Moravian Christiansfeld]. Aabenraa: Historisk Samfund for Sønderjylland, 1965.

Petersen, Steen Estvad. *Christiansfeld: Herrnhuternes by i Sønderjylland* [Christiansfeld: The Moravian town in Southern Jutland]. Copenhagen: Fonden Realdania, 2002.

Poulsen, Rasmus Rask. "Like Living Stones: An Anthropological Study of How the Recognition of Christiansfeld as a World Heritage Site Implicated the Life of the Moravian Brethren in Christiansfeld, Southern Denmark." Master's thesis. University of Copenhagen, 2017.

Ravn, Thomas Bloch. "Håndværk og fabriksvirksomhed" [Tradesmanship and industry]. In Thyssen, *Herrnhuter-samfundet i Chrisiansfeld*, 143–274.

Ravn, Thomas Bloch. "Kostskolerne 1774–1832" [The boarding schools, 1774–1832]. In Thyssen, *Herrnhuter-samfundet i Christiansfeld*, 513–40.

Realdania. *Værdiskabende udvikling af kulturmiljøer—en undersøgelse med udgangspunkt i Christiansfeld* [Creating value in the development of cultural environments: A study based on Christiansfeld]. Copenhagen: Realdania, 2018.

Reventlow, Sybille. "Musik og sang" [Music and song]. In Thyssen, *Herrnhuter-samfundet I Christiansfeld*, 633–708.

Rønnow, Helge. *Brødremenigheden—en levende tradition* [The Moravian congregation: A living tradition]. Christiansfeld: Forlaget Savanne, 1980.

Rønnow, Helge. "De liturgiske former og deres forudsætninger" [The liturgical forms and their prerequisites]. In Thyssen, *Herrnhuter-samfundet i Christiansfeld*, 709–70.

Rønnow, Helge. *Niels Johannes Holm—et levnedsløb* [Niels Johannes Holm: A memoir]. Christiansfeld: Forlaget Savanne, 1995.

Smith, Laurajane. *Uses of Heritage*. New York: Routledge, 2006.

Smith, Valene L., ed. *Hosts and Guests: The Anthropology of Tourism*. Philadelphia: University of Pennsylvania Press, 1977.

Stasch, Rupert. "Primitivist Tourism and Romantic Individualism: On the Values in Exotic Stereotypy about Cultural Others." *Anthropological Theory* 14, no. 2 (2014): 191–214.

Thyssen, Anders Pontoppidan. "Det store og det lille herrnhutersamfund" [The universal and particular Moravian community]. In Thyssen, *Herrnhuter-samfundet i Christiansfeld*, 11–102.

Thyssen, Anders Pontoppidan, ed. *Herrnhuter-samfundet i Christiansfeld* [The Moravian community of Christiansfeld]. Vols. 1 and 2. Aabenraa: Historisk Samfund for Sønderjylland, 1984.

Tunbridge, J. E., and G. J. Ashworth. *Dissonant Heritage: The Management of the Past as a Resource in Conflict*. Chichester: Wiley, 1996.

Varming, Niels Chr. "Salshuset" [The hall]. In Thyssen, *Herrnhuter-samfundet i Christiansfeld*, 491–512.

Waterton, Emma, and Laurajane Smith. "The Recognition and Misrecognition of Community Heritage." *International Journal of Heritage Studies* 16, no. 1–2 (2010): 4–15.

Wertsch, James V. *Voices of Collective Remembering*. Cambridge: Cambridge University Press, 2002.

Chapter 7

Being and Becoming World Heritage
Exploring the Materialization of the Deliciously Sweet
Christiansfeld Honey Cake

Marie Riegels Melchior

Christiansfeld is now a UNESCO World Heritage site. Its designation was announced in 2015 and celebrated on 29 August of that year with festivities in the presence of Her Majesty Queen Margrethe II of Denmark. It was a remarkable event in all respects and an auspicious moment for the town's future. The day's many speeches and reflections expressed an awareness of both the honor and responsibilities that accompany the town's new identity as a World Heritage site. The queen even returned home with a piece of local history, as she was presented with beautiful heart-shaped honey cakes—a specialty for which Christiansfeld has long been noted—decorated with the names of her grandchildren. In 1986, long before the town obtained World Heritage status, the confection made it into the Guinness Book of World Records when local baker Aage Schmidt baked the world's largest heart-shaped honey cake, measuring about two square meters and weighing 113 kilograms.[1]

The World Heritage designation was the culmination of more than ten years of strategic work by a core partnership consisting of the Moravian Brethren in Christiansfeld; the philanthropic association Realdania, which works through the built environment to improve living standards in Denmark; and the local municipality, Kolding Kommune. In order for the town of Christiansfeld to be both preserved and developed, the partnership believed that four themes had to be kept in focus—its story, its history, its heritage, and its symbolism—and they articulated this vision in a number of publications documenting their ambitions for the town.[2] With the World Heritage designation, UNESCO legitimized the ambitions for the town at the international level by supporting the work to create a thriving Christiansfeld in all its aspects: the religious community, the built environment, the everyday life of the town's inhabitants, and the local business community.

But what did the partnership actually mean by choosing to focus on the story, the history, the heritage, and the symbolism of Christiansfeld? I shall attempt to explain this, as well as to propose how the town's deliciously sweet honey cakes play a significant role in the way Christiansfeld has come to be acknowledged as a UNESCO World Heritage site—in other words, as a representation of human creative powers, displaying what humans can do at their best.[3]

Of the four focus areas, the partnership began by asserting the importance of what they termed "the story" of Christiansfeld. To them, this meant the story of the Moravian Brethren in Denmark, particularly in Christiansfeld from its settlement in 1771–73 and up to the present.[4] There was a special emphasis on the complexities arising from its location in the border region, where it was part of the former Danish duchy of Schleswig until 1864, part of Germany from 1864 to 1920, and part of the southern region of Denmark since 1920. Second, by presenting the town's history in this context, the partnership meant to show respect for the materializations of the past, especially when interacting with the very deliberately conceived buildings and town planning that provide a kind of proof of the past. Third, what the partnership meant by "heritage" is a demonstration of the customs of the Moravian Brothers and Sisters over time. For instance, the craftsmanship traditions performed by the Moravians in their original built environments draw attention to the modern craftsmanship that sustains the historic buildings today, while also pointing to the relationship among Moravian settlements around the world. Finally, the partnership intended "symbolism" to mean the very literal accentuation of religious symbols present in the streets of Christiansfeld in order to make visitors aware of the original market town and its religious foundations.[5]

It is in the context of Christiansfeld becoming a UNESCO World Heritage site that the present analysis of the meaning of its honey cake takes place. What follows will explain not the story of the honey cake but rather the many stories of the honey cake. This is to illustrate that it is not the normative story of the honey cake that is important; instead, it is the various ways stories are told and materialized as part of the process of being heritage, and becoming "World Heritage"—to show, in other words, how these cakes have become the sweet glue that helps bind the vision and designation of UNESCO World Heritage, as they are practiced and experienced in real life and represent an entanglement of story, history, heritage and symbolism.

The chapter is based on an ethnological approach to the study of cultural history and everyday life, which combines contemporary field-work in the form of observations and qualitative research interviews (see the list of interviews at the end of the chapter) with historical studies.[6] Through such methodology, the chapter draws on the view within critical heritage studies of heritage as practice[7] and is in line with anthropologist and heritage scholar Sharon Macdonald's ideas about how the past is performed in the present and becomes the past, captured in her concept of "past presencing."[8] To understand the Christiansfeld honey cake as the "sweet glue" that makes it possible for both tourists and residents to experience the town's legacy and religious foundation is a kind of past presencing, since the various honey cakes available in Christiansfeld are not identical—that is, not made from exactly the same ingredients—but they do share a claim to history with the locality of Christiansfeld and with the Moravian Brethren's values regarding fine craftsmanship.

Experiencing Honey Cake Heritage

It is Wednesday morning in Christiansfeld on a February day in 2020, under a surprisingly clear sky after weeks of rain in most of Denmark. The sun shines low along Lindegade, creating a spectacular view from east to west toward the greening farming land and forest on the hori-zon, which was the backdrop of the original Tyrstrupgård property that the Moravian Brethren bought from King Christian VII's estate in 1772. On what was then called "the long field" to the east of the farm, the Moravian settlement would erect the town of Christiansfeld in a layout they believed reflected God's utopian ideal.[9]

On this February morning, the town is peaceful; many locals will tell me today that this is characteristic of the place. Around eight o'clock, a few children on bikes pass by on their way to Tyrstrup public school. An hour later, the few shopkeepers along Lindegade and Prætorius Square make their way to their shops to prepare for their first customers. On the corner of Lindegade and Kongensgade, the Moravian Honey Cake Bakery—Brødremenighedens Honningkagebageri—opens at ten. This bakery and café has a large Herrnhut star hanging out front, as do many other buildings in Christiansfeld. But the back of the building has been busy for quite some time already, with people making chocolates. The company that has held the lease and run the place since 2012 is the fine chocolatier Xocolatl, originally founded in Haderslev, a market town about twenty kilometers south of Christiansfeld. At half past ten, tourists

Figures 7.1. and 7.2. The Moravian Brethren Bakery, Lindegade 36 in Christiansfeld. Photographs by Marie Riegels Melchior, February 2020.

arrive in the streets, changing its aspect. Perhaps they have stayed over-
night at the Brethren Hotel across the street from the bakery, or perhaps
at the inn—Tyrstrup Kro—a few kilometers outside Christiansfeld, or
perhaps they are just passing through on a tour of southern Denmark,
which holds not one but a cluster of three UNESCO World Heritage
sites and tourist destinations: Kongernes Jelling, the Wadden Sea, and
Christiansfeld.

The bakery's doorbell rings. An elegantly dressed woman in her sixties enters the shop and enthusiastically addresses the shopkeeper with
her pressing question: "What is the most authentic honey cake here?"

The shopkeeper responds promptly: "The one with apricot. Would
you like to taste it? It is made from the original recipe!"

The customer does and then replies, "Mmm, this tastes delicious. I
have never been here before. I will take one of these and a sample for my
husband waiting outside. We are on our way around Southern Denmark.
Thank you. Goodbye."[10]

The shopkeeper tells me afterwards that I have just witnessed what
is for her a regular occurrence. Since the 2015 UNESCO World Heritage
declaration, sales of honey cakes in the bakery have increased by approximately 40 percent. Every day, tourists stop in to buy honey cakes, which
is indeed good for business. On weekends, the bakery even welcome
buses full of cruise passengers from the harbor in Fredericia, approximately forty kilometers to the north. These tourists spend about an hour
in Christiansfeld, coming to the bakery at the end of their visit to receive
their prepaid takeaway coffee and two small heart-shaped honey cakes
for their return trip to Fredericia. For the tourists, the honey cake is a bite
of world heritage, a way to taste the heritage of the Moravian settlement,
the shopkeeper explains.[11]

Ironically, however, honey cake is not considered a traditional food
among the Moravians themselves, nor even among the locals as such. The
shopkeeper, in her early sixties, was born and raised in Christiansfeld
and is not member of the Moravian congregation, though her pater-
nal grandmother was. She says, "We were never stuffed with honey
cake, nor do we have any traumas about honey cake. Coming from
Christiansfeld, you just live with the honey cakes."[12] But, as explained
by Christiansfeld Centeret, the visitor and communication center established as part of the UNESCO World Heritage application process in
2009, honey cake from Christiansfeld is a commodity—and more
recently, a World Heritage commodity—and as such, it has become part
of the living tradition of the place. Visitors to Christiansfeld, including
those who take the tour offered by the Christiansfeld Center's guides,

are told the story of the skilled artisans of the Moravian Brethren and the tradition of making honey cakes. A tourist brochure offers more about the tradition of heart-shaped honey cakes: "In the old days, before young couples could choose their own partners, honey cake hearts were used to declare an engagement. The couple would each eat one half of the cake in the presence of the minister as an official blessing of the engagement."[13]

The center has even recently developed an activity for children in which they have to help the honey cake baker find his recipe by answering questions while walking through the heritage site. The reward for completion is an apron, a baking mold in the shape of a heart, and a recipe for honey cake to take home.[14]

Today, there are three honey cake bakers in Christiansfeld: the Moravian Honey Cake Bakery, located at Lindegade 36; the Honey Cake House, located just outside the UNESCO heritage site at Haderslevvej 21; and finally, the Brothers' House Bakery, located outside the UNESCO heritage site at Industrivej 32, in an industrial area of Christiansfeld established in the 1970s when a bypass road was built to reduce car traffic in the historic town.

Why Honey Cake in a Moravian Settlement?

It seems fair to ask why honey cakes are connected to this place at all. According to the narratives offered by the three present-day honey cake bakers and by the website www.honningkager.dk, the tradition is linked to the early years of the Moravian settlement in Christiansfeld. The Moravian Honey Cake Bakery tells its story on a sign on its front door that reads, "The Moravian Honey Cake Bakery. Founded in 1783 by Immanuel Martin Achtnich."

The Brothers' House Bakery prints its story in both Danish and English on the packaging of their honey cakes:

> Since 1776, the bakery of the Moravian Brethren in Christiansfeld, "Brødrehusets Bageri," has been making honey cakes. It all started when an Evangelical community, The Moravian Brethren, settled in Christiansfeld in 1772.
>
> And it is still the good old recipes from then that provide the basis of production today. 18 different types of honey cake are made in the bakery, "Brødrehusets Bageri." The traditional form of honey cakes is the honey loaf, on which you spread butter. Since then, the production range has been expanded, introducing various kinds of crème and other goodies. There is something to please

every palate. An outstanding feature of the genuine Christiansfeld honey cake is their excellent keeping qualities. Special packaging keeps the cakes fresh and delicious. Honey cake should be consumed at room temperature.

Only the Honey Cake House does not highlight its historical legacy with a written story, since this bakery was founded later, in the early 1970s. Opened by a baker trained at the Brothers' House Bakery, it is currently run by Torben and Tove Jørgensen. Nevertheless, it is the only one of the three bakeries to mark its honey cakes as *Christiansfeld World Heritage*, and a logo saying "Authentic Christiansfelder Honey Cake" is printed on their shopping bags and honey cake products.

In the book *Herrnhutersamfundet i Christiansfeld* (The Moravian Community in Christiansfeld)—which the guides at the Christiansfeld Center call their "bible," as they perceive it to be the most thorough historical description of the Moravian Brethren's settlement in Christiansfeld—it is clear that the origin of honey cake making in Christiansfeld is a story of a tradition, arising from coincident and entrepreneurial initiative on the part

Figure 7.3. The Honey Cake House promotes its honey cake in terms of world heritage. Here it becomes obvious that consuming honey cake is consuming heritage. Photograph by Marie Riegels Melchior, February 2020.

of the people who chose to settle in the community. It was an initiative that would make it possible to earn a living while sharing and practicing their religious beliefs with others who saw their daily work as a tribute to God.[15]

As the book explains, once the congregation chose to accept the offer to buy Tyrstrupgård and build the settlement of Christiansfeld, scouting for business opportunities in the region began. One immediate observation was that the high-quality craftsmanship and skills that the Brothers and Sisters brought with them from the various German settlements would be considered valuable assets in the region. A report from 1771 by Brother Peter Henningsen, from Egernsund near the market town of Sønderborg, states that the crafts produced by the congregation's members would be of interest to the region's wealthy inhabitants: notably, their leather, fine woven linen (which was not produced locally), and woolen cloth from the fine local wool would be superior to what was otherwise available for purchase in the region. Most importantly, the report underscores that the high quality of the congregation's crafts would create a competitive advantage, since the region's existing craftsmen were serving the market for less expensive, less refined goods.[16]

In the first years following its founding, Christiansfeld's craftsmen were focused on the production of common goods for the settlement. In this light, it made sense to establish a bakery to provide bread for the young community.[17] A key element in the sustainability of the workshop and small businesses to which they gave rise were the privileges granted to the settlement in a Royal Concession in 1771. The craftsmen were granted the right to export and trade their goods all over the country, a right that no one else in Denmark and the duchies enjoyed on the same scale.[18] In addition, the economic organization of the congregation made it possible for artisans in the congregation to apply for seed capital from community funds, a practice that strengthened the craftsmen and helped their small-scale industries grow in a way that was difficult for others to compete with at first. Obviously, the neighboring market towns were unhappy with this situation, and, as Thomas Bloch Ravn has shown, historical documents reveal disputes and discontent with Christiansfeld and the privileges given to the religious community, as these advantages were perceived to demonstrate contempt for the surrounding society.[19] In hindsight, however, Christiansfeld, its surrounding market towns, and other emerging kinds of organization and privilege (like the guild system) were all part of a broader change taking place in crafts and trade in Denmark as it transformed from a feudal economy to that of a liberal market.[20]

It is within this context that the Brothers' House Bakery was established. According to the bakery itself, it was started in 1776 to provide for the inhabitants of the Brothers' House, where the settlement's unmarried

Figure 7.4. These honey cakes made by the Brothers' House Bakery are sold nationwide through the supermarket Netto. This is how, today, many Danes get to know and consume Christiansfeld. Photograph by Marie Riegels Melchior, February 2020.

men lived according to the collective lifestyle of the religious community, as was the norm until the latter part of the nineteenth century. Exactly when this bakery began baking honey cake is unclear. However, the Moravian Honey Cake Bakery dates from 1783, when the congregation accepted Brother Rasch, a pastry chef, into the young community. According to Bloch Ravn's research, the records of the congregation state that Brother Rasch from Herrnhut sought permission to come to Christiansfeld to set up a "sugar bakery" (*Zuckerbeckerey*).[21] Very little else is known of the activities of the pastry bakery, but the records of the community's board of supervisors reveal that it was difficult to secure a supply of honey for the production of so-called pepper cakes (*Pfeffer-Küchlerey*) in the bakery's first years owing to competition for the ingredient from the Brethren's more profitable beer brewery.[22]

Sources relating to the market trade over the course of the nineteenth century show a widening distribution of honey cakes beyond Christiansfeld, as the Brethren's honey cakes became a familiar commodity nationwide. An 1868 advertisement from the local newspaper of the market town of Sorø (approximately eighty kilometers west of Copenhagen) demonstrates this fact:

> Christiansfeld honey cake. As I will attend the upcoming market with a wide and attractive selection of the famous and celebrated Christiansfeld honey

cakes, I recommend myself to its visitors. The tent will have my name on it. C. Schrøder, pastry chef.[23]

Tax registrations and censuses from 1789 and 1810 tell us further that in 1789 there was one pastry shop and one bakery in Christiansfeld. By 1810, the number of bakeries had increased to three. It is not known whether all three bakeries produced honey cakes at this time, nor whether the pastry shop also made bread and/or other ordinary bakery items.[24]

Brother Rasch, the first pastry chef, died in 1799. According to sources collected by Hans Gorrsen, a typesetter and history enthusiast (1916–1986), Rasch's pastry shop was not a great success at first, and he died as he had arrived in Christiansfeld, a poor artisan. The next to take over the Moravian Honey Cake Bakery was Immanuel Martin Achtnich, who arrived in Christiansfeld in 1785 as a wigmaker. However, since wigmaking was not a viable business at that time and place because of changing fashions, the congregation appointed Achtnich to take over the pastry shop. He managed to establish a business he could hand down to his son, Heinrich Immanuel Achtnich, in 1820. According to sources visited by Gorrsen, Heinrich was successful, apparently experimenting to develop a more efficient, industrialized method of producing the honey cakes. The third-generation baker, Carl Anton Achtnich, managed the bakery from 1866 until 1887, entering into the generational leases offered by the congregation. The fourth and last generation of Achtnichs to run the bakery was Emil Achtnich, who gave up the lease of the bakery in the early twentieth century. He also held the job as mayor of Christiansfeld from 1905 to 1920, and he transferred the lease to his brother-in-law.

Emil Achtnich was known to have promoted his honey cakes as "the original" (*originale*) Christiansfeld honey cakes, while at the same time his competitor Johannes Schmolke, the tenant of the Brothers' House Bakery from 1899 until 1940, advertised his as "the authentic" (*ægte*) Christiansfeld honey cakes. These initiatives can be explained by the competition that had arisen because of the changing border between Denmark and Prussia. In the 1864 war, Denmark lost the three duchies of Schleswig, Holstein, and Lauenburg to Prussia, moving the border between the countries three kilometers north of Christiansfeld. This created a market opportunity for others in Denmark to produce honey cakes and sell them as Christiansfeld honey cakes, while the bakeries in Christiansfeld fought to distinguish their claim to the history and legacy of producing the "original" and "authentic" Christiansfeld honey cakes.

Just as the Moravian Honey Cake Bakery was managed by generations of the same family during the nineteenth century, the Brothers' House

Bakery enjoyed a similar family legacy in the twentieth century. Johannes Schmolke obtained the lease to the bakery in 1899 and continued in business until 1940, when his son Herman Schmolke took over; he in turn passed the lease and business on to his son Gottfred, who ran the bakery from 1967 to 1986. As Gottfred Schmolke's sister, Käte Thomsen, tells it, the bakery was very much a family business. Her grandmother managed the bakery during the First World War, while her husband served in the German army. Since handling the stiff and heavy honey cake dough is physically demanding, she sold honey cakes from the Moravian Honey Cake Bakery alongside her own bread and other cakes.[25]

In Thomsen's father's time, honey cakes from the Brothers' House Bakery were sold all over Denmark, and as children, she and her brother helped with sending promotional material to customers and packing honey cakes for special occasions. She remembers the "Holiday box," the "Christmas box," the "Christiansfelder box," and the "Children's box." A box might contain a honey bread decorated with five almonds, a fancier bread with cream, and honey cake hearts glazed with chocolate. It was her brother who specialized the bakery in the 1980s, narrowing the production exclusively to honey cakes in various shapes and combinations with cream and marmalade. According to Thomsen, these developments were due to a refinement of the original recipe. Unfortunately, in 1986 bad luck struck the bakery: it burned down along with part of the historic Brothers' House in Lindegade at the center of the historic site of Christiansfeld. This came as a shock to the congregation. Gottfred Schmolke still had his business but no longer had a lease or a shop. He decided, therefore, to take the opportunity to develop his business by building a modern cake factory in the recently developed industrial area of Christiansfeld, on Industrivej 32. His ambitions were grander than his budget, however, and without the revenue obtained from selling ordinary bread and other bakery goods, the business went bankrupt after a year. The last Schmolke's skills in refining the honey cake recipe were not enough to secure the transition to an independent business model no longer attached to the Brethren. In the early 1990s a cake company bought the secret recipe for the honey cakes from Gottfred Schmolke, and it later bought the factory from an investor who had taken over the bankrupt bakery. This company, Willy F Kager, continues to bake honey cakes under the Brothers' House Bakery brand name, though no further connection to the congregation remains.[26]

As this history suggests, it was the business mindset of the Moravian congregation that made honey cake production a more and more integrated part of the Christiansfeld Moravian Brethren. As it became evident that honey cakes were in demand in the region and the market matured for buying them, the cakes became a source of income for the Brethren through the lease of its bakery facilities. For approximately 200 years, the Brethren leased two bakeries whose tenants were obligated to produce Christiansfelder honey cakes. Today there is only one lease with this obligation, but three honey cake producers still operate in Christiansfeld, as described above.

An awareness of the history of the Christiansfeld honey cakes, and the repetition of this history, can be seen as a past presencing act that has made it part of the visual and tangible heritage of Christiansfeld, despite the cakes' lack of religious significance. As such, the UNESCO World Heritage designation has yet again made Christiansfeld honey cakes into an asset for the Moravian congregation, as well as for the development of tourism and the experience economy in the wider region. One could even say that privilege seems to follow the Christiansfeld settlement, though accompanied by much hard work and sacrifice, and now Christiansfeld is again blessed with the privilege of being a World Heritage site. The settlement's values of continuity, sustainability, and a higher mission than one's individual prosperity—the prosperity of the congregation—can be argued to be of importance for the tradition of honey cake making as well.

The Three Bakeries: How to Uphold Tradition

What is learned through the history of honey cake baking in Christiansfeld is much like what can be learned through studying most traditions: at some more recent point, they were invented! British historians Eric Hobsbawm and Terence Ranger made this point clear in their 1983 book, *The Invention of Tradition*, in which they demonstrated through case studies how traditions are comparatively recent processes of formalization of practices, which are then able to create a sense of continuity with a suitable historic past. In the case of the honey cakes, the history of their invention is part of their legacy as a world heritage product. But what, then, is the actual content of this tradition—the content of the honey cake that today is consumed (sold and eaten) as world heritage?

The answer may be found in Käte Thomsen's story of the so-called "original recipe" that was handed down from one generation to the next, and from one holder of the bakery lease to the next, and how this recipe was not performed exactly but rather refined by each baker according to his present time and sense of taste. It is this act—not the act of change but that of refinement—that is the essential heritage of Christiansfeld's craftsmanship and honey cakes. Thomsen explains:

In 1773, when the Moravian Brethren settled in Christiansfeld, it was with the ambition to make their craftsmanship and business demonstrate their right to be there. This ambition could only be fulfilled if their craft and the products they produced were qualitatively better than their competitors'. Refinement was and still is a necessity, an essential part of how the craftsmen and businesses of Christiansfeld have to work.[27]

This "refinement strategy" has not only been at the root of the honey cakes' sustainability; it can also explain the variations in taste and execution exemplified by the assorted honey cakes available on the market today. It is relatively easy to see that, conceptually, Christiansfeld honey cakes are alike but also differ in their parts, shape, and taste. So, when the bakeries claim that their honey cakes are "original" or "authentic," it does little more than draw additional attention to the product for sale. The experience of tasting the honey cake will not bring you closer to the past, to the first Christiansfeld honey cake recipe in the young Moravian Brethren's settlement. Instead, eating a Christiansfeld honey cake has the potential to allow you to experience and taste years of bakers' efforts to refine their cakes in the struggle to gain market share and court consumer taste at any given historical moment.

Not surprisingly, given this history and their ongoing competition, the three bakeries in contemporary Christiansfeld make honey cakes that are rather different—not only in appearance but in their ingredients as well. Take, for instance, how much honey a Christiansfelder honey cake contains. One might be surprised to learn that this differs significantly among the bakeries. A basic recipe for honey cake dough is about 25 percent honey (see Appendix 1). However, at the Moravian Honey Cake Bakery, honey is prominently listed as the first ingredient on the label, making up 45 to 47 percent of each cake. The honey even comes from a local honey producer near Haderslev in order to ensure its quality, which is evident in the taste of the cake. Indeed, according to the bakery's sales assistant, it is even possible to taste whether summer or autumn honey was used in a cake's production. Furthermore, the high percentage of honey in the dough makes the cake less shelf-stable, and thus it is appropriate to sell these particular honey cakes as both high quality (because of the quality of the ingredients) and exclusive (because of their perishability, high price, and limited production).

The honey cakes from Brothers' House Bakery and Honey Cake House also contain honey but in significantly lower amounts. At the Honey Cake House, the amount is 8 percent, while the Brothers' House Bakery does not disclose the amount of honey used. As the Moravian Honey Cake Bakery points out, the other bakeries substitute invert sugar for honey, making their cakes less perishable and therefore more suitable as a shelf-stable supermarket product.[28]

The spices added to the honey cake dough are where further differences are found—or perhaps where the secret of making honey cake lies. Here again, the exclusive Moravian Honey Cake Bakery recipe sets itself apart. In addition to cinnamon, cardamom, and allspice, the bakery adds ginger and anise to refine its honey cake (see Appendix 2).

Any two honey cakes are not alike, even when they both come from Christiansfeld and share the same historical legacy and heritage. The town's honey cake history, one might claim, is performed differently by the different bakeries.

Toward a Conclusion: Becoming World Heritage Honey Cake

In this chapter, the story of the Christiansfeld honey cake has been told through the lens of becoming heritage, with heritage viewed as a past-presencing activity. To this end, it has been shown that heritage is only not a thing—in this case, a honey cake—but a practice, a way of making honey cake through refinements that adjust the past to the present.

The Christiansfeld honey cake might at first seem to be a secondary feature of the otherwise impressive heritage site—including the settlement's layout, its residences, and its formidable church building. However, the honey cake has nevertheless become a symbol of the site, a token for both the queen of Denmark and tourists to taste while experiencing southern Denmark and the region's World Heritage sites and a part of the collective memory of the local community.

The idea that the honey cake should be more than just a deliciously sweet treat was always the Moravian Brethren's intention, just as it was with the other goods produced by craftsmen originally granted permission to operate in Christiansfeld. Christiansfeld was established and began to grow as a consequence of the Royal Concession that gave its inhabitants special privileges and competitive advantages until the community came under German rule in 1864. Mercantile capitalism thrived in Christiansfeld, but members of the congregation were obliged not only to use their privileges to increase trade but also to support the community and its religious mission. Striving for the finest craftsmanship to win market share was part and parcel of the congregation's missionary work.

The honey cake can still be understood as part of this missionary work, recently reinforced by UNESCO's World Heritage site designation. The cakes participate in the visibility of the Christiansfeld site as well as of the Moravian Brethren, adding value—both literally and

Figure 7.5. Heart-shaped honey cakes have become a symbol of Christiansfeld. Here a photo shoot is taking place for a publication for the Region of Southern Denmark Annual Report. Photograph by Inger-Marie Børgesen, February 2020, Christiansfeld, Museum Kolding.

symbolically—through the lease of the bakery at Lindegade 36, as well as through the municipality's guided tours operated by the Christiansfeld Center. The religious community is the foundation of the locality and everything else that has arisen from this place. Becoming world heritage, even for a honey cake, is part of the mission and the work to make Christiansfeld and the Moravian Church sustainable in the present and into the future.

Hopefully this brief chapter has demonstrated how even humble things—in this case, honey cake and its refinements in taste—can become precious and important "sweet glue" over time, connecting substance and texture not only to something as grand as the UNESCO World Heritage mission but also to the distinguished mission of the Moravian Brethren in Christiansfeld.

Marie Riegels Melchior is an associate professor in European ethnology at the University of Copenhagen. Her research interests concern mainly fashion and design culture, cultural history from the nineteenth century onward, and heritage and museum studies. She has written extensively on Danish fashion and design history in the twentieth- and twenty-first centuries as well as on museological issues when fashion enters museums. She is on the editorial board of the journal *Ethnologia Scandinavica: Journal of Scandinavian Ethnology.*

Notes

1. Else-Marie Hjorth, interview by the author, 26 February 2020.
2. For example, Frandsen, *Christiansfeld.*
3. Hafstein, *Making Intangible Heritage,* 1.
4. Frandsen, *Christiansfeld,* 45.
5. Frandsen, 48.
6. Kaijser and Öhlande, *Etnologiskt Fältarbet.*
7. Smith, *Uses of Heritage.*
8. Macdonald, *Memoryland.*
9. Frandsen, *Christiansfeld,* 22–23; Bøytler, *Gribe og begribe.*
10. Field notes, 27 February 2020.
11. Winnie Kroløkke, interview by the author, 27 February 2020.
12. Kroløkke interview.
13. "Walking Tour in Christainsfeld," Christiansfeld Centret & Christiansfeld Turistudvalg.
14. Inger-Marie Børgesen, interview by the author, 26 February 2020.
15. Thyssen, *Herrnhuter-samfundet i Christiansfeld.*
16. Bloch Ravn, "Håndværk og fabriksvirksomhed," 153–54
17. Bloch Ravn, 153.
18. Bloch Ravn, 148.
19. Bloch Ravn, 159.
20. Bloch Ravn, 166.
21. Bloch Ravn, 169.
22. Bloch Ravn, 170.
23. *Sorø Amts Tidende,* 30 June 1868.
24. Bloch Ravn, "Håndværk og fabriksvirksomhed," 174.
25. Käte Thomsen, interview by the author, 27 February 2020.
26. John Frandsen, interview by the author, 8 April 2020.
27. Thomsen interview.
28. Kroløkke interview.

Bibliography

Bøytler, Jørgen. *Gribe og begribe. Liv og tradition i brødremenigheden* [Grasp and comprehend: Life and tradition in the Moravian Congregation]. Christiansfeld: ProRex, 2015.

Frandsen, Søren, ed. *Christiansfeld—en levende by* [Christiansfeld: A living town]. Kolding Kommune, 2014.

Hafstein, Valdimar. *Making Intangible Heritage*. Bloomington: Indiana University Press, 2018.

Kaijser, Lars, and Magnus Öhlander. *Etnologiskt Fältarbete* [Ethnological field work]. Lund: Studentlitteratur, 1999.

Macdonald, Sharon. *Memoryland: Heritage and Identity in Europe Today*. London: Routledge, 2013.

Ravn, Thomas Bloch. "Håndværk og fabriksvirksomhed" [Tradesmanship and industry]. In Thyssen, *Herrnhuter-samfundet i Christiansfeld*, 143–274.

Smith, Laurajane. *Uses of Heritage*. London: Routledge, 2006.

Thyssen, Anders Pontoppidan, ed. *Herrnhuter-samfundet i Christiansfeld* [The Moravian community of Christiansfeld]. Vols. 1 and 2. Aabenraa: Historisk Samfund for Sønderjylland, 1984.

Interviews

Käte Thomsen, former chairperson of the congregation administration, Christiansfeld. 26 February 2020.

Else-Marie Hjorth, guide for the Christiansfeld Communication Center. 26 February 2020.

Inger-Marie Børgesen, guide for the Christiansfeld Communication Center. 26 February 2020.

Winnie Kroløkke, sales assistant at Xocolatl, Lindegade 36, Christiansfeld. 27 February 2020.

Hans Schmith, member of the congregation administration and antique tiled oven specialist, Christiansfeld. 18 March 2020.

Gitte Minck, owner of Xocolatl. Email. 1 March 2020.

John Frandsen, Willy F Kager / Brødrehusets Bageri i Christiansfeld. 8 April 2020.

Chapter 8

The Moravian *Lebenslauf*
Tradition and Sustainability

Jill E. S. Vogt

In Per Olov Enquist's novel *Lewi's Journey*, the narrator describes a funeral at the Moravian congregation at Christiansfeld in Denmark. Although some of the details vary from actual practice, and this is indeed a fictional account of an event that never actually happened, he captures the essence of one of the central parts of a Moravian funeral when he describes the following event in the course of the service:

> From his briefcase the pastor took out a folder containing a stack of papers that must have been ten centimeters thick. He placed it on the pulpit, cast a somber look over the congregation, opened the folder, paused and began to read.
>
> It was the first time I encountered a Lebenslauf. It belonged to Efraim Markström. And, as I understood much later, to Lewi.
>
> It was actually quite simple: Every member of the Unitas Fratrum congregation, every Moravian, was expected to keep a running chronicle of his life. Life was a novel that had to be written down, life was a "work in progress," in which chapter should be added to chapter, as if life were the Bible itself and each person an evangelist. And when a person's life was over, the chronicle of that life would be read before the congregation, a more or less symbolic reading of excerpts, but the entire text would be available.
>
> A Lebenslauf. Recorded while life lasted.
>
> And now he was holding Efraim's Lebenslauf in his hand, reading from it.[1]

The reading of a *Lebenslauf* has formed a central part of burial practices in the Moravian Church for more than 275 years. In many cases, these memoirs have been autobiographical accounts, written by church members in view of their own funeral. Unlike Enquist's description, however, a Lebenslauf is not a running diary of events but a personal narrative of what was important in one's life, which generally includes biographical details as well as reflections on one's spiritual walk. Christiansfeld belongs to the group of many Moravian congregations in the European Continental Province where the writing and reading of Lebensläufe continues to be practiced as a cherished and meaningful tradition. Unfortunately, in other areas, such as the United States and Great Britain, Lebensläufe have given way to the more common cultural practice of a memorial written by the pastor with the help of input by family and friends. Currently there is interest in the British Province of reintroducing the practice, which is seen particularly as a way of capturing the unique life stories of older members who have lived through a period of rapid change and remarkable progress. Drawing on my firsthand experience with the Lebenslauf practice as a Moravian pastor, I want to use the opportunity of this chapter to explore the particularities of this tradition and to address the question of its sustainability.

Enquist is not the only one to find Lebensläufe fascinating. From scholars such as Katie Faull, Pia Schmid, and Gisela Mettele we hear quite a bit about the Lebenslauf tradition, especially their significance as sources that provide important first-person accounts of historical periods.[2] The existence of tens of thousands of archived memoirs is a treasure and a great heritage of the Moravian Church, as well as a gold mine of source material for historians. The Lebenslauf tradition, however, is not simply text in the archives. It is the ongoing practice in the life of the congregations, where church members hear Lebensläufe being read at funeral services and are writing Lebensläufe themselves for their own funerals. It is this living practice that raises the issue of sustainability: Will the practice continue to be a living and meaningful tradition in the future?

This living practice is also what interests me as the pastor of the Herrnhut Moravian congregation, where funerals are a regular part of my ministry. Because the practice of writing Lebensläufe and having them read at funerals is still very much a part of our spiritual life, I see the great potential of the Lebenslauf to facilitate communication and self-reflection. A Doctor of Ministry project has given me the opportunity to explore these aspects in depth, and in this chapter I want to address the question of sustainability from my particular pastoral perspective.[3]

Moravian Memoirs in the Context of Moravian Funerals

The practice of the Lebenslauf belongs to the Moravian traditions surrounding death and funerals. Before we talk about the meaning of the

Lebenslauf, it is important to consider the understanding of death in Moravian tradition and spirituality. From the early time of the Herrnhut community, death was approached with a relatively positive outlook.[4] Theologically, Moravians believe that death is the door to eternal life, which unites the believers with their Savior. So, it has been customary in the Moravian Church that we do not say a person has died, but rather that he or she has "gone home."[5] In the United States I have heard it said that someone "has entered into the more immediate presence of their Savior." Originally, in the early eighteenth-century Moravian communities, the death of a person was seen simply as a transition to the "higher congregation" and therefore little mention was made of it. And yet, as the church grew and members began to move between congregations, there was an increased sense that it would be important to remember the life of a deceased person and what God had done in his or her life, so the reading of a short memoir was introduced, usually written by a third person. The Lebenslauf thus functioned initially as a kind of death announcement, remembering, connecting, and placing the deceased in the life of the congregation.

Today, the Lebenslauf still plays an important role in Moravian funerals but in a different way. A typical Moravian funeral in the European Province today begins in the *Saal* (Moravian sanctuary). The body is not present but outside in a small chamber where people stop to visit before they go in to the service. A funeral is always an event for the whole congregation, not just the family. The service places particular emphasis on hope and resurrection and the atmosphere generally reflects this; for example, hopeful scripture passages are read and the hymns are played relatively quickly. Sometimes these readings and hymns have been chosen in advance by the deceased. But it is the Lebenslauf that forms the central part of the service. It is read by the pastor, who is sitting behind a small table in front of the congregation. If the memoir was written by the deceased, it will be read as it stands, using the first person, for example: "I was born in 1930, the first child of John and Mary Smith." When no autobiographical memoir has been written, one is usually composed by family members. When a memoir is too long, the pastor will shorten the version read in the service; otherwise, no editing occurs. The ending of the Lebenslauf is usually completed by the family, bringing it up to date and often including a brief description of the circumstances surrounding the death. The reading of the Lebenslauf is usually followed by a verse sung by the choir or a congregational hymn and is not commented upon. The sermon or address by the pastor then takes up the biblical text, sometimes highlighted by examples from the Lebenslauf or connecting themes to the life of the deceased but mainly focusing on the biblical and theological understanding of death and resurrection. It is relatively short and should definitely not overshadow the Lebenslauf. In no way is it seen to be a eulogy or even a memorial of the deceased since this has already been provided through the Lebenslauf. Following the service in the church, the congregation reassembles outside and follows the white coffin in a funeral procession, often led by a brass choir, to the cemetery, which is known as God's Acre. Members are laid to rest in rows instead of family graves because of the belief that, as congregants are Brothers and Sisters, the entire cemetery is a kind of family grave site. Afterward, it is customary to hold a "Lovefeast" or coffee reception where people are invited to share stories and remembrances of the deceased. It is not unusual for these stories to reflect or expand on events mentioned in the Lebenslauf. Overall, the experience of a Moravian funeral is generally one of hope, fellowship, and a strong sense of the identity of the deceased.

One important detail of the tradition is the fact that a copy of the Lebenslauf is stored in the congregational archives. It is also possible to provide additional copies to those who could not be present for the service. All congregations have their own collections of Lebensläufe of all their deceased members, which, in a way, represents the collective memory of the congregation. For families who mourn the loss of a loved one, it may be a source of comfort to know that his or her life story is preserved in the archives.

At Herrnhut, a surprisingly large number of people still write a Lebenslauf. When someone has died, one of the questions a pastor has for the family is, "Is there a Lebenslauf?" There is still a sense of duty to write one's Lebenslauf, especially among older members, because many people have listened to Lebensläufe during funeral services all their lives. It is the way things are done in the Moravian community. At the same time, writing a Lebenslauf is a profoundly personal experience and, for some, a daunting task.

Historically speaking, the tradition that members compose their own memoirs to be read at their funerals goes back to the eighteenth century. The idea of writing a spiritual autobiography was not a new idea for those in the Pietist tradition. There are many examples of conversion narratives in seventeenth- and eighteenth-century renewal movements, which often served to corroborate the author's state as a true, converted believer.[6] For Moravians, however, the emphasis was not so much on a particular conversion moment; instead, the Lebenslauf was supposed to be an account of one's whole life as spiritual testimony. In Herrnhut, this tradition began to take shape as the community began to grow and spread and not all members were able to know one another well. According to the late Bishop Hellmut Reichel, in 1747 Count Nikolaus Ludwig von Zinzendorf suggested that a brief memoir of deceased members be read after funeral services.[7] A few years later, we find an instance in which Bishop Matthaeus Hehl, working in the Pennsylvania field, expressed a desire for better information about the members of the congregations and thus sent out some kind of questionnaire for personal testimonies.[8] It seems possible that some of these autobiographical reflections were later used as a commemoration during funeral services. During the second half of the eighteenth century, the number of autobiographical memoirs increased, so that the practice of writing one's own Lebenslauf to be used at one's funeral became the established tradition.[9]

Although the style and focus of Lebensläufe have changed over the centuries, the main idea remains constant. The point of the Lebenslauf is not to brag about one's life accomplishments but instead to tell the story of one's life in relation to one's faith and experiences of God's leading, providing a spiritual testimony to be read at one's funeral. Rather than having a family member or pastor deliver a eulogy, the reading of the Lebenslauf holds the central place in the service, allowing the deceased to have the last word, as it were, to tell their own story. The words of the Lebenslauf serve to connect their life story to the story of the congregation and to the story of God. At the Lovefeast, in turn, church members have the opportunity to tell stories that connect to the story of the deceased. By placing the Lebenslauf in the archive, the memory of that story is preserved, adding to the collective memory of a Moravian congregation, which forms an important part of its historical heritage.

There is no set age for writing a Lebenslauf. Some say seventy, some sixty. Interestingly, there is also no official set of rules for writing a Lebenslauf, such as a list of topics to include or format to follow. Instead, most people learn or are influenced by hearing other Lebensläufe read. While we may think that the writing of one's Lebenslauf is the core of the Lebenslauf tradition, repeatedly hearing Lebensläufe being read is an equally important aspect of this tradition as a living practice. I am convinced that when people sit down to write their own Lebenslauf, they usually have the sound of other Lebensläufe in their ear. With a strong Moravian emphasis on humility and the belief that everyone is equal before God, it is understood that Lebensläufe are not intended to be used for boasting, nor are they an opportunity to reveal secrets or get back at others who might have hurt the writer. But the construction and content of the memoir are left to the writers, who probably can reference other Lebensläufe they have heard to decide exactly what they will write and what the tone should be.

Assessment of the Tradition

I have found that most church members consider the Lebenslauf tradition to be important, valuable, and uniquely suited to honor their deceased and express their faith. The Moravian Lebenslauf tradition has also, as I pointed out above, enjoyed a great deal of attention from scholars. In addition, there is some renewed interest from Moravian provinces where this tradition has subsided over time to re-establish the practice, as church leaders have come to realize the Lebenslauf tradition's unique contribution to Moravian heritage and identity as well as to the collective memory of a congregation. From a pastor's point of view, I feel it is important to keep the tradition of writing Lebensläufe alive and to appreciate its full potential as a spiritual practice. The following unique attributes of the Lebenslauf practice, I think, lend to its distinction and make this tradition worthy of preserving.

- *Power over one's own story.* In the Moravian funeral tradition, the deceased gets the last word. Instead of others making comments or sharing their memories, in the Lebenslauf tradition the deceased gets to define himself or herself. In a community that stresses the equality of all members, it means that we hear from all people, no matter their ethnic or economic background, their gender, or their race. If we look at the archived Lebensläufe from previous centuries, we will find accounts from people who in other situations would have been silenced. Since Lebensläufe are not commented upon, the authors are free to share what they feel is significant in their lives, and they are able to find their own voice. Given the Moravian emphasis on humility and the intent of these memoirs, the Lebensläufe do not usually serve to glorify the writer but to explain honestly a context and a journey, thereby giving insight into the lives of people who may otherwise be overlooked.
- *Recognition of important trends and events.* The flow of the Lebenslauf can also reveal much about the writer. When we spend time listening to a Lebenslauf, we may note that the author seems to get stuck at a certain point or often returns to some event—the loss of someone, forced evacuation from his or her home, or the war in general. This usually reveals that in this person's life, this was a situation that defined everything that followed it. We understand the writer better, just by seeing what the writer chooses to include in their Lebenslauf. This also helps us to understand the impact of historical events and to see how important life experiences can affect the rest of our lives. By comparing Lebensläufe from similar time periods,

we may learn much about certain events and how they shaped not only an individual but a community.

- *The communal experience of listening.* The Lebenslauf invites people to connect. It also reveals missed opportunities, even surprises. The stories connect people through shared relationships, memories, or anecdotes. At funerals when a memoir is being read, there are often smiles, laughter, heads nodding, or signs of recognition. When a name is mentioned, the hearers immediately connect that to their own stories ("Yes, I remember Brother XY, I have a story with him too"). Hearing a Lebenslauf read causes us to form images, to connect stories, bringing the congregation closer together.
- *Emphasis on emotion.* The Lebenslauf prohibits the possibility of eulogizing—that is, raising someone up over others; it is subjective rather than objective. Instead of simply listing what someone accomplished, a self-written Lebenslauf allows us the possibility to hear how the writer felt about the things that happened in his or her life. This offers us a completely new perspective to events and allows the community in the future to know not just what happened but how the writer responded emotionally to it.
- *The discipline of self-reflection.* The writing of a Lebenslauf provides the believer with an opportunity to reflect and to think spiritually and theologically about his or her own life, identifying and becoming familiar with God's movement in that life. Self-reflection is an important tool for mental and spiritual health, and the discipline of writing a Lebenslauf helps members to be intentional about asking questions about their lives and seeing their lives narratively, making connections and discerning various movements and themes.
- *Preservation of memory.* The Lebenslauf allows the deceased to be remembered as they would like to be remembered. Their story is not lost; it is preserved in context and it is shared with others now and archived for the future. My story, as I want it told, is still available to those who want to hear it. It is an interesting experience to compare one's own memory or experiences of someone with their Lebenslauf. Having a first-person self-written account in addition to a biography written by someone else can be very illuminating.
- *A web of relationships.* A side effect of the Lebenslauf reading occurs after the funeral when we gather for the Lovefeast. Often those in attendance tell stories that relate in some way to the Lebenslauf, fleshing it out with more examples. We weave the stories of the deceased together with our own stories and share them in a way that becomes our common story. I recall a recent Lebenslauf read at the funeral of a pastor where she mentioned the variety of pastoral

duties she had performed, including visits in hospitals and prisons. At the reception following the burial, a man, unknown to most, stood up and said, "When our Sister referred to visiting those in prison, she was talking about me." He then went on to tell a bit of his own story as a political prisoner in the German Democratic Republic and how this Sister's faithful and courageous visits had helped him to survive the experience.

Question of Sustainability

Let us now turn to the question of sustainability. What can be done to sustain the Lebenslauf tradition as a living practice? The most important thing, in my opinion, is the recognition that a great deal of interest already exists. Most members of our congregations value this tradition and find it profoundly meaningful. Perhaps the greatest hindrance is that people feel overwhelmed by the project or do not know how to get started. I can see several ways in which this problem can be addressed. First, it is important to provide an opportunity for people to share their stories. I have had great success with something called the *Erzählcafé*: a method of social interaction where people sit in small groups in a comfortable setting to share their life stories. A helpful addition is the use of cards containing leading questions to help people remember past events, places, and people they may have forgotten. Second, it can be very effective to read Lebensläufe in small group meetings. Our women's circles enjoy hearing Lebensläufe read and then talking about them, which often leads to more personal sharing. It can also be helpful to use church newsletters to offer guidelines regarding the writing of a Lebenslauf. Several years ago, the late Bishop Theo Gill published a short essay for the Moravian Church newsletter in which he developed a framework for the appreciation of life stories. His main point was that everyone has a story to tell and that telling the story is, in a way, ministry to others.[10] Perhaps the most effective way to encourage people to write Lebensläufe is through seminars where participants can learn from one another and be supported in the process. As part of a research project for my Doctor of Ministry, I held such a seminar in Herrnhut in 2016. I present the positive results of this experience below.

The Project of a Lebenslauf Workshop

My workshop was based on the idea that the Lebenslauf may be used as a tool for helping people to talk with others about their own stories, to deepen their ability to identify the movement of God in their lives, and to learn more deeply about others as those stories are shared. When I began designing my project, I was interested in seeing how writing one's Lebenslauf and sharing it with others would affect one's ability and comfort in regard to speaking about matters of faith—something we call *Sprachfähigkeit* in German. To research this, I gathered a group of ten people between the ages of thirty-six and seventy-eight to write their Lebensläufe in a workshop setting. I offered sessions on the history of the Lebenslauf as well as giving practical tips for writing and invited them to share their Lebenslauf with members of the group. We met weekly for three weeks and then, after a two-week pause for writing, we came together again to share what they had written. In addition, I conducted personal interviews with each member before and after the seminar to assess their expectations and their experiences. I also read all of the Lebensläufe that the participants produced.

My working hypothesis was that the Moravian Lebenslauf practice would be an effective tool to help people improve their *Sprachfähigkeit*, or their ability to speak about their faith. Now, reflecting back on the workshop experience as well as on the conversations I had with the individual participants, I can attest that this is indeed the case, although in ways that are more complex than I had expected. I discovered, first of all, that people enjoyed telling their stories. Everyone opened up, albeit to different degrees, and was eager to talk. With each meeting, the stories flowed more easily and the participants were reluctant to leave when time was up. They were particularly pleased to remember things long forgotten and recalled them with wonder and shared happily. Not only did they talk, but they also listened to one another. Especially in the small groups, they entered into conversation about both life experiences and faith. When asked in the pre-interview if they were comfortable speaking about faith to others, most participants responded with "it depends." Within the group setting, "it depends" took a positive turn toward speaking and sharing openly. In this respect, it appears that the *Sprachfähigkeit* here is conditional. Whether participating in such a course helps people to approach strangers and talk about faith is doubtful, but the results would seem to suggest that such a workshop experience could prove useful in a congregational setting to build trust and a better spiritual base for congregational life.

It was interesting for me to find that the workshop not only helped to improve people's *Sprachfähigkeit* but also facilitated experiences that could be described as emotional therapy and spiritual growth. Clearly, for some participants the group work had a therapeutic effect. There were moments of healing in remembering and expressing deeply meaningful personal experiences, as well as in receiving affirmation and empathy from the other members of the group. Moreover, the process of getting to know one another on the basis of each person's self-definition, rather than on preconceived notions, formed a positive transformative experience for the group. Individuals shared important information about themselves, which helped the other participants to change their perceptions and to make new connections. In one case, a couple remarked that their sharing of stories was like "marriage therapy" for them, drawing them closer together and deepening their mutual understanding.

Regarding spiritual growth, I observed that the task of writing a Lebenslauf offered a welcome opportunity to reflect on the question of God's presence and leading in one's life. Many participants shared that they had endured experiences of severe conflict, loss, sickness, or other hardships in their life and had struggled with the question of why those things had happened to them. Reflecting on one's life in its entirety allowed people to gain a broader perspective and to place moments of crisis into the larger framework of their faith journey. As one participant wrote, "So I continue to go hand in hand with God. I have seen how he held us closely through difficult times, and he has accompanied our daily life with his love and grace and given me deep roots." In sum, the practice of writing a Lebenslauf in a group setting has the potential to serve as a vehicle for growth and transformation, both personal and social as well as emotional and spiritual.

During the course of my project, I discovered two other dimensions of *Sprachfähigkeit*, which I had not expected when I began. The first discovery was the role of memory exercises and memoir writing for those who are struggling with dementia and for their friends and families. This experience has motivated me to reflect on the usefulness of the Lebenslauf as an empowering tool for those with dementia or any other progressive illness. Even while such individuals may be slipping away from us day by day, it is important to give them the opportunity to tell their own story. They may be able to reflect and, hopefully, find meaning in the path their lives have taken. Seeing traces of God's leading over the course of their lives, they may find comfort, strength, and hope in the knowledge that God is with them still. My experience of the group is that sharing stories can also be validating for people who feel their power or identity slipping away from them. Even if they know they may forget what they have said in a year or a few months, knowing that they have said it and it has been heard is significant. Additionally, in the context of a group, sharing stories may also provide strength, courage, and insight as others share their faith journeys during difficult times.

The other unexpected insight is that the writing and sharing of memoirs can also be a vehicle for talking about a difficult shared history, in our case experiences of living as Christians under East Germany's social-ist regime. Of course, this brings up the question of using Lebensläufe to address difficult events, so-called dark memories, so that a community can talk about issues that may be painful to address.

The experience of my workshop clearly underscores the relevance and potential of the Lebenslauf tradition. In analyzing the interviews I carried out, my observations of the group, and the Lebensläufe written by the participants, I have come to the following conclusions:

- There was a widely shared sense that listening to one another's stories helped people to get to know one another on a deeper level and understand the forces that had made them who they are. As one participant said, "People became more real."
- Many participants stated that they had gained a better perspective on their own lives.
- Sharing life experiences created a sense of trust, which in turn opened up a safe space for people to talk about faith issues.
- In some cases, people felt their own faith was strengthened through the witness of another person's life story.
- Some people acknowledged that writing their memoir had helped them to discern and name traces of God's presence and leading in their lives.
- It was evident that over the course of the workshop series, the relationships between participants changed and developed in a positive way.

Being invited to tell one's life story was a new experience for most of the participants, and all of them found it meaningful. The established tradition of the Lebenslauf, in which a person's life is seen in relation to God, provided a format that enabled people to talk about God as they related their life stories. The degree to which people spoke about their faith varied, but it was clear that talking about faith would be acceptable. In this way the Moravian Lebenslauf can be seen as a helpful and effective tool for spiritual growth, small group process, and congregational development.

Conclusion

The Moravian Lebenslauf tradition is an important cultural heritage practice in that it comprises first-person accounts of people from all walks of life who share their stories not with the intention of drawing attention to their achievements but as a simple testimony of a lived faith.

These autobiographies, when considered together, represent a tradition that has evolved and changed over time but that also reflects a continuous appreciation of individual life stories in the communal context from the eighteenth century to the present. The relevance of the Lebenslauf tradition is its ability to connect the individual life story with the larger story of the Moravian community and the even larger story of God. The sustainability of this tradition requires, on the one hand, ensuring that the practice continues to be carried out, that Lebensläufe continue to play a role in funerals, but also, on the other hand, that church members see the meaning of their life in a spiritual narrative context. In my view, the use of a Lebenslauf in a funeral is a very appropriate way to honor a person who has died and to provide comfort to those who mourn. Furthermore, these testimonies can be inspirational for those who read them, and the practice of writing and self-reflection can assist people today to understand their lives more clearly and to be able to talk more openly with others about their faith.

I found it interesting that Enquist, the novelist, looked at a Lebenslauf as a novel, to which chapter after chapter is added. This description may easily lead to a misunderstanding, namely that a Lebenslauf is a running chronicle of events in which people describe everything they experience. Frankly, such a voluminous text would be a pastor's nightmare. What I find much more important is that people are able to reflect on what was important in their life and tell their own story. Some Lebensläufe are not much longer than one page, and still they are able to capture what a person's life was about. Moreover, Enquist suggests that the writing of a Lebenslauf should be carried out "as if life were the Bible itself and each person an evangelist." While I like the idea that a person who writes a Lebenslauf is an evangelist, I would put the emphasis somewhere else: the Lebenslauf, in which we tell our own story, does not take the place of God's story but connects us to God's story. Through our own life narrative we find our place in the larger narrative of God. This, at least, is the ultimate goal of autobiographical writing in the Moravian tradition.

In April of 2016, the Moravian congregation in Herrnhut was honored by a visit from Germany's then president Joachim Gauck and his partner, Daniela Schadt. Because we had a limited amount of time to explain as much as possible about the Moravian Church, my husband and I decided to use the lot (a practice that has been a distinctive tradition for Moravians, still used in the selection of the Moravian *Daily Texts*) to choose which topics would be covered. When President Gauck drew the topic "Lebenslauf," I could not have been happier to have the opportunity to explain this wonderful practice to him. I pointed out that Moravians have been writing and collecting personal memoirs for more than 250 years, noting that there are tens of thousands of life stories in the archives and more added every year. When I had finished, Mr. Gauck smiled and replied, "What a wonderful treasure this is and a gift to German culture." I could not agree more. The Moravian Lebenslauf tradition is a treasure indeed. But while President Gauck was probably thinking about the past, I am thinking about the future. A Lebenslauf is not only a helpful historical document; it can be used as a tool for assisting people to reflect spiritually on their lives and to strengthen their appreciation of others. The Lebenslauf's contribution to understanding our past is important, but I am convinced that, for members of the Moravian Church, it also holds great potential for shaping and deepening our spiritual life in the future.

Jill E. S. Vogt is a minister in the Moravian Church in Germany and currently serving the Herrnhut congregation. She received her bachelor's degree in religion and sociology/anthropology from Denison University, her Master of Divinity from Harvard Divinity School, and a Doctor of Ministry degree from Acadia Divinity College and is a graduate of the Ecumenical Institute of Bossey, Geneva. Her academic interest is narrative theology, especially as it relates to the tradition of Moravian memoirs.

Notes

1. Enquist, *Lewi's Journey*, 21.
2. See, for example, Faull, *Moravian Women's Memoirs*; Schmid, "Moravian Memoirs"; Mettele, "Constructions."
3. Vogt, "This Is My Story."
4. Atwood, "Joyfulness of Death."
5. Peucker, *Herrnhuter Wörterbuch*, 32.
6. See, for example, Hindmarch, *Evangelical Conversion Narrative*.
7. Reichel, "Ein Spiegel der Frömmigkeit."
8. See McCullough, "Most Memorable Circumstances."
9. See Vogt, "Spiritual Autobiography."
10. Gill, "Der Lebenslauf," 4.

Bibliography

Atwood, Craig D. "The Joyfulness of Death in Eighteenth-Century Moravian Communities." *Communal Societies* 17 (1997): 39–58.
Enquist, Per Olov. *Lewi's Journey*. New York: Harry N. Abrams, 2005.

Faull, Katherine. *Moravian Women's Memoirs: Their Related Lives, 1750–1820.* Syracuse, NY: Syracuse University Press, 1997.

Gill, Theodor. "Der Lebenslauf" [The memoir]. In *Gemeindezeitung der Brüdergemeine Herrnhut*, November 2014, 4.

Hindmarch, Bruce. *The Evangelical Conversion Narrative: Spiritual Autobiography in Early Modern England.* Oxford: Oxford University Press, 2007.

McCullough, Thomas J. "The Most Memorable Circumstances: Instructions for the Collection of Personal Data from Church Members, circa 1752." *Journal of Moravian History* 15 (2015): 158–175.

Mettele, Gisela. "Constructions of the Religious Self: Moravian Conversion and Transatlantic Communication." *Journal of Moravian History* 2 (2007): 7–36.

Peucker, Paul. *Herrnhuter Wörterbuch. Kleines Lexikon von brüderischen Begriffen* [Moravian dictionary: A small lexicon of Moravian terms]. Herrnhut: Unitätsarchiv, 2000.

Schmid, Pia. "Moravian Memoirs as a Source for the History of Education." In *Self, Community, World: Moravian Education in a Transatlantic World*, edited by Heikki Lempa and Paul Peucker, 168–86. Bethlehem: Lehigh University Press, 2010.

Reichel, Hellmut. "Ein Spiegel der Frömmigkeit und des geistlichen Lebens: Zur Geschichte des brüderischen Lebenslaufes" [A mirror of piety and spiritual life: Contribution to the history of the Moravian memoir]. In *Der Brüderbote*, no. 464 (March 1988): 4–7.

Vogt, Jill. "This Is My Story: Autobiographical Writing as a Tool for Spiritual Reflection, Christian Witness and Group Building." Doctor of Ministry Dissertation, Acadia University, 2018.

Vogt, Peter. "Spiritual Autobiography and Ecclesiology: The Social Dimension of Individual Life Stories in 18th Century Pietism and the Moravian Church." In *Moravian Memoirs: Pillars of an Invisible Church*, edited by Christer Ahlberger and Per von Wachenfeldt, 35–57. Gothenburg: Artos and Norma Bokförlag, 2017.

Chapter 9

Tangible and Intangible Heritage
Impacts of the World Heritage Inscription of Christiansfeld on the Moravian Church

Jørgen Bøytler

After the UNESCO World Heritage inscription, the question remained as to what impact the listing would have on the Moravian congregation in Christiansfeld. In this chapter, I will explore the situation of Christiansfeld in terms of the legacy and sustainability of the settlement and what it means for the Moravian Church congregation to be included on the UNESCO World Heritage list. UNESCO distinguishes between tangible and intangible cultural heritage, and Moravian Christiansfeld is formally inscribed as tangible cultural heritage. However, I will argue that intangible cultural heritage (ICH) is also important for understanding Christiansfeld, as Moravian Christiansfeld is much more than its buildings. Furthermore, I will discuss the concept of ICH and debate whether it makes sense to differentiate between tangible and intangible heritage when it comes to Christiansfeld.

My perspective is theological, as I am the minister of the Moravian Brethren in Christiansfeld and was highly involved in the process of Christiansfeld's inscription as UNESCO World Heritage. I believe that the continuing legacy and the future sustainability of Christiansfeld is tightly connected with both tangible and intangible heritage.

The UNESCO Convention for the Safeguarding of the Tangible and Intangible Cultural Heritage

Understanding the distinction between tangible and intangible cultural heritage is important in order to appreciate the process of the inscription of "Christiansfeld, a Moravian Church Settlement" on the UNESCO World Heritage list. The tangible heritage of Christiansfeld is obvious: the buildings, the squares, the town plan, and so on. But, as I will demonstrate, a Moravian Church settlement also includes intangibles, such as the ideas of communal life in the settlement, the everyday life practices, and the religious understandings and ideas of the congregation of Christiansfeld. I argue that a prerequisite for understanding how a Moravian settlement came to be "cultural heritage" is the fact that there is a living Moravian Church congregation that embodies both tangible and intangible heritage. It is not either/or but an entanglement of both.

In 2003, thirty-one years after UNESCO's Convention concerning the Protection of the World Cultural and Natural Heritage, the General Conference of UNESCO adopted the Convention for the Safeguarding of the Intangible Cultural Heritage (ICHC). The convention was adopted to meet a number of needs concerning ICH, including its importance as a mainspring of cultural diversity, the deep-seated interdependence between ICH and tangible cultural and natural heritage, and the awareness of a universal will and common concern to safeguard the ICH of humanity. The ICHC explains in detail what "intangible cultural heritage" means and how it is manifested. The overall purpose of the convention is to safeguard, ensure respect for, and raise awareness of the importance of ICH.[1] This all is important and relevant in the case of the Moravian settlement being accepted as tangible and intangible cultural heritage.

Polish heritage scholar Iwona Szmelter offers the following definitions: "Tangible heritage [is]: movable/immovable (the movable including libraries, archives, and objects; the immovable including archaeology, buildings, landscape and heritage sites). Intangible heritage [is]: identity, memory and unique crafts, stories etc."[2] Further, Szmelter speaks about the term "identicity" as a combination of the words "identity" and "authenticity," which is interesting for Christiansfeld.[3] The question in Christiansfeld is whether tangible and intangible cultural heritage each has authenticity in its own right. I suggest that defining Christiansfeld in terms of "identicity" helps in understanding the two dimensions of its cultural heritage: obviously tangible, yet only understandable if seeing the intangibles. One day, I overheard a visitor in Christiansfeld remark, "I wonder why this is UNESCO World Heritage; there are just some yellow brick buildings." The person had observed the tangible heritage, without being overly impressed, but had evidently missed the intangible heritage. The explanation of the identity of Christiansfeld was missing. This serves as an example of the importance of an explanation of the spiritual aspect of and the ideas behind the settlement, which would assist visitors in truly appreciating Christiansfeld as a site of cultural heritage.

As late as 2015, UNESCO published a list called "Ethics and Intangible Cultural Heritage."[4] The document contains twelve ethical principles for safeguarding ICH. Among these principles, the aspects relevant to the situation of Christiansfeld are as follows: The ethical principles focus on the rights of the community as being the principal stakeholder in the ICH. The community should have the primary role in safeguarding its own ICH, with the implication that outsiders are less likely to be able to safeguard ICH. The community must always retain the right to continue the practices, representations, expressions, knowledge, and skills necessary to ensure the viability of the ICH. Respecting the dynamic and living nature of the ICH is underlined. Authenticity and exclusivity should not constitute concerns and obstacles in the safeguarding of ICH. Another important ethical principle in safeguarding ICH is that the community should play a significant role both in determining what constitutes threats to its ICH—including the decontextualization, commodification, and misrepresentation of that heritage—and in deciding how to prevent and mitigate such threats.

The importance of considering ethics, as defined by UNESCO in relation to ICH, is further accurately exemplified in the preface to the description of the recent European Research Council–funded research project Heriligion: The Heritagization of Religion and Sacralization of Heritage: "often what is now considered heritage was and still is seen as religious in nature and possibly sacred."[5] Heritagization is the process through which objects, places, and practices are turned into cultural heritage,[6] or, put more simply, in discussing heritagization, the ethics mentioned can serve as guidelines in dealing with ICH. This point, I argue, is relevant to Christiansfeld as a World Heritage site and as a living church congregation and community at the same time.

Intangible and Tangible Values or Intangible and Tangible Heritage

The term "intangible cultural heritage" is defined in the ICHC as, in part, "the practices, representations, expressions, knowledge, skills—as well as the instruments, objects, artefacts and cultural spaces associated therewith—that communities, groups and, in some cases, individuals recognize as part of their cultural heritage."[7] However, the meaning of the less frequently used double term "tangible and intangible values" is less obvious. Australian heritage and museum scholars Laurajane Smith and Gary Campbell explore the contradictions of the advent, dissemination, and use of the terms "intangible value" and "tangible value." The tautological phrase "intangible value" and its contradictory companion "tangible value" have become ubiquitous in anglophone academic writing, public policy documents, and practice.[8] The late professor Herb Stovel, former secretary general of the International Council on Monuments and Sites (ICOMOS), who was an adviser for the Christiansfeld Initiative, uses the term "intangible values."[9] Smith and Campbell discuss political reasons for using the two terms, which were also used quite frequently in the process leading to Christiansfeld's inscription. Smith and Campbell state, "Bringing 'intangible' and 'value' together does two things. Firstly, it creates a tautology by the fact the terms are really redundant to each other—of course, 'values' are 'intangible.' Secondly, and this is important to what heritage professionals do, it weakens any sense of the positive values the intangible might have, as not being tangible makes it difficult, impossible, vague, abstract and of a value not precisely measurable."[10]

In a Moravian Church understanding, the term "tangible and intangible heritage" is highly relevant. However, instead of indicating the "what" of tangibles/intangibles by referring to a noun, like "heritage" or "value," it serves the understanding to simply say "tangibles" or "intangibles." This keeps the terminology open for interpretations and helps avoid any tautology, such as the meaningless idea of a value (or other intangible) as tangible. Refraining from qualifying tangible/intangible by culturally commoditizing terms like heritage or value, one is left in a state of intellectual freedom of the hermeneutics of deciphering the "cultural" of the heritage. This offers space for a less black-and-white interpretation, in fact fusing some of the cultural heritage as having both tangible and intangible aspects.

There is a problem, however: one of the most important reasons for using the term "heritage"—both "tangible" and "intangible"—is that it is often understood as something left behind by a deceased person or by a religious community that no longer exists. In missiological terms, a church can live through three simple categories, which objectify the sequential stages of a church's rise and fall: movement, monument, mausoleum. The problem is that a Moravian Church like the one in Christiansfeld is not simply a heritage, not a mausoleum. It sees itself as a living organism that exists today. This provides another reason for using the terminology of tangibles and intangibles, for it leaves space for a self-understanding of the Moravian Church being alive, a vibrant community, and yet bearing its heritage of brick and mortar in mind.

The Understanding of Intangible Cultural Heritage in the Process Leading to Christiansfeld's UNESCO World Heritage Status

Between 2000 and 2007, the Christiansfeld Initiative undertook numerous activities, working toward the inscription of Christiansfeld on the UNESCO World Heritage list. In a publication from 2005, *Conservation of Living Religious Heritage*, the International Centre for the Study of the Preservation and Restoration of Cultural Property (ICCROM) paid special attention to "living religious heritage" through a number of articles, including one article on Christiansfeld.[11] The article in that publication, by Japanese heritage scholar Nobuko Inaba,[12] prompts the following insight found in the book's introduction: "In all cases, the tangible and intangible manifestations of the heritage carry intangible values, expressing the significance of the heritage for the communities who consider it important."[13] Inaba's article, like the whole book, was written in 2003, the same year that UNESCO adopted the ICHC.

In September 2000, the so-called Christiansfeld Document appeared. It came out of the first Christiansfeld Initiative Conference leading to the application to become UNESCO World Heritage and included participants from Christiansfeld Municipality, national government authorities, UNESCO, ICCROM, Harvard University, and the Moravian Church. The "Christiansfeld Document" operated with the idea of "spiritual values, expressed in buildings and their spatial organization in landscape."[14] Note that the term "intangible heritage" was not used, but "spiritual values, expressed in buildings" obviously refers to intangibles expressed in tangible cultural heritage.

The second Christiansfeld Initiative Conference took place in March 2003 and the draft founding document, aimed at formalizing the "Christiansfeld Initiative, a network of municipalities of the Moravian heritage," mentioned as the first of the guiding principles that it should "ensure continuity of the whole of material and immaterial Moravian Heritage in the civil societies of the settlements that have been founded or strongly influenced by Moravian Brethren."[15] The terms "material" and "immaterial" were used as synonyms for tangible and intangible Moravian (cultural) heritage.

"The World Heritage Convention Tentative List, property Christiansfeld, January 2003," notes that justification of "outstanding universal value" was based on two cultural UNESCO criteria: representing a masterpiece of human creative genius; and being an outstanding example of a type of building, architectural or technological ensemble, or landscape that illustrates (a) significant stage(s) in human history.[16]

The latter calls Christiansfeld "a testimony of a religious community with high standards for its towns and buildings."[17] The mention that a religious community has erected the town, implies, in my understanding, the presence of ICH being expressed in the tangible heritage.

What became the Moravian Heritage Network, Christiansfeld Initiative, had its second international conference in Bethlehem, Pennsylvania, in October 2004, counting participants from the Bethlehem and Christiansfeld Municipalities, the Moravian congregations in Bethlehem and Christiansfeld, UNESCO, ICCROM, and other Moravian Church settlements. The conference document noted that "the members of the Network, [hereby] agree to initiate, take part in and support inter-disciplinary research on the relationships between tangible and intangible heritage of the Moravian communities and the underlying Moravian values."[18]

During these years, the distinction between tangible and intangible heritage appears to have become a key to understanding the outstanding universal values of Christiansfeld. The increasing understanding of the value of intangible cultural heritage was supported through the adoption of the ICHC and through interest from other bodies such as ICCROM.[19] A turning point came when the director of the Danish Monument Department in the Ministry of Culture, in a meeting with representatives of the newly established Kolding Municipality and the Moravian Church, clarified the Danish government's understanding of Christiansfeld as living religious cultural heritage, consisting of tangible and intangible heritage.

The Moravian Church in Christiansfeld

The Moravian Church in Christiansfeld is part of a worldwide organization, Unitas Fratrum, or the Worldwide Moravian Church. The Moravian Church's congregations are organized within provinces. The Unity consists of twenty-four unity provinces[20], five mission provinces, and close to twenty mission areas. A unity province is self-governing through a synod and a provincial board. Christiansfeld is part of the European Continental Province,[21] which consists of Moravian Churches in Germany, the Netherlands, Switzerland, Denmark, Sweden, Estonia, Latvia, and Albania.

In terms of legal status, the Moravian Church in Christiansfeld is an Evangelical Lutheran Free Congregation, not a "recognized religious community" (*Anerkendt trossamfund*). The leadership is conferential; the congregation is led by a Board of Elders, which is democratically elected for a six-year term. The Board of Elders calls and employs the minister and is responsible for operations.

The legal status of the Moravian Church in Christiansfeld is unique, because the term "free congregation" in Denmark was invented to facilitate the establishment of the Moravian Church when founding Christiansfeld in 1772. The Moravian Church is not in a category with other religious communities but legally known as a "§8a association," enjoying tax exemption like many other Danish associations and non-governmental organizations. The Moravian Church has expressed no interest in obtaining the right to perform legal marriages. The Moravian Church in Christiansfeld receives no state support other than the exemption from property tax on the listed houses, as is the case for anyone owning a listed house. The funeral authority is given by the local folk church to the Moravian pastor in each individual case of a funeral for a Moravian member. All in all, the Moravian Church is keen on not being part of the state authority.

We can look at the intangible heritage of Moravian Christiansfeld's theological basics in order to describe some of the fundamentals of the Moravian Church, which may help frame the contents of its tangible and intangible heritage.[22] First, there is Christocentrism, which means that an understanding of Christ as redeemer is the epicenter of the preaching, which may be seen as an intangible. This is to some extent a legacy of the theological understanding of the founder of the Renewed Moravian Church, Count Nicolaus von Zinzendorf (1700–1760),[23] who from childhood was rooted in Hallensic Pietism and influenced by mysticism. Zinzendorf developed a rather extreme focus on the wounds of Christ on the cross, employing both blood-erotic terms and diminutives to describe Christ—among other theological excesses. Moravian Pietism to some extent distanced itself from Hallensic Pietism, which emphasized personal faith and called for penitential remorse against the main Lutheran Church's perceived emphasis on doctrine and theology at the expense of Christian living. While Moravian Pietism agreed with Halle in stressing piety and Christian living, it had less time for remorse and favored preaching that Christ's atonement was the only requisite for salvation. Freedom in Christ was important for the Moravians and is still a key to understanding the notion of faith as a conviction of the individual, while also living in a community together, being active and joyful, being part of a fellowship that lives together in equality. The Moravian movement has also shown many signs of being an Enlightenment movement.[24]

Moravians have a strong ecumenical identity. Ever since the Ancient Moravian Church was founded in 1457 in Kunvald, Bohemia, ecumenism[25] has been part of the fabric of the Moravian Church. In the sixteenth century, Moravians even saw themselves as bridge builders between the European Reformation movements. Later on, Zinzendorf's idea of "the Heart Religion," which focused on the importance of having Christ in the heart rather than encapsulating Christ and Christianity in the church as an organization, was decisive for the ecumenical conviction. Zinzendorf developed a set of mission principles, which in contemporary language includes contextualization, indigenization of the Gospel, self-reliance for new Christian groups or congregations, and self-propagation of the Gospel. Finally, one may also mention equality as a principle of the Moravian Church, which was the basic reason for electing Christ as the Chief Elder, or leader of the church.

Impact on Some of the Intangibles of a Living Religious Tangible Heritage

I will now examine some of the intangibles mentioned in the Advisory Board Evaluation by ICOMOS[26] of the World Heritage nomination of Christiansfeld. ICOMOS and a portion of the academic—and maybe also commercial—agents connected with Christiansfeld operate with a less precisely defined concept of intangible heritage. This is, however, not always compatible with the concepts of intangibles of the Moravian community. Since the intention of UNESCO and of some of the other Moravian settlements is to propose a transnational nomination of Moravian Church Cultural Heritage, it is important to identify the intangibles in the Moravian Church's understanding of the Moravian settlements. The following are a couple of examples of potential friction or collision between understandings of intangibles.

First, one could mention the church, including worship, prayer, faith, and spirituality. The obvious place for a spiritual encounter is the church building, the Saal House.[27] Probably more than 90 percent of visitors to Christiansfeld visit the Saal House. Generally, visitors are respectful of the worship space. They often seem to take it in, enjoying its aesthetic qualities, which make them satisfied and grateful. The Saal is open year round for prayer and contemplation. The congregation mainly sees it as positive that many visit the church. Sunday morning can be a slight challenge: on the one hand, participation in the worship service is open to everybody; on the other hand, it is preferred that tourists avoid entering the worship space during the service to watch the churchgoers, take photos, and leave.

The fellowship of the members of the congregation is a living intangible, and it can be argued that this intangible has various tangible implications,

including the church services, the congregational feasts, mutual visits on
birthdays, and volunteer work together. It is a more complicated task to
communicate tangible expressions of the fellowship to visitors, unless they
decide to join a church service or another event. Rituals or rites defined as
religious and symbolic actions with a fixed structure, celebrated in connection with initiation or transition in the individual phases of life or society's
most important celebrations and ceremonies, are part and parcel of most
Christian churches. Several of the rites, especially the sacraments, have
tangible and intangible parts. In baptism, for example, the water is a tangible; the religious meaning of the baptism is intangible. Concerning rituals,
the Moravian Church is not very different from most other churches. One
Moravian Church assembly, however, is rather unique: the Lovefeast,[28]
which is understood as a liturgical meal and also a church service (song
service). It is not a sacrament[29] but, in accordance with a New Testament
term, understood as an *agape* meal. The tea and buns served are tangibles,
while the intangible is the Lovefeast's symbolization of the loving fellowship of the congregation.

A further intangible element highlighted in the heritage documents
is the Moravian world view. The design, the town plan, the craftsmanship of the buildings, the architecture—all reflect the world view of the
Moravians, who erected the town. This world view is to some degree
shared by present-day Moravians but it is the twenty-first-century version
of a Christian, Danish, democratic, pluralistic world view. The eighteenth-
century Moravians who built the settlement were people of their era, but
they also had distinctive ideas concerning the creation of a Moravian
settlement, ideas that displayed a specific world view and made a statement about the faith of the Moravians. This was also expressed in the
physical structures erected to be the base of congregational life, overseas
mission work, and diaspora work in Denmark. The twenty-first-century
Moravians aim to continue to live a life based in the Moravian Church
world view but aligned with the twenty-first-century context.

The world view, as the Moravian ideas behind the settlement, has
tangible implications on the design, the town plan, and the architecture.
Going into further details of design, I find that ideas are presented in
the design of the houses, in the very existence of choir houses, including
the dormitories. The same goes for the Saal, with its stringent, elegant,
simple, and white appearance, as well as for God's Acre and the church
square, with its strong aesthetic values. The fundamental notion of
everything in daily life being connected to God resulted in well-known
quality craftsmanship. The design of the church communicates equality
and simplicity, as does the design of God's Acre. The choir houses show
the importance of fellowship and communal life. Many of these values

exist today; craftsmanship is still important, and volunteer work by the members is important for the general economy of the church community.

The testimony of a Christian church can be described as giving testimony to the Christian faith and life in a broad sense. Bearing testimony to the Gospel is a general Christian responsibility, based on the final words of Christ in Matthew 28, also known as "The Great Commandment." The tangible Christiansfeld should, according to the Moravian Church understanding, communicate the essence of the Gospel. The intangibles in this case include the mission work, the internationality of the Moravian Church, being tangible in social and diaconal action and development work in the Third World.

The congregational structure is the one intangible that has the greatest impact on the tangibles of the town. Without the tangible implications of the congregational structure, it is difficult to imagine that Christiansfeld would have been inscribed on the UNESCO World Heritage list. It is a goal for the congregation that the testimony of some of the other intangibles — including the aims of equality, simplicity, and communality — gain tangible implications through the presence of the congregation, which by no means feels superior or perfect but is inspired to seek some of these qualities in the framework of the physical structures, the tangibles of the town. Since the founding of the congregation in Christiansfeld, the continuous change in society and culture has prompted a certain adjustment of principles, whether religious, social, or ethical. However, the tangibles of the settlement are pretty much a given.

Consider the following example of using principles to maintain qualities and to avoid commodification of the intangible heritage.[30] On Sunday mornings on the church square, there is often a special atmosphere, best described as the Sunday morning silence and tranquility. To maintain this deeper intangible sense, the Moravian Church asks that guided tours be avoided on Sunday mornings. One could argue that we use the Christian principle of the day of rest to maintain the peace on Sunday mornings and, by doing so, give people an opportunity to experience the Sunday morning tranquility of the town center. Visitors are more than welcome to be present at the square, including on Sunday mornings, but more for contemplation than for a guided tour.

A key concept regarding "adaptation" and change in cultural heritage terminology is "authenticity." This is not without reason: without authenticity, there is no real heritage, only a replica. In Christiansfeld, it can be argued that we look at objective authenticity based on the originality and genuineness of the town.[31]

While there is a high degree of objective authenticity in many of the intangibles present, questions have been raised concerning the authenticity of the tangibles. The UNESCO decision to include Christiansfeld on the World Heritage list stated, "In some cases, architectural renovations could have been implemented with more respect for authenticity. At times architects have aimed for modern interiors of a high aesthetic standard and refinery which have unfortunately reduced traces of historic construction materials and techniques."[32]

Another important part of the identity is cross-cultural practice and thinking, which is tangibly accessible in the mission and development work in the Third World. It is also evident in architectural details such as broad staircases in some of the houses, including the choir houses and the parsonage. Apart from the visible mission office, its organization, and its employees, quite a few members of the Moravian Church past and present have begun work as missionaries and, after coming back, have stayed and lived in Christiansfeld. The museum bears witness to these missionaries, who brought with them artifacts from abroad.

Atmosphere is an intangible, which in many ways depends on personal sensation. The tangible framework for the atmosphere is virtually the whole town—the town's plan, the green areas, the houses, and the squares. Atmosphere is also elusive. A few tourist buses on the church square will change the atmosphere.[33] Too many visitors in the town center at the same time will do the same. The upkeep and repair of the buildings, and strict rules on what can be done to the buildings, helps to maintain the atmosphere.

Identity can be said to consist of several intangibles. In relation to Christiansfeld, a specific Christian identity would include the theology communicated in a church service, and in the texts, but also in living together as a congregation. The Moravians have understood themselves, and are probably also understood by others, as *Die Stillen im Lande* ("the quiet in the land").[34] A small piece of a description of Herrnhut, from 1922, reads,

> The small patch lies pleasantly there, in the green of its orchard. The structural center of the whole is the unassuming little church with its ridge turret. And just as far as the little tower can overlook what belongs to it, the houses and small houses of the place arrange themselves around the church into a homely, closed world that seems to lead a quiet, separate and remote life [my translation].

This small text captures in some ways the identity of a Moravian settlement: a quiet place. I argue that this quietness is an element in the identity of the Moravian Church, which can be challenged by a large influx of visitors as a result of the UNESCO World Heritage inscription. If looking for the tangibles of that part of the identity, one would look at the church square, the gardens, the garden houses, and possibly the way in which the Moravian fellowship is lived out.

Tangibles and Intangibles Impacting Life in Christiansfeld

Often, a Moravian Brother or Sister will express that part of his or her identity is embedded in being a member of the Moravian Church. Some of the keywords typically used to describe this identity include fellowship, equality, joy, faith, and responsibility to the group. In the contemporary Moravian Church of Christiansfeld, one will find a group of people, comprising some very active and dedicated persons—and some not quite as active but still very dedicated.

Within the worldwide Moravian Unity, only a small minority of Moravians live in Moravian settlements. Most live in villages or cities, where the only physical Moravian structure is a church building. Most of the Moravian traditions were developed within the settlements, and today it is primarily in the settlements that most living traditions are found.

Daily life in Christiansfeld is in a way quite ordinary: people live in a middle-class Danish neighborhood; they work, they study, or they are retired, much like the rest of the population. Yet, daily life in Christiansfeld is in some respects also extraordinary. Life is spent living in historical buildings; the aesthetic values of the houses, the squares, and the Saal House are not easily overlooked. At the same time, thousands of visitors converge on Christiansfeld, listening to tour guides, wandering around town, perusing the many shops—indeed, there are more shops in Christiansfeld than in many other small towns in Denmark.[35]

By and large, the impact of World Heritage status on the congregation of Moravian Christiansfeld has turned out to be relatively limited. It must be acknowledged that the awareness of the tangible heritage of Christiansfeld has led to significant investment, from both private and public funds, for the restoration of the historic buildings and their surroundings.[36]

For the Moravians it can at times feel quite strange to be "living cultural heritage," for Moravians see themselves as quite ordinary citizens. Moravian culture and identity are not loud and self-promoting; rather, they are quiet—but also efficient. The value and notion of efficiency is, in my opinion, rooted in the fact that the Moravian Church settlements were erected by Moravian artisans, who need to work efficiently in order to make a living. The efficiency is mirrored in the liturgical tradition. The *Singstunde*,[37] the Sunday morning church service, and other assemblies in church are as a rule relatively short. Formerly, the Moravians in

Christiansfeld would assemble on a daily basis for prayers, singing, and at times teaching sessions in various groups. The sessions were normally quite short, so people could then get back to work.

Liturgy continues to play a strong role in the church service in Christiansfeld. In some parts of the worldwide Moravian Unity, the liturgical tradition is weaker. In architecture as in the church service, simplicity is an ideal. *Schlicht und vornehm* ("simple and noble") describes some of the fundamental architectural principles applied in the Moravian settlement, and the same principles are found in liturgical expressions in the church service. The music is an important part of the spiritual life in the settlement congregation but also in congregations unrelated to settlements. Christiansfeld has a music archive,[38] which is a collection of music by known and unknown composers, and contemporary music scholars are paying attention to this resource. The congregational archives are much larger, representing the common memory of the congregation.[39] Included in the archives are the biographies of the Moravians (*Lebenslaüfe*), an extraordinary source of biographical, anthropological, and social history over a span of almost 250 years.[40] Numerous other handwritten and printed documents are kept in the archives, which are seen as an integrated part of the living congregation. The idea is that the archives document for the Moravians what God has been doing through the Moravian Church over the years. For many years, the Moravians documented life in detail and there was a system of exchanging letters and reports on the work between the overseas mission fields and the settlement congregations and between the settlements.

Toward a Conclusion: The Heritagization of Christiansfeld

A quick look at Christiansfeld can result in the question that I overheard some years ago. Standing in the church square, a tourist asked, "So where is the cultural heritage?" He looked at the buildings and was not impressed. He looked at tangibles alone and had no conception of the history of the town. This illustrates that unless one understands that the cultural heritage of Christiansfeld is both tangible and intangible, one may fail to understand why Christiansfeld is on the UNESCO World Heritage list.

I return to the question of heritagization, through which objects, places, and especially practices become heritage, objects of the past, relics. This heritagization can become a challenge, for example, in the context of the Sunday morning worship service or that of the funeral. A church service is generally understood as the epicenter of the work and life of a Christian church. However, the worship service risks being heritagized when tourists enter the church (Saal) during a service, take a few photos, whisper, and walk out again. In that situation, the church service is heritagized, is seen as a relic to be observed. Any person is most welcome to take part in the service, but there is a fine line between taking part in a church service as a guest and being a tourist witnessing a church service as a spectator. The case of the funeral is more complex. Clearly this attracts attention, but even though it could be understood as a heritagization of the funeral, the attention drawn to a funeral procession is not particularly connected to Christiansfeld being cultural heritage, since this attention is commonplace at any other funeral procession.

As a UNESCO World Heritage site, the tangible as well as the intangible heritage can come under various pressures. These include wear and tear, as well as a devaluation or at least a challenge to some values. The religious legacy can come under pressure through disturbances in church services and through a feeling among worshippers of being on display. The atmosphere of Christiansfeld, especially its tranquility and quietness, can be endangered if the tourism is not sustainable. UNESCO defines sustainable tourism as "tourism that respects both local people and the traveler, cultural heritage and the environment."[41] The Moravian congregation in Christiansfeld would prefer to use the term "guest" than "tourist," since a tourist is basically a spectator, often viewing the world through a camera lens, while a guest in principle interacts with the hosts, who are also supposed to show hospitality. As a congregation this is our goal and approach in order to show appreciation of Christiansfeld—our church settlement—being named UNESCO World Heritage.

Jørgen Bøytler holds a PhD in Theology. Since 1997 he has been pastor of the Moravian Church in Christiansfeld; from 2007 to 2010 he was director of the European Continental Province of the Moravian Church, and since 2010 he has been the Unity Board administrator. Bøytler was active in the process for including Christiansfeld on the UNESCO World Heritage list (2015).

Notes

1. "Text of the Convention for the Safeguarding of the Intangible Cultural Heritage," UNESCO, 17 October 2003, accessed 18 May 2020, https://ich.unesco.org/en/convention.
2. Szmelter, "New Values," bullet point 7.

3. A number of authors, thinking in traditional terms, have used the term "authenticity" when referring strictly to the material constitution of a work and proposed "identity" as a term suitable for the character of the contemporary cultural legacy. Unfortunately, identity is not included in the conservation normative frame. In 2010 Iris Kapelouzou proposed a new term, "identicity," which "may be introduced in the place of 'authenticity' as a concept including 'authenticity' as well as 'identity' as criteria for decision making. 'Identicity' includes artwork and heritage identities, defined in terms of ontology and in terms of the relative hierarchy of the heritage values attributed to a work of art respectively." Szmelter, "New Values," bullet point 40.
4. "Ethics and Intangible Cultural Heritage," UNESCO, accessed 18 May 2020, https://ich.unesco.org/en/ethics-and-ich-00866.
5. "The Heritagization of Religion and Sacralization of Heritage in Contemporary Europe: Heriligion," HERA (Humanities in the European Research Area), accessed 24 December 2021, https://heriligion.eu/.
6. Sjöholm, "Heritagisation," abstract.
7. The explanation of "intangible cultural heritage" continues: "This intangible cultural heritage, transmitted from generation to generation, is constantly recreated by communities and groups in response to their environment, their interaction with nature and their history, and provides them with a sense of identity and continuity, thus promoting respect for cultural diversity and human creativity. For the purposes of this Convention, consideration will be given solely to such intangible cultural heritage as is compatible with existing international human rights instruments, as well as with the requirements of mutual respect among communities, groups and individuals, and of sustainable development." "Text of the Convention," Article 2.1.
8. Smith and Campbell, *Tautology*, 26.
9. Stovel, "Introduction," 9.
10. Smith and Campbell, *Tautology*, 31.
11. Bøytler, "Christiansfeld," 19.
12. Inaba, "Ise Shrine," 44
13. Stovel, "Introduction," 9.
14. Christiansfeld Dokumentet, 1.
15. Draft founding document for the Christiansfeld Initiative, a network of municipalities of the Moravian heritage.
16. The decision to inscribe Christiansfeld on the UNESCO World Heritage was list based on criteria (iii) and (iv). UNESCO, "Christiansfeld, A Moravian Church Settlement, Denmark," Decision 39 COM 8B.20, 2015, https://whc.unesco.org/en/decisions/6370. This was suggested by us in the group doing the application.
17. *Denmark—Tentative List 2003.*
18. Christiansfeld Dokumentet, 1.
19. See, for example, Eleonora Lupo, "Intangible Cultural Heritage Valorisation: A New Field for Design Research and Practice" (paper presented at IASDR 07 [International Association of Societies of Design Research 2007], Hong Kong, 12–15 November 2007), https://pdfs.semanticscholar.org/c11e/20b5f414187813f72b5f57729b57df165764.pdf; Lucas Lixinski, "A Framework for the Protection of Intangible Cultural Heritage in International Law" (PhD diss., European University Institute, 2010), https://cadmus.eui.eu/handle/1814/15384. The Advisory Body Evaluation (ICOMOS) does not reveal any deep understanding of many of the specific intangible heritage elements found in Christiansfeld. The intangible heritage seems to be understood only to a certain degree, and a better understanding of the identity and theology of the Brethren would have been desirable.
20. Church Order of the Unitas Fratrum (COUF), 36ff.

21. "An International Organisation," Unitas Fratrum, accessed 19 February 2020, http://www.unitasfratrum.org/.
22. Bøytler, "Religious Cultural Heritage," 13.
23. It could be argued that it is not totally precise to name Zinzendorf as the founder of the Renewed Moravian Church; however, in many aspects he played an important role in terms of ideas, theology, liturgy, poetry, and mission. See Bøytler, *Eccelsiology and Culture*, 101ff.
24. Bredsdorff, *Den brogede oplysning*, 49, 73, 83, 88, 90.
25. Ecumenism is the principle or aim of promoting unity among the world's Christian Churches.
26. "Christiansfeld, a Moravian Church Settlement," UNESCO, accessed 22 February 2022, https://whc.unesco.org/en/list/1468/.
27. Saal House, or Saal, is the term often used for the Moravian Church building. It is a German word and often not translated into English, even in an English text.
28. Lovefeasts originated in the first gathering of Christians after Pentecost. The early believers met and broke bread together, thereby signifying their union and equality. These meals of the church family were associated with the celebration of the Lord's Supper, which followed them. They were called *agape*, from the Greek word for love, that is, for the highest type of spiritual love. "The Lovefeast," The Moravian Church, accessed 22 February 2022, https://www.moravian.org/2018/11/the-lovefeast/.
29. A sacrament is a religious ceremony recognized by the Christian church, or a rite of passage that infers some blessing or grace on the people who receive it. Baptism and Holy Communion are Protestant sacraments. The Lovefeast is not a rite or a ceremony but a meal of Christian love (*agape*) that builds fellowship among the participants.
30. Kim, Whitford, and Arcodia, "Development."
31. Kim, Whitford, and Arcodia, 423. Apart from objective authenticity, Kim, Whitford, and Arcodia look at staged authenticity, normally a limited range of culture "on the front stage," while the genuine authentic culture occurs more hidden, not readily available for the tourists. Further, they mention constructive authenticity as well as existential authenticity, meaning that the authenticity displayed to tourists has no absolute originality and the heritage tourism is to offer identification to the tourists of their "real self." Space here does not permit further investigation of the nature of authenticity displayed in Christiansfeld, but it is certainly a relevant topic.
32. UNESCO, "Christiansfeld." On some restored doors and windows, conservators have removed several layers of paint, layer by layer, showing all the colors that have been used over the more than two centuries. In the parsonage, twelve to fourteen different colors are displayed on one door. It is a fifteen by fifteen centimeter square that tells, in the most authentic way possible, the history of Christiansfeld.
33. If constructive or existential authenticity was furthered in Christiansfeld, the first victim would be the atmosphere.
34. Baudert and Steinmann, *Der Welt die Stillen im Lande*, 5.
35. See chapter 7 in this volume.
36. Since about 2002, investments in the houses and squares including God's Acre have totaled about DKK 250 million (approximately USD 40 million), financed partly through contributions from private foundations, partly through the Moravian Church's own investments, and to a smaller extent by contributions from the Ministry of Culture and the Kolding Municipality. Most of the investments were made before Christiansfeld's inscription on the UNESCO World Heritage list.
37. *Singstunde* is a lirtugical service that predominantly entails singing a number of stanzas from Moravian hymns. The stanzas are arranged such that a message can be received through the singing. A reading and a prayer will often be part of the *Singstunde* as well. The German word *"Singstunde"* is usually not translated into English.

38. See chapter 4 in this volume.
39. See chapter 10 in this volume.
40. See chapter 8 in this volume.
41. *Bæredygtig Turisme Strategi Christiansfeld,* 12.

Bibliography

Atwood, Craig D. *The Community of the Cross: Moravian Piety in Colonial Bethlehem.* University Park: Penn State University Press, 2004.

Atwood, Craig D., and Peter Vogt, ed. *The Distinctiveness of Moravian Culture: Essays and Documents in Moravian History in Honor of Vernon H. Nelson on his Seventieth Birthday.* Nazareth, PA: Moravian Historical Society, 2003.

Baudert, S., and Th. Steinmann. *Der Welt die Stillen im Lande. Bilder aus zwei Jahrhunderten herrnhutischer Geschichte und brüderischen Lebens* [The world of the quiet in the lands: Images from two centuries of Moravian history and life]. Berlin, 1922.

Bæredygtig Turisme Strategi Christiansfeld [Sustainable Tourism Strategy for Christiansfeld], 2019.

Bøytler, Jørgen. "Christiansfeld: A Religious Heritage Alive and Well." In Stovel, Stanley-Price, and Killick, *Conservation of Living Religious Heritage,* 19–30.

Bøytler, Jørgen. *Ecclesiology and Culture in the Moravian Church.* Aarhus: Aarhus University, 2009.

Bøytler, Jørgen. "Religious Cultural Heritage, the Intangibles: A Theological Reading of the Decision 39COM 8b.20 and Advisory Board Evaluation (ICOMOS) for the Inscription of Christiansfeld." Paper presented at Bethlehem Conference on Moravian History and Music, 2018.

Bøytler, Jørgen. "Unity in Diversity: Challenges to the Worldwide Moravian Church." *The Hinge* 21 (Fall 2015): 3f.

Bredsdorff, Thomas. *Den brogede oplysning* [The multifaceted Enlightenment]. Copenhagen: Gyldendal, 2003.

Christiansfeld Dokumentet, signed 26 September 2000. Christiansfeld Kommune, Byfornyelsesselskabet Danmark smba, signed by Jørgen From, Mayor Christiansfeld, Jelen Janos, ambassador UNESCO, Hungary, Jørgen Bøytler, pastor of the Moravian Church Christiansfeld.

Christiansfeld Forvaltningsplan [Christiansfeld management plan], *2019–2022.* Advisory Body Evaluation (ICOMOS), Christiansfeld (Denmark), No 1468.

Church Order of the Unitas Fratrum (COUF). Published by order of the Unity Synod held in Montego Bay, Jamaica 12–19 August 2016. Christiansfeld 2017. ISBN 978 87 7068 133 9.

Freeman, Arthur J. *An Ecumenical Theology of the Heart: The Theology of Count Nicholas Ludwig von Zinzendorf.* Bethlehem, PA: Moravian Church in America, 1998.

Inaba, Nobuko. "The Ise Shrine and the Gion Festival." In Stovel, Stanley-Price, and Killick, *Conservation of Living Religious Heritage,* 22–57.

Kapelouzou, I. "Contemplating Integration: Modern Art and the Conservation System." In *Art and Science,* vol. 8. Proceedings of a Special Focus Symposium in Art and Science, Baden-Baden, 2–6 August 2010, edited by G. E. Lasker, H. Schinzel, and K. Boullart, 39–44. Tecumseh, ON: International Institute for Advanced Studies in Systemic Research and Cybernetics, 2010.

Kim, Soojung, Michelle Whitford, and David Arcodia. "Development of Intangible Cultural Heritage as a Sustainable Tourism Resource: The Intangible Cultural Heritage Practitioners' Perspective." *Journal of Heritage Tourism* 14, no. 5–6 (2019): 422–35.

Meyer, Dietrich. *Zinzendorf und die Herrnhuter Brüdergemeine* [Zinzendorf and the Moravian Brethren]. Göttingen: Vandenhoeck and Ruprecht, 2009.

Sjöholm, Jennie. "Heritagisation, Re-heritagisation and De-heritagisation of Built Environments: The Urban Transformation of Kiruna, Sweden." PhD diss., Luleå University of Technology, 2016.

Smith, L., and G. Campbell. "The Tautology of 'Intangible Values' and the Misrecognition of Intangible Cultural Heritage." *Heritage and Society* 10, no. 1 (2017): 26–44.

Stovel, Herb. "Introduction." In Stovel, Stanley-Price, and Killick, *Conservation of Living Religious Heritage*, 1–11.

Stovel, Herb, Nicolas Stanley-Price, and Robert Killick, eds. *Conservation of Living Religious Heritage*. ICCROM Conservation Studies, no. 3. Rome: International Centre for the Study of the Preservation and Restoration of Cultural Property, 2005.

Szmelter, Iwona. "New Values of Cultural Heritage and the Need for a New Paradigm regarding Its Care," *CeROArt*, HS (2013). https://doi.org/10.4000/ceroart.3647.

Chapter 10

The Community Archive in Christiansfeld between Local and Global

Christina Petterson

As anyone working with Moravian archival material will know, the Moravian archives are veritable treasure troves of historical information dating back to the early eighteenth century. The archives were formally established in 1764, but materials pertaining to the history of the Moravian Brethren had accumulated steadily since the foundation of Herrnhut in 1722.[1] The reasons for this comprehensive archival tradition are manifold. Count Nicolas Ludwig von Zinzendorf's aristocratic background and the manorial archival tradition are but one. Another is Zinzendorf's legal training and subsequent appointment as councilor to the court of the Elector of Saxony, a training and task that both emphasized documentation. Finally, the growing movement and its flourishing missionary activity meant an increase in correspondence and records.[2] Together these aspects fed into the establishment of the Moravian archives, which were transported around Europe until the establishment in 1764 of the formal archive. Since then, the central Unity archive of the Moravian Brethren is situated in Herrnhut, Germany. In addition to this central archive, which also constitutes the provincial archive of the European Continental Province, the individual settlements and congregations have their own congregational archives, of which the archive in Christiansfeld, discussed in this chapter, is one. Such an archival structure reflects the relationship between the local Moravian communities and the Moravian Church as a global fellowship.

The present chapter is based on my schooling in theology and cultural studies and is structured as follows. I begin with a section on the restructuring of the Christiansfeld archive according to Herrnhut's directives in the late nineteenth century. These directives requested a particular ordering of the local archival material—an organization that was to be followed in all local communities. The following main section looks at how this organization of the local archival material is parallel to the communal structure of Christiansfeld and how this relates to global Moravian aspects. Finally, the chapter considers the representation of this history in the heritage process. Thus, the first two sections deal with the common Moravian aspects of Christiansfeld, while the third looks at the reception of these elements in the UNESCO World Heritage inscription.

Cataloging and Organizing

The archive of the Moravian Congregation in Christiansfeld is currently housed in the Single Sisters' House in Christiansfeld and is managed by the congregation. In contrast to the central archive in Herrnhut, the local community archives, such as those in Niesky, Christiansfeld, Gnadau, and Neudietendorf, do not have a full-time archivist employed; instead, the minister or an elder serves this function. The archive in Herrnhut is centrally funded by the Unity Board, while the local archives are not. The archive in Christiansfeld is a local archive and as such differs in scope, purpose, and structure from the central archive in Herrnhut.

At the General Synod in 1879,[3] it was decided to produce catalogs of the archives of the communities and the missionary stations, as well as to construct a secure location for the central archive.[4] This was discussed and decided at the behest of the archivist, Alexander Glitsch, in order to secure, complete, and index the core collections of the Unity archive.[5] To this end, the various leaders of the local congregations were asked to send in a list of what materials—if any—they had in their charge. The correspondence included instructions as to how to organize the material in various groups[6] and a list of questions. The two main groups into which to organize the material were the *Gemeinarchiv* and the *Vorsteherarchiv*, the community or congregational archive and the supervisor's archive. The latter was to be divided into *Acta Publica*, which was to include all negotiations with governments and authorities, and *Acta Domestica*, which should include all internal legal issues, such as bills of sale, contracts with local authorities and legal negotiations, and communication between members. Then a pattern was suggested for dividing the congregational archive into a number of subgroups, to which we return below. Questions were posed to the local pastor regarding whether there were any archival records (and which ones), whether there was a special room for storing them and enough shelves, whether there was some order or structure to the collection, whether there was an accurate register, and how much time would be needed to bring it to order.

Pastor Becker in Christiansfeld wrote back and responded diligently to each question: Indeed, they had manuscripts in Christiansfeld—diaries, memoirs, letters, and meeting records. They were kept in the church, in the small hall under the Brothers' gallery, and yes, there would enough space to store them, but they were not in any particular order. Becker himself had roughly sorted the manuscripts recently; that had been impossible to do earlier because of the previous very narrow quarters of the archives. Finally, in respect to the last question, he said that if it was a question of only the manuscripts, and if one person was working on it from morning till night, it could be done in a couple of months.

This correspondence was part of the Unity Board's project, as indicated above, to organize and catalog the local community archives according to the same registry as the Herrnhut local congregational archive (as distinct from the central archive in Herrnhut). This is presumably why the German terms are retained, to secure conformity. While the overall manager of the project was Alexander Glitsch, the archivist in the central archive in Herrnhut (from 1875 to 1905), the reorganization of the Christiansfeld archive was carried out by Glitsch's son, Hermann. Hermann Glitsch arrived in Christiansfeld in mid-June of 1903 and completed his task in autumn of that year with the *Katalog des Gemeinarchivs*. In the correspondence arranging his visit and stay he estimated that he would be in Christiansfeld for seven weeks, spending two days on the Widows' material, four days on the Sisters' House material, up to two weeks on the Brothers' House material, and the remainder on the institutional archive (*Anstaltsarchiv*), the pastoral archive (*Predigerarchiv*), and the supervisor's archive (*Vorsteherarchiv*). Today, all local congregational archives are (ideally) arranged according to this structure.

Archive and Community

Christiansfeld's archival collection is divided into five unequally sized parts, as indicated in the correspondence:

> *Predigerarchiv* (PA),
> *Vorsteherarchiv* (VA),
> *Brüderchorarchiv* (BA),
> *Schwesternchorarchiv* (SA),
> and *Anstalts Archiv* (AA).

Each of these collections has several subgroups. The *Predigerarchiv*, or pastoral archive, is the archive for matters pertaining to the "inner" workings of the community. Its first subgroup, "General" (*Allgemeines*), illustrates the relationship of Christiansfeld to the wider Moravian unity, in that it contains minutes from the general synods held after Zinzendorf's death in 1760, beginning with the synod in Marienborn in 1764,[7] and the meeting minutes from the provincial synods beginning in 1856.[8] Generally, the mix of documents in this group shows the local and global nature of the Moravian community in Christiansfeld, in that a subgroup such as "Mission" (P.A.I.R.5) is divided into General/*Allgemeines* (A) and Local/*Örtliches*, as is the subgroup on community statutes (P.A.I.R.8). Turning to the local aspect of the pastoral archive, these contain the minutes of the various leadership conferences in Christiansfeld, the diaries of the congregation, and the *Lebensläufe* (memoirs). We also find the *Prediger*'s correspondence from 1772 to 1946 and instructions for the various pastoral leadership positions in the community.[9] Here we find the documents relating to the Married choir and the Widows' and Widowers' choirs. While the Single Brothers and the Single Sisters have their own archival collections, the archive of the Widows' House, with its diaries, catalogs, house rules, speeches, correspondence, and so on, is contained in the pastoral archive. Furthermore, the pastoral archive contains all the documents pertaining to the foundation and growth of the community in Christiansfeld and some papers from the Scandinavian societies (Copenhagen, Bergen, Göteborg, Trondheim). The final collection in the pastoral archive is a rather substantial collection called *Versammlungs-Akten*, or meeting records, where we find, among many other items, the hymns that are sung at various Lovefeasts. Two bundles relate to two special occasions, namely 13 August and 13 November. These two dates are significant in the global Moravian community in that 13 August (1727) marks the birth of the community during communion in the church in Berthelsdorf and Christiansfeld's "birthday,"[10] and 13 November (1741) celebrates the appointment of "the Savior" to the office of Chief Elder in the community.[11] As we see from their presence in the Christiansfeld archive, these days are celebrated in the global Moravian community. Another bundle includes the hymns sung at the various choir days, which was an annual celebratory day for each choir,[12] with the major "Day of all Choirs" celebrated on 25 March. These are also good examples of the global dimension in the local community.

The *Vorsteherarchiv* is the collection of all matters economic in Christiansfeld. The *Vorsteher* was the manager of the assets of the individual community, and his archival collection is thus a gathering of every item (e.g., correspondence, taxes, bequests, ledgers, account books) that pertains to collective finances, property in land and buildings, insurance, and communal industry.

As mentioned, this local archive in Christiansfeld matches the organization of all other local Moravian archives around Europe and North America. Formally, it is a global structure, but some of the content is local and relates specifically to the Moravian community in Christiansfeld. This global/local distinction is a constitutive feature of Moravian self-perception and is reflected in the archival distinctions between "general" and "specific." Another equally important distinction is that between "inner" and "outer" things. Ordering in terms of *innerliche* and *äußerliche Dinge*, while present in earlier years, became an increasingly prevalent organizational feature in post-Zinzendorf Moravian administration. The inner things are connected with community organization, congregational practice, liturgy, and mission; the outer things relate to business and enterprise. We see this distinction in the division between the *Predigerarchiv*, which deals with inner things, and the *Vorsteherarchiv*, which deals with outer things.

The *Brüderhausarchiv* is the archive from the Single Brothers' House. All but one of the European and North American settlements had separate dwellings, for example, choir houses for the Single Brothers and Single Sisters, and many had a separate house for the Widows.[13] This is also the case in Christiansfeld. The houses were distinct economic units and had their own industries. The archive of the Single Brothers' House is divided into the archive of the *Pfleger*, the person in charge of the (inner) pastoral care of the choir, and the *Vorsteher*, the person in charge of the (outer) assets of the choir. The *Brüderpfleger* archive contains diaries of the choir, meeting minutes, lists of the members (Single Brothers, Youths, and Boys), principles and rules, correspondence, and so forth. The *Brüdervorsteher* archive contains documents relating to military issues, taxes, bequests, bonds, ledgers and accounts, landed property, industry, and contracts. To give an idea of the scope of industry in the charge of the Brothers' House, there was baking, turning, metalworking, shoemaking, clothes-making, soap-making, starch boiling, coopering, weaving, carpentering, stocking weaving, tanning, oven-making, butchering, spinning, and dyeing. There are records for all these industries in the archive of the Brothers' House.[14]

The archive of the Sisters' House is not quite as detailed as that of the Brothers' House but follows the same structure. As noted in Glitsch's letter, he estimated four days to organize the Christiansfeld Sisters' House archive and one and a half to two weeks for the Brothers' House archive. One of the reasons for this is that the Sisters' archive does not have an independent subgroup on business and industrial activities, in correspondence with the Herrnhut blueprint. These activities must be found by digging a little bit deeper into the *Vorsteherarchiv* of the Single Sisters. Here we see that the account books from Christiansfeld do have separate sections for the main industries in the Sisters' House, namely embroidering, weaving, ribbon making, laundering, tambour-working, and spinning. Added to that, some members' catalogs from the Sisters' House actually contain catalogues of women's labor. One list mentions tailors, laundresses, spinners, seamstresses, maids, ribbon-weavers, and cooks, among others. In the Sisters' House, the main industries were tailoring, lace-making, knitting, embroidery, and spinning. Then there are the service tasks such as cooking and working as maids (milkmaids, housemaids, nursemaids, etc.). Finally, there are the various choir professions, such as nurse, overseer, and caretaker. From the wages earned, the women paid room and board to the Sisters' House.

The *Anstaltsarchiv* contains the archival matters pertaining to the two boarding schools in town, one of which was for the boys and one for the girls.[15] The materials mainly date from the mid-nineteenth century to the first two decades of the twentieth century. There are some documents from the eighteenth century, such as some correspondence from individuals to the house father, conference minutes, account books, inventory, and building matters, but the main bulk is from the nineteenth century.[16]

The organization of the archival materials reflects the organization of the Moravian community as it had been honed over more than a century. The distinction between inner and outer things and their management, the choir structure and its gender segregation, the labor system, and the institutions for children were all aspects of Moravian life and had been since the 1740s—with the exception of the children's institutions which began in 1723.[17]

Inner and Outer Things

The distinction between inner and outer things is not set out in any document or explained explicitly. It is assumed or ingrained and has not been the object of research as such.[18] From my own archival work, I offer a couple of examples that demonstrate that the inner/outer distinction is made both in reference to a person and within a community.

One of ways in which the Brothers and Sisters were subjectified was through choir speeches, which were speeches given to the individual choirs by the leader of the choir or of the congregation. A choir speech would typically be given at individual choir gatherings, which often took place in connection with a worship service. The nature of the speeches may be reprimanding, encouraging, or an exposition of scripture, for example.[19] Zinzendorf gave around 430 choir speeches in Herrnhut between 1744 and 1760, with which I have worked extensively. In these speeches, especially the ones to the Single Sisters and the Single Brothers, Zinzendorf emphasizes the difference between the outer and inner nature of a Sister's and a Brother's life. The outer Single Sister-ness is circumstantial and is connected to her duties within the congregation, while the inner—sometimes expressed as "maiden hearts," or "choir-mind"—is essential and eternal. In the speeches to the Single Brothers this is expounded a bit more, with the emphasis that the ideal inner human is totally saturated by the Savior. In external matters, the Brothers are subject to the will of the Savior and are expected to demonstrate unconditional obedience. However, once the inner connection is in place, this is not an issue, because the outer will follow naturally. Once one is a true and whole Brother, which means to be as similar as possible to the Savior, one acts just as the Savior did when he was on earth. When such a connection has been established, then it is no matter to let the Lamb have his way with the choir and the members of the choir, be it death, missionary, marriage, or a profession in Herrnhut or, say, in Niesky. An interesting example is Gottlieb Oertel (1714–1767), a clothmaker from Steinkunzerdorf (Silesia) who joined the Moravian community in 1741. During his twenty-six years of membership, he established three factories for the Moravian Brethren, but he stated that he always wanted to do something more meaningful or "inner" (*innerlich*), instead of the external business (*äußerliche Dinge*) to which his skills were being devoted. It was a dissatisfaction that followed him until his death. Such self-determination would have been undesirable in the community.[20] A Brother must follow the path the Savior has set out for him, be it marriage or evangelization, spinning or managing the choir. All of these services are in service of the Savior. Commercial undertaking, evangelization, and marriage are all cogs in the machine of the divine plan, and the Savior may have this or that plan for this or that person. It is just as important to be married in Neuwied as it is to be building an oil mill in Bethlehem or sent out as a missionary to Paramaribo. The significant thing is the inner relation to the Savior.[21] This is a good example of the Christocentric anthropology so characteristic of eighteenth-century Moravian theology, as mentioned in the introduction.

At a community level, the distinction seemed to gather strength in the reorganization of the Moravian Brethren after Zinzendorf's death. As mentioned earlier, these two aspects should always be seen as complementary, the outer enterprise always in service of the inner. In Bethlehem, Pennsylvania, for example, the General Economy, to which two-thirds of the congregation contributed, provided structural and financial support to the missions to the Native Americans, but this was to be separated into a European-style organization with outer and inner spheres after 1760.[22] Oldendorp's history of the Moravian mission to the West Indies has an appendix on the mission's outer and inner conditions.[23] Several archival documents are named as such, for example, the collection of reports on the "inner and outer course of the community in Neuwied" between 1750 and 1759, which was organized in the decades after Zinzendorf's death. The documents themselves, from that period, do not operate with the distinction, but the archivist, Erich von Ranzau, who was in charge from 1769 to 1796 (with a four-year hiatus from 1775 to 1779) gave this title to the collection.[24] Finally, as the memoir of Gottlieb Oertel indicated, the establishment of factories in the German states was regarded as an external thing in contrast to inner service. This distinction moved from the most general level down to each choir, as we saw in the archival distinctions between *Pfleger* and *Vorsteher*.

Choirs

Choirs are groups within the congregation segregated according to sex and marital status and, for the children, in terms of development. In Christiansfeld there were, as mentioned, three choir houses but (at least) five choirs. In Herrnhut, there were eight choirs (Children, Boys, Girls, Single Brothers, Single Sisters, Married Couples, Widows, and Widowers), with corresponding houses. These choirs formed the central units of the communities and functioned as units of labor, worship, and subjectification—the process by which the members became Brothers and Sisters of the Moravian community. Not only the choir houses but also the *Saal*, with its separate entrances, and the God's Acre with its segregated graves (in many settlements) testify to the gendering of members of the Moravian community—as in Christiansfeld.

The choir structure was not part of the Moravian organization from the beginning. It grew out of, and further developed and adapted, the earlier voluntary *Banden*, which were smaller groups that formed according to gender and marital status to talk through matters of faith.[25] They served to mediate various experiences and backgrounds, melding these into a community. The founding members of Herrnhut were German-speaking peasants and artisans from Moravia, but the community grew and grew with an influx of members from the surrounding areas of the Oberlausitz, the German states, Bohemia, Denmark-Norway, and so on. These members were peasants, artisans, and nobility, and it took the leadership in Herrnhut many, many years to work out a way of managing these very different groups and integrate their ways of life, customs, and expectations into a coherent whole. During its first twenty years, the community in Herrnhut went through a number of purges, or, as they were called, "siftings" (from Luke 22:31 where Satan has demanded permission to sift the disciples like wheat), where less desirable or problematic members where either asked to leave or sent elsewhere, to the missions (e.g., Greenland) or to other settlements (e.g., Herrnhaag or Niesky) or other congregations (e.g., Rixdorf).[26] The system of choirs, as an overarching structure, was conceived in the late 1730s and consolidated in the early 1740s as the most successful way of managing this social challenge. Once it was in place, the system went full steam ahead. Thus, the years of experimentation had well and truly passed by the 1770s, when Christiansfeld was founded; the parameters were in place and the leadership now knew what worked and, more importantly, what did not.

The choirs were also followed by an innovative approach to labor in the Moravian communities. In these so-called choir houses, the members had to "earn their own bread," that is, each house was regarded as a discrete economic unit that had to support itself. In 1745 in Herrnhut, many of the apprentices were moved into rooms in the Single Brothers' House, where each craft was given a separate room. This replaced the more traditional workshop structure in the houses of the masters. In the Single Sisters' House, many rooms functioned as spinning rooms, where up to fifteen women and children per room were working with spinning and needlework. This means that the innovation was not really one of labor organization or technical skill (at this stage) but only an increase in the *scale* of crafts and trades that were already in practice. Another innovation was the establishment of the communities and the movement of labor. In the case of the founding of Christiansfeld, for example, before any agreement was settled, careful investigations of the area were made, to estimate the impact that the Moravians would be able to make and whether it would be a worthwhile, profitable venture.[27] Add to this the generous subsidies, tax exemptions, and freedom of trade granted by the Crown, and the Moravian leadership were convinced that northern Schleswig was a good place to settle. In time, the rest of the world caught up with and overtook the Moravian enterprises. As Moravian bishop Karl Müller notes, "In the second half of the nineteenth century, the Brothers' Houses were brought down by the changes in modern economic life."[28]

Inner and Outer Cultural Heritage

As this organization of the archival material has demonstrated, the individual Moravian congregations such as Christiansfeld were

distinct manifestations of general Moravian institutions and sociothe-
ological organization. The distinctiveness of the individual congregations was determined by specific political, cultural, and economic
contexts. Christiansfeld, established in the duchy of Schleswig, experienced great prosperity until the mid-nineteenth century and the wars
between Denmark and Germany, which culminated in the Danish loss of
Schleswig-Holstein in 1864. We now turn to something slightly different,
namely how these inner and outer things are present in the UNESCO
inscription text and in the World Heritage application document. We thus
move from the eighteenth and nineteenth centuries into the twenty-first
century, after it has been decided that these things are now cultural
heritage.

From the point of view of a scholar who has worked extensively with
the Moravians in the eighteenth century, the following description of
Christiansfeld and Moravian town planning is curiously one-dimensional:

> The Moravian town plans and architecture were developed in parallel with
> the development of the congregational structure and the evolution of the
> denomination's understanding of the good Christian life and how society
> ought to be designed. The Moravian societal structure, town plans, and
> architecture had been 50 years in the making by the time Christiansfeld was
> planned. Christiansfeld is a result of the town planning, architectural, and
> cultural experiences that the Moravian Church had had through the establish-
> ment of earlier settlements. Christiansfeld thus reflects the Moravian Church's
> needs and values. This is quite concretely expressed through the town's place-
> ment in an open agricultural landscape, the town plan's compass orientation,
> the central square with tangential streets, the location of God's Acre in the
> landscape, the placement of the Hall alongside Kirkepladsen, the division of
> the town into brothers' and sisters' sides, and the open circle of construction
> consisting of family houses. Christiansfeld contains all of the functions that are
> so characteristic of the Moravian Church's colonies.[29]

This quote is taken from the UNESCO application, which was submit-
ted in 2014. However, planning a settlement for the Moravians in the
eighteenth century was much more than merely producing the blue-
prints of the town and its streets. By the time the Moravian leadership
had reached the stage of "town planning," it had already surveyed the
area, assessed the capacities of the surrounding towns and their industries, planned which industries to establish and whom to put in charge,
negotiated concessions from the government in terms of taxes and trade
permissions, and decided on which members to send where. In short, to
return to the terminology of the archives, all the outer things had already
been organized and planned by the time they got to the architecture. This
detailed economic nous, the extensive skills, and the mobile membership

made the Moravian Brethren an entrepreneurial powerhouse, and it seems to me curiously reductive to refer to this as architecture, town planning, and craftmanship. And yet, how else is it possible to convey such a monumental history in what essentially are mere traces? Furthermore, is this only the case in the application document, or is this a broader historical problem, a compression of time?[30] The application document does mention the industrial history of Christiansfeld, but how are we to fathom the impact of Christiansfeld in its heyday? Our current categories both analytical and descriptive cannot convey such a history in full and can only do so by designations such as "world heritage," by which tangible monuments and buildings are seen as embodying a value that is nearly impossible to articulate.

Another example is from the section "Justification for Inscription," in which the Moravian Church's archives in Christiansfeld and Herrnhut are mentioned as *documentation* of the authenticity necessary to justify the inscription.[31] Specifically mentioned are:

> the royal concession for the establishment of Christiansfeld, preliminary designs, and later maps and views of the town. These are complemented by personal accounts of the lives of Moravian Church members as well as numerous original items that are preserved in the town including the interiors, musical instruments, etc., which provide testimony as to the craftmanship and skill involved in religious and secular life in Christiansfeld.[32]

The focus here is on the individual members and on the town itself. Again, in light of the earlier section's analysis of the archives and the institutional framework to which they refer, we may note that the specific Moravian mediating institutions, such as choirs and schools, are not mentioned. This is presumably because the choir system is no longer part of Moravian life, and the boarding schools are closed, evident in the use to which the buildings are put today. The former Brothers' House is now rental accommodation, the Sisters' House the administrative center for both the Moravian Church and the Museum of Kolding and their respective exhibitions. It also houses the archives, as well as the local archive, which is unconnected with the Moravian archive. The Widows' House is undergoing renovation but is used for residential purposes and has housed the museum with artifacts collected from the missions. The boarding schools, closed in 1890 (girls) and 1891 (boys), have been sold and are currently under redevelopment.

The disappearance of these mediating institutions from the community raises an important question: Where did they go? Or, more precisely, what happened to their functions? The schools were eventually absorbed into the Danish school system. Christiansfeld School is today a public school, raising the question as to whether the heritage, or Moravian effects, are to be found in Christiansfeld itself or in Danish society at large. As Tine Damsholt demonstrates in chapter 3 of this volume, the emerging Danish bourgeoisie sent their children to Christiansfeld for schooling. The choirs were, as we have seen, sites of communal and individual subjectification, innovative production, and pre-industrial labor organization during the eighteenth and the first half of the nineteenth century. While these were new and groundbreaking features in the small rural societies of eighteenth-century Schleswig, industrialization and the subsequent implementation of civil society, individual rights, and wage labor made this particular structure redundant. In all cases of Moravian settlements, the choirs and their functions also were absorbed into or overtaken by the various industrialized societies where the Moravians were settled.[33]

So, what is left? From the outside, the bus leaves the freeway and takes us into town. We are taken on a walk, shown the church, the Sisters' House, the God's Acre, and several of the older houses, and then taken to the hotel for lunch, and then off again. Is this what we are left with? As Rasmus Rask Poulsen points out in chapter 6, these tours raise questions of representation for the residents of Christiansfeld, who take issue with some of the more fanciful stories told about themselves to outsiders.

There is of course much more to Christiansfeld than a UNESCO stamp, town plans, pretty houses, craftmanship, and even the church and its congregation. The German word *"Gemeinde"* contained in the German name for the Moravians, *Brüdergemeine*, means both congregation and community.[34] And indeed, the communal aspect has always been a strong feature of the Moravians, and an attractive one at that. The congregation is not one of individual believers; it is a community with a long-shared history. What tourists see are outer fragments of an inaccessible entity, which contains both the inner and outer history of the Moravian community in Christiansfeld. Perhaps this is the result of zoning, a well-known practice in the administration of natural World Heritage, where the most ecologically sensitive areas are protected from access.[35] Or is it a result of our current historical illiteracy, where we remember particular things in certain fragmented ways and forget about others, more or less disabled to attain or strive toward a more comprehensive historical consciousness?[36]

Conclusion

In this chapter, I have examined the close relationship between archival categories and community organization in Christiansfeld. Through this, I looked at how the community structure in Christiansfeld mirrored that of Herrnhut, and what understanding of community is present therein. Finally, I questioned the ability of the UNESCO world heritagization process to comprehend or articulate these aspects of Moravian history, in that the fullness of this history is flattened in the presence of heritage. But this problem is not limited to Christiansfeld and Moravian history; it is an issue of the consciousness of the present and our relationship to the past.

Christina Petterson is a visiting research fellow at the Australian National University and at the Department of Church History, University of Copenhagen. Her background is in theology (M.Th.) and cultural studies (PhD) and her research interests concern the relationship between Christianity and social history in the eighteenth century both in the colonies and Europe. She is on the editorial board of the *Journal of Moravian History* and recently published *The Moravian Brethren in a Time of Transition: A Socio-Economic Analysis of a Religious Community in Eighteenth-Century Saxony* (2021).

Notes

1. For a good presentation of the history, organization, and contents of the Unity Archive in Herrnhut, see Kröger, Mai, and Nippe, *Das Unitätsarchiv*; Peucker, "Pietism and the Archives."
2. Mettele, *Weltbürgertum oder Gottesreich*.
3. The General Synod is the highest decision-making body of the Moravian Church, where all the provinces are represented. In the nineteenth century it met every ten years, and currently every seven years.
4. The matter was discussed at the German provincial synod in 1878 and suggested to the General Synod the following year. The request as formulated by the provincial synod may be found in the Unity Archive in Herrnhut (UA) UA.R.2.B.70 A (Verlaß der Provinzial-Synode der deutschen Unitäts-Provinz gehalten in Herrnhut vom 27. Mai bis 6. Juli 1878), p. 84, and the discussions thereto in UA.R.2.B.70.B, (Druckschriften der Provinzialsynode 1878) E: 109–111.
5. Kröger, Mai, and Nippe, *Das Unitätsarchiv*, 27.
6. "Anweisungen und Bemerkungen zum Zweck der Abfassung von Kataloge für die Archive der Brüdergemeinen, Diaspora- und Missionsposten."
7. The synod in Marienborn in 1764 was the first constitutional assembly of the Moravian Church and the one where the archive was formally established.
8. The synod in 1857 decentralized the global Moravian community by establishing provinces, each with its own synod.
9. For example, choir helpers. See the introduction in this volume.

10. While the town of Herrnhut was founded on 17 June 1722, the community as a whole was constituted on 13 August 1727, when divisions were healed and factions overcome. See Sommer, introduction to *Serving Two Masters*, 1–9. Furthermore, the concession to found Christiansfeld was signed on 13 August 1772.

11. The office of the chief elder was in 1741 held by Leonhard Dober, one of the first missionaries to the West Indies and a leading figure in the Moravian community. When Dober resigned from office, the lot was cast to appoint a new leader, and the lot fell on "the Heiland," which for the Moravian community was an indication that the Savior himself wanted to take leadership of the Moravian Church. Meyer, *Zinzendorf*, 46.

12. The Married choir had its annual celebration on 7 September, the Widows and Widowers on 31 August, Single Brothers on 2 September, Single Sisters on 4 May, and so forth. Peucker, *Herrnhuter Wörterbuch*, 19.

13. The published application for the World Heritage nomination considers twenty-seven towns built by the Moravians between 1722 and 1807 in Europe and North America. Fifteen settlements had a minimum of three choir houses (Sisters' House, Brothers' House, and Widows' House), nine settlements had two choir houses (Sisters' House and Brothers' House), two had only one house, and one had none. See the table in Berg, Marcussen, and Stocklund, *Christiansfeld*; see p. 315 for the criteria and p. 325 for the statistical list.

14. Thomas Bloch Ravn has an excellent chapter on the industries of Christiansfeld; see Ravn, "Håndværk og Fabriksvirksomhed."

15. See also chapter 3 in this collection.

16. In 1710, Zinzendorf was sent to Halle to attend the Paedagogium Regium, one of several schools in Francke's Halle. Apart from the Paedagogium Regium, the school for the sons of the nobility, Francke's Halle also included an orphanage, the *Waisenshaus*, where poor children were schooled, as well as a *Lateinschule* for the boys of the bourgeoisie and a girls' school. In his pedagogical ideology, August Hermann Francke (1663–1727) was strongly inspired by Johann Amos Comenius, who died in 1670 but whose works were sent to Halle by his grandson, Daniel Ernst Jablonski, where they were published. Meyer, "Von Herrnhut in die Neue Welt," 194. The first schools in Herrnhut were built in the image of Halle. With the increase of the Moravian settlement, the influence of Comenius was brought to Zinzendorf's attention, and he began to undertake studies of Comenius's works, especially from 1727, when he had to step in and bring order to the out-of-control situation in Herrnhut. Modrow, "Daniel Ernst Jablonski," 334. Through these influences, and Zinzendorf's personal relationship with Jablonski, the institutions in Herrnhut were founded and developed and would later partially overlap with the choir system but, in the last quarter of the eighteenth century, develop into boys' and girls' schools proper. Bechler, *Ortsgeschichte*, 196. Again, Christiansfeld was founded after all of these initial experimental phases were over, and the boarding schools for boys and girls were ready for opening in 1774, complete with plan as well as budget. Both schools were originally contained in already existing buildings: the boys' school in the Brothers' House until 1775 and the girls' school in the first congregational building until 1784. Ravn, "Kostskolerne," 515–17. See chapter 3.

17. Bechler, *Ortsgeschichte*, 190–98.

18. This emergence of a taxonomical approach in sorting out one's practices and possessions is a central feature of the eighteenth century as analyzed by, among others, Foucault, *Order of Things*.

19. These speeches to the choirs as collectives should not be confused with the individual speakings between choir helper and individual member, as Tine Damsholt discusses in chapter 3.

20. UA R.22.109.9. Memoir of Gottlieb Oertel. An amended and printed version may be found in *Nachrichten*, 771–80.

21. This argument is taken from and unfolded further in Petterson, *Moravian Brethren*, 129–233.
22. Erbe, *Bethlehem, Pa.*; see also Engel, "Evolution." For a very good analysis of the end of the communal organization of Bethlehem known as the General Economy and the particular missionary system it supported see Engel, *Religion and Profit*. In his notebook outlining the fundamentals of the transition, Johannes Arbo, leader of the Single Brother's choir, had a section titled "von der äußerlichen Oeconomie überhaupt" that outlined the new economic and industrial organization of the community. Moravian Archives, Bethlehem BethSB.7, section B. Memorandum book, kept by Johann Arbo, warden of the Single Brothers, relating to the dissolution of the General Economy, especially in regard to the choir of the Single Brothers 1761–1765.
23. Oldendorp, *Historie der Caribischen Inseln*, 1913–2059.
24. Discernible by his handwriting. Thank you to Olaf Nippe for pointing this out for me.
25. The best study of this early period and the role of the *Banden* and their role in early Herrnhut piety is Wollstadt, *Geordnetes Dienen*.
26. There was a very large purge in Herrnhut in 1744 and 1745, in which three Single Sisters were beaten and sent into servitude in the neighboring village of Berthelsdorf, five families were expelled, and several other couples and twenty single members were advised to leave.
27. Fischer, "Wirtschaftliche Prosperität." See also Ravn, "Håndværk Og Fabriksvirksomhed."
28. Müller, *200 Jahre Brüdermission*, 11, unnumbered footnote.
29. Berg, Marcussen, and Stocklund, *Christiansfeld*, 155.
30. For a good analysis of the problem of history and heritage, see Salemink, "History and Heritage."
31. Berg, Marcussen, and Stocklund, *Christiansfeld*, sec. 3.
32. Berg, Marcussen, and Stocklund, 166.
33. On the industrial function, see Ravn, "Håndværk og Fabriksvirksomhed," 11; Müller, *200 Jahre Brüdermission*. On the family, see Petterson, "'Plague.'"
34. *Gemeinde* is the modern spelling, while the Moravians use the older spelling *Gemeine*.
35. UNESCO, ICCROM, ICOMOS, and IUCN, *Managing Natural World Heritage*, 47.
36. Again, this is in reference to Salemink's article that engages this question in relation to cultural heritage in Vietnam. Salemink, "History and Heritage."

Bibliography

Bechler, Theodor. *Ortsgeschichte von Herrnhut mit besonderer Berücksichtigung der älteren Zeit* [Settlement history of Herrnhut with special focus on older times]. Herrnhut: Verlag der Missionsbuchhandlung, 1922.

Berg, Annemette Løkke Borg, Lene Lindberg Marcussen, and Karen Stocklund, eds. *Christiansfeld: A Moravian Settlement* (Danish World Heritage Nomination). Kolding: Kolding Kommune, 2014.

Engel, Katherine Carté. "The Evolution of the Bethlehem Pilgergemeine." In *Pietism in Germany and North America, 1680–1820*, edited by Hartmut Lehmann and James Van Horn Melton, 163–81. London: Routledge, 2009.

Engel, Katherine Carté. *Religion and Profit: Moravians in Early America*. Philadelphia: University of Pennsylvania Press, 2009.

Erbe, Hellmuth. *Bethlehem, Pa. Eine Kommunistische herrnhuter Kolonie des 18 Jahrhunderts* [Bethlehem, Pennsylvania: A communist Moravian settlement of the eighteenth century]. Stuttgart: Ausland und Heimat Verlags-Aktiengesellschaft, 1929.

Fischer, Ole. "Wirtschaftliche Prosperität und religiöse Erweckung. Das Handwerk in der Herrnhutersiedlung Christiansfeld" [Industrious prosperity and religious awakening: Tradesmanship in the Moravian settlement of Christiansfeld]. In *Aus der Mitte des Landes. Klaus-Joachim Lorenzen-Schmidt zum 65. Geburtstag* [From the middle of the land: In honor of Klaus-Joachim Lorenzen-Schmidt's sixty-fifth birthday], edited by Detlev Kraack and Martin Rheinheimer, 175–94. Neumünster/Hamburg: Wachholtz Verlag, 2013.

Foucault, Michel. *The Order of Things: An Archaeology of the Human Sciences*. New York: Vintage Books, 1973.

Kröger, Rüdiger, Claudia Mai, and Olaf Nippe, eds. *Das Unitätsarchiv. Aus der Gesichte von Archiv, Bibliothek und Beständen* [The Unity Archives: From the history of the archive, the library and the collections]. Herrnhut: Comenius Buchhandlung, 2014.

Mettele, Gisela. *Weltbürgertum oder Gottesreich: Die herrnhuter Brüdergemeine als globale Gemeinschaft 1727–1857* [Citizenship of the world or kingdom of God: The Moravian Brethren as global community, 1727–1857]. Bürgertum Neue Folge series. Göttingen: Vandenhoeck and Ruprecht, 2009.

Meyer, Dietrich. *Zinzendorf und die herrnhuter Brüdergmeine* [Zinzendorf and the Moravian Brethren]. Göttingen: Vandenhoeck and Ruprecht, 2009.

Meyer, Dietrich. "Von Herrnhut in die neue Welt. Jablonski als Begleiter Zinzendorfs und der Mährischen Exulanten" [From Herrnhut into the New World: Jablonski as companion of Zinzendorf and the Moravian emigrants]. In *Brückenschläge. Daniel Ernst Jablonski im Europa der Frühaufklärung* [Building bridges: Daniel Ernst Jablonski in early Enlightenment Europe], edited by Joachim Bahlcke, Bogusław Dybaś, and Hartmut Rudolph, 189–201. Dößel: Verlag Janos Stekovics, 2010.

Modrow, Irina. "Daniel Ernst Jablonski, Nikolaus Ludwig von Zinzendorf und die herrnhuter Brüdergemeine" [Daniel Ernst Jablonski, Nikolaus Ludwig von Zinzendorf, and the Moravian Brethren]. In *Daniel Ernst Jablonski: Religion, Wissenschaft und Politik um 1700* [Daniel Ernst Jablonski: Religion, science, and politics around 1700], edited by Joachim Bahlcke and Werner Korthaase, 331–43. Wiesbaden: Harrassowitz, 2008.

Müller, Karl. *200 Jahre Brüdermission I: Das erste Missionsjahrhundert.* [Two hundred years of Moravian mission I: The first century of mission]. Herrnhut, 1931.

Nachrichten aus der Brüder-Gemeine [News from the Moravian Brethren]. Gnadau: C. E. Genft, 1825.

Oldendorp, C. G. A. *Historie der caribischen Inseln Sanct Thomas, Sanct Crux und Sanct Jan: Insbesondere der dasigen Neger und der Mission der Evangelischen Brüder unter denselben* [History of Caribbean Islands St. Thomas, St. Croix, and St. John: In particular the Negros there and the Mission of the Evangelical Brethren among them]. 2 vols. Berlin: Verlag für Wissenschaft und Bildung, 2000.

Petterson, Christina. *The Moravian Brethren in a Time of Transition: A Socio-Economic Analysis of a Religious Community in Eighteenth-Century Saxony*. Historical Materialism Book Series 231. Leiden: Brill, 2021.

Petterson, Christina. "'A Plague of the State and the Church': A Local Response to the Moravian Enterprise." *Journal of Moravian History* 16, no. 1 (2016): 45–60.

Peucker, Paul. *Herrnhuter Wörterbuch. Kleines Lexikon von brüderischen Begriffen* [Moravian dictionary: A small lexicon of Moravian terms]. Herrnhut: Herrnhut Unitätsarchiv, 2000.

Peucker, Paul. "Pietism and the Archives." In *The Brill Companion to German Pietism*, edited by Douglas H. Schantz, 393–429. Leiden: Brill, 2015.

Ravn, Thomas Bloch. "Håndværk og Fabriksvirksomhed" [Tradesmanship and industry]. In *Herrnhuter-samfundet i Christiansfeld I* [The Moravian community of Christiansfeld], edited by Anders Pontoppidan Thyssen, 143–273. Aabenraa: Historisk Samfund for Sønderjylland, 1984.

Ravn, Thomas Bloch. "Kostskolerne 1774–1832" [The boarding schools, 1774–1882]. In *Herrnhuter-samfundet i Christiansfeld I* [The Moravian community of Christiansfeld], edited by Anders Pontoppidan Thyssen, 513–40. Aabenraa: Historisk Samfund for Sønderjylland, 1984.

Salemink, Oscar. "History and Heritage, Past and Present: Thinking with Phan Huy Lê's Oeuvre." In *Nhân Cách Sử Học* [A historical personality: A book to celebrate Prof. Phan Huy Lê's eightieth birthday], edited by Trần Văn Thọ, Nguyễn Quang Ngọc, and Philippe Papin, 547–68. Hanoi: NXB Chính trị Quốc gia, 2014.

Sommer, Elisabeth W. *Serving Two Masters: Moravian Brethren in Germany and North Carolina, 1727–1801*. Lexington: University Press of Kentucky, 2000.

UNESCO, ICCROM, ICOMOS, and IUCN. *Managing Natural World Heritage*. World Heritage Resource Manual series. Paris: UNESCO, 2012.

Wollstadt, Hanns-Joachim. *Geordnetes Dienen in der Christlichen Gemeinde* [Ordered service in the Christian congregation]. Göttingen: Vandenhoeck and Ruprecht, 1966.

Chapter 11

Digital Humanities and Cultural Heritage
Updating the Eighteenth Century

Katherine M. Faull

Introduction

In her landmark monograph, *The Uses of Heritage*, Laurajane Smith defines heritage not as a thing or a set of things but as a social and cultural process. "Heritage" she argues, "is a multilayered performance—be this a performance of visiting, managing, interpretation or conservation—that embodies acts of remembrance and commemoration while negotiating and constructing a sense of place, belonging and understanding in the present."[1] Residing therefore in the act of reception, the process of heritage depends not on the tangibility of its objects but rather on the discourse that surrounds it, a discourse or sets of discourses that allows interpretations of the past to be instrumentalized in the construction of a national or localized identity.

This concept of heritage as an intangible process runs, for the most part, perhaps counter to our experience of it. Cultural institutions, such as museums, art galleries, and archives, seem to adhere to a notion stemming from the nineteenth century: that the construction of heritage resides in the building, artwork, manuscript, statue, and even landscape that is being passively observed and received by the visitor. Heritage societies and national trusts recognize, through purchase or declarative statements, what are considered to be significant buildings and tracts of land to be preserved, conserved, and visited because they exemplify or literally embody narratives of the past that serve the present. Smith uses the term "authorised heritage discourse" (AHD) to describe the process of validation of dominant discourses of history, nation, and identity, where the practice of this discourse is limited to such authoritative bodies of cultural heritage as trusts, historical societies, and museums. Smith's intervention into this dominant AHD consists of a call to subvert this discourse through the introduction of the memories and narratives of the subaltern, for example, Aboriginal peoples in Australia or the residents of a working-class neighborhood in Northern England.

Published in 2006, Smith's important intervention predates the advent of Web 2.0, the development of the interactive World Wide Web that we know today, in which the previously passive viewer can become an (inter)active author, in what was perceived at the outset to be the ultimate democratization of (social) media. The ubiquitous ability to post photos, comments, and blogs and then share them widely may have subsequently manifested its dangers, from the incitement to violence to the spread of misinformation, but Web 2.0 also originally had the potential to effect the kind of subversion of AHD that Smith calls for. So, what happens to the experience of cultural heritage when the place of encounter is online? How does the visitor interact with and react to digital objects of heritage? Can the digital offer a way of opening up exploration of the past in a non-hierarchical way, or does the medium of the digital "dilute" the experience of the archival or museum object to such an extent that is rendered a pale replica of the original? How does the digital experience modulate the role of cultural and collective memory in the framing of heritage discourse? And how might the very process of archival digitization contribute to the sustainability of a cultural community?

The case study that will help to address some of these questions is the international digital humanities (DH) project "Moravian Lives," which is the result of a collaboration between scholars of religion and theology, archivists, and digital humanists in the United States, Sweden, and Germany and which aims to make available for study the *Lebensläufe* (memoirs) of members of the worldwide Moravian Church from the eighteenth to the twentieth century. The theoretical underpinnings of this project are questions rooted in recent work on autobiography, the history of Pietism, gender studies, and textual scholarship.

A survey of recent publications in English and German reveals a healthy, vibrant, and multidimensional set of inquiries. Over the last twenty-five years the genre of the Moravian memoir has attracted renewed interest in many scholarly fields, fueled by the recognition that autobiography is a genre worthy of critical scrutiny and aided also by the increased accessibility of the main repository of the manuscript sources in the Unity Archives in Herrnhut, Germany. Print publication of collections of smaller corpora of memoirs has deepened specific communities' needs for historical discourses of the Moravian self, whether it be memoirs from the Sorbian minority in Upper Lusatia or the textual exploration of the people whose gravesites rest in the God's Acre in Neudietendorf.[2] Furthermore, conceptual models in social and religious history and gender and critical race theory recognize these "ego documents" as valuable primary sources for a perspective from the social classes that do not usually have a voice in the writing of history, such as women and men of the artisan classes and non-Europeans.

One constant focus of critical attention within this genre is the question of the freedom allowed each individual to express authentic and unique reflections on lived experience. Whereas some critics have argued that the very institutional edict to write a self-narration necessarily limits that act in terms of form, formulation, and individuality, others have argued that the Pietistic environment in which these self-relations were created encouraged, at least in the eighteenth century, a balance between the demands of the community and the self. As Peter Vogt has so aptly stated, the Moravian memoir constitutes "a dynamic of reciprocity between individual witness and community identity."[3] Within the theory of autobiography, such reciprocity in the narration of the self folds into itself the recognition that without a story there is no self. In the age of the digital, this self is "not only reported but performed, certainly by any of us as we tell or write stories of our lives, and perhaps to a surprising degree by the rest of us as we listen to them or read them."[4]

Spanning the divide between the private and public—or, in Jan Assmann's terms, between communicative and cultural memory[5]—autobiography allows the writing subject to examine her or his own past, to (re)shape that history, and to interrogate the reasons for action and examine personal conscience. For the reader, the genre provides an opportunity to view these processes within another human subject, to witness the relation of authentic (or inauthentic) experience and emotion.

This idea of the self being one that is created in the act of telling one's story is deeply redolent with Zinzendorf's own concept of the role of the individual life in creating and sustaining the "invisible church." From the mid-eighteenth century on, each member of the worldwide Moravian Church has been asked to write a memoir, intended to articulate and preserve each individual's path from a state of ignorance of grace to his or her rebirth in Christ. Because of the worldwide reach of the Moravian Church, Moravian archives preserve some of the earliest "ego documents" produced by eighteenth-century Africans and Native Americans. And archiving these documents has fulfilled a twofold purpose: storing and ordering them in the institutional archival memory of the church and, for those who access this archival memory, functioning as a locus of presence and interactivity in the lived memory of the church.[6]

As noted above, the relation of the lives of exemplary believers, as Vogt argues, helped to create "a tangible impression of the invisible church community."[7] The extraordinarily large number (over 60,000) of *Lebensläufe* in the worldwide archives of the Moravian Church presents both opportunities and challenges for researchers who wish to draw on this large corpus, to access the archival memory for the purposes of lived memory. Accessibility to these documents has, however, severely curtailed the ability of researchers to conduct comparative analyses between time periods, places of composition, ethnicities, or genders. With digital access to such a large corpus of ego documents (and their metadata) from around the world that spans social class, race, and gender over the last 270 years, then, scholars could ask and attempt to answer major research questions in many fields.

The question of digitization is itself fraught with ethical questions. In his comprehensive overview of the archives of Moravian materials, Paul Peucker identifies and discusses the most important repositories of the Moravian Church, namely the Moravian Archives in Bethlehem, Pennsylvania, and the Unity Archives in Herrnhut, Germany.[8] These two major archives participate to varying degrees in the digitization of their holdings. Since the acquisition of its own high-quality scanner, the Moravian Archives in Bethlehem, Pennsylvania, is able to digitize selected materials in-house, attaching thumbnail images featuring a digital "watermark" to its archival catalog. High-resolution versions of these images, without the watermark, are available for purchase by researchers. Specific collections are digitized according to ongoing significance of the source (for example, the Bethlehem Diary) and also in response to funded research projects by external parties (the Eastern Caribbean collection for the Digital Library of the Caribbean [http://www.dloc.com/] and the Labrador materials for the University of Newfoundland). In addition, specific areas of interest to the archivists are also being digitized (for example, the Travel Diaries). The Unity Archives in Herrnhut (https://www.unitaetsarchiv.findbuch.net) has digitized individual collections since 2004. These holdings are primarily of a visual nature, such as images of landscapes, buildings, plans, maps, and portraits of people. Now, also with the acquisition of a high-resolution scanner, specific collections are being digitized and a fee schedule has been developed that allows for the delivery of high-resolution images of materials upon request.

The increasing availability of Moravian sources in a digital format enables researchers, students, and interested laypeople to have much easier access to the collections, which also allows new approaches such as digital analysis. During the COVID-19 pandemic and ensuing lockdown, the existence of these digital archives meant that researchers could continue their work and archives could continue to bring in much-needed funds from digitization requests. However, there are many smaller archives across the Moravian world that have not begun the process of digitization, and indeed even resist it, expressing a fear regarding the loss of control over the contents of their archives. This fear of what might happen to materials once they are digitized and made available online mirrors in many ways the anti-Reformation fears of what would happen to religious and scientific knowledge once it was printed and put in large circulation.[9]

However, smaller portions of the memoir collection have been digitized for specific projects, such as the Sorbian collection (https://www.sorabi con.de/). Responding to the cultural and historical need to sustain Sorbian cultural heritage, readers can find a Sorbian cultural lexicon alongside Moravian Sorbian voices from the past. Awakening a broader awareness of Sorbian history and culture, the Sorabicon project serves as an excellent example of how digitization can support the sustainability of a cultural and linguistic minority and promote cultural heritage.

Looking through the Digital Lens

The development of tools in the field of digital humanities affords researchers a way to not only approach these questions but also think in new ways about how to conceptualize notions of self, narrative, and language. In many ways reenacting the archival drive of the Moravians in the eighteenth century—that is, their desire to keep a record of the activities and lives of the members of the church for the purpose of creating "a history from below"—the methods of DH permit analyses of both the metadata and the text of large amounts of information that allows the other function of memoir to be fulfilled: the function of lived memory in which the archived materials of the past become present and interact with others.[10] The Moravian Lives project realizes the potential of DH approaches to opening up the memoir corpus, namely through the construction of a searchable database of the memoir metadata of all the holdings in the main archives of the Moravian Church in Bethlehem, Pennsylvania, and Herrnhut, Germany, and also linking the metadata visualizations with the facsimile and transcribed memoirs and their extracted named entities.

How might the act of digitally reading thousands of religious memoirs be understood as participating in Smith's subversion of AHD in the Moravian Church and beyond? How does the medium of the digital affect the conceptualization of selfhood, both historically in terms of accessing "archival memory" and also phenomenologically in terms

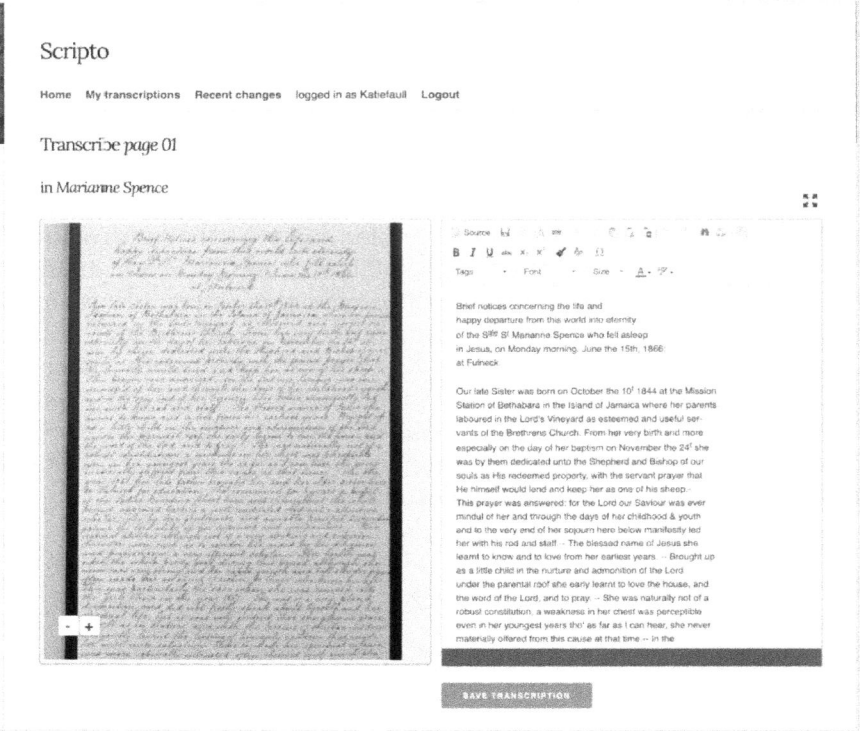

Figure 11.1. The digital interface of the transcription desk. Photograph by Katherine M. Faull.

of participating in "lived memory"[11] Recently, scientific research has revealed that St. Augustine's notion of memory as a repository archive is only partially accurate. An additional concept adheres to the "connectionist" paradigm by which the past is understood as not only stored but re-created and re-constructed every time it is invoked by the present subject in a new associative context: "Every memory … is a new memory because it is shaped (or reconsolidated) by changes that have happened to our brain since the memory last occurred to us."[12] If we apply José van Dijck's insights into the working of memory and autobiography to the reading of thousands of digitally transcribed memoirs, then how might the experience of reading a digitized material manuscript of a Moravian man or woman's life substantively change the re-presentation of that life? Will the existence of the digital archive of memoirs bring these memoirs back into a lived present? If the original Zinzendorfian tradition of writing a memoir was conceived theologically, does the digital medium transform and make immediate that particular instantiation of the word and kingdom of God? In other words, how does the digital framework affect meaning? And how does it affect the sustainability of the tradition?

In his seminal essay "The Work of Art in the Age of Its Technical Reproducibility," Walter Benjamin critiques the notion of authenticity and genius in the production of value of the work of art. The time of the publication of this essay, in 1934–35 while Benjamin was in exile, coincided with both the rise of Fascism in Germany and the rise of cinema; indeed, his essay contains many of the founding aesthetic principles of the discipline of film studies and cultural critique of mass media. However, can Benjamin's concepts of the ethics of reproducibility and the question of authenticity be helpful in an analysis of the transformations of digitization of historical artifacts? Often, the question of digitization asks what technology can bring to an appreciation of the original artifact. In the case of the Moravian Lives project, the original manuscript can be captured digitally; this digital reproduction can allow the magnification of detail; the zoom/pan function permits discovery of details that might have previously not been seen; the act of transcription (whether performed by human or artificial intelligence) can be made faster and more accurate; and texts can be semantically tagged, revealing the occurrences of patterns of people and places, times, and organizations across a corpus of texts. Digital text analysis can reveal patterns of lexical usage that might adhere or not adhere to the norm. In Benjaminian terms, the technical reproduction of the religious memoir via digitization creates an "afterlife" of the work and thus allows it to perform different roles in different time periods and places than the original. As mentioned above, such an afterlife can help to sustain threatened cultural histories and identities (including those belonging to linguistic and ethnic minorities, such as the Sorbs of Lusatia or the cultural narratives of Indigenous peoples).

Furthermore, the afterlife of the digitized cultural artifact can constitute a "translation" of the original into a completely new heritage environment and thereby subvert the earlier AHD. The resistance to such recontextualization can be seen in the recent debate about the UK National Trust's new interpretive narratives of objects within its stately homes. In this initiative, the creation of a new narrative of cultural heritage that focuses on the enslaved human cost of objects, such as a mahogany Chippendale cabinet, has evoked resentment and pushback from certain members of the public.[13]

As Smith posits in her work, and as this example from the National Trust highlights, the action of heritage is a discourse around objects, and I would argue that this holds true whether those objects are physical or digital. The *function* of that discourse, however, is part of a larger "memory culture," or *"Erinnerungskultur,"* as Assmann would term it within the

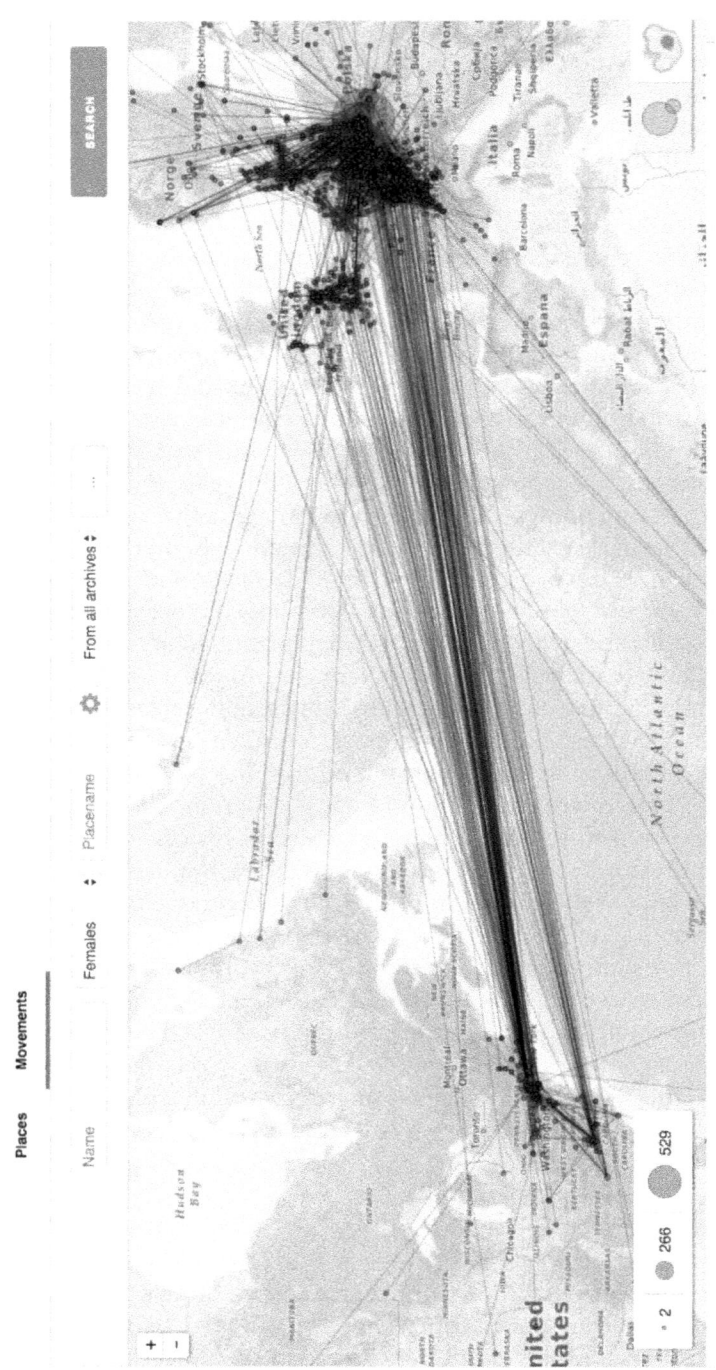

Figure 11.2. Visualization of the birth and death places of all female authors of Moravian memoirs from 1700 to 1800. Source: http://moravianlives.org.

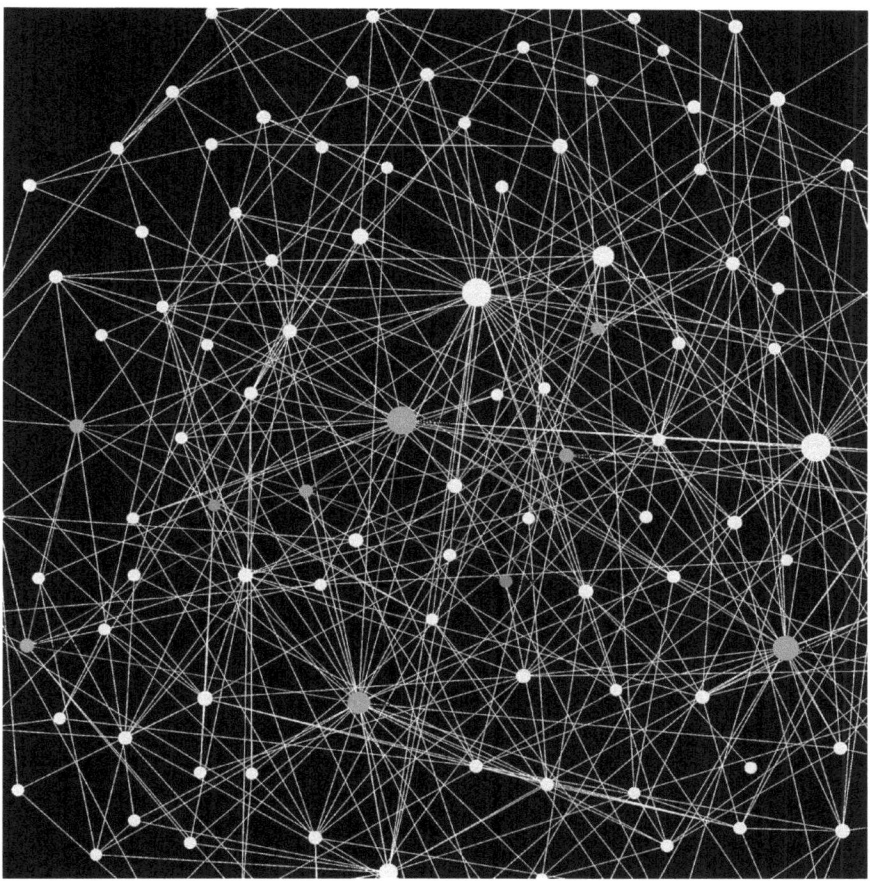

Figure 11.3. Word vector of Fulneck memoirs. Rendered 31 May 2020 with InfraNodus by Katherine M. Faull (https://infranodus.com), a web-based tool that presents text analysis as a network visualization to reveal co-occurrence of terms.

Moravian Church. Building out Smith's notion of AHD, Assmann argues that this cultural memory, like the massive corpus of Moravian memoirs in analog and digital form, "encompasses the age-old, out of the way and discarded, and in contrast to collective, binding memory, it includes the non-instrumentalizable, heretical, subversive and disowned."[14] Therefore the importance of accessibility to the *whole* corpus of the memoirs, and not just a selection of those deemed most interesting, important, edifying, or paradigmatic (that were perhaps already sanctioned as such by their publication in the *Gemeinnachrichten*), permits access to a cultural memory that does not act as a restrictive and potentially enslaving heritage narrative.[15]

The question then remains, how do we as digital scholars and Moravian historians ethically navigate the afterlives of the memoirs? In these new digital environments, where the original document is detached from its moment and place of creation, how have we maintained what Benjamin calls its *Kultwert*—the artifact's function within a specific ritual of cultural memory?[16] Recognizing that copyists transcribed texts for hundreds of years before the invention of print, and the print medium itself revolutionized the way in which we think about the sanctity of a holy text, what new ontological transformations does digitization bring?

Two of the founding DH scholars in the field of text analysis, Geoffrey Rockwell and Stefan Sinclair, ask similar questions in a 2016 essay on the history of computer-assisted text analysis. They pose this question: What are we doing in an attempt at digital replication, where replication is defined as "an iterative and interpretive practice that can serve heuristic and epistemological purposes that extend beyond our horizons of understanding"?[17] A digital heuristic is a way of experimenting with old (analog) methods that are made new through the translation of the archival artifact into the digital realm. In this way Moravian Lives, as a digital platform, can provide insight into the records of Moravian lives contained within the archived memoirs, leading to interpretive and analytical texts that can illuminate the rich and varied ways in which personal history becomes universal history. The digital archive also makes available the recorded lives of artisans, women, enslaved peoples, and Indigenous peoples. Applying a new phenomenological reading to the function of the archive, therefore, has enormous implications for theology and religious history. In this new digital way, Moravian memoirs might achieve their truly Zinzendorfian purpose: to create a living history of the church that consists of the lived history of all its members. Or, in the words of Assmann, "the text is the sum of its variations, it is in flux." I would argue that the digital text or texts, in the case of the memoirs, displays "*mouvance*," to borrow Paul Zumthor's term, in that it possesses a deep structure that can manifest itself in an ever-changing set of appearances.[18] Could we thus understand the digital manipulations of the text in this way? Whether it is in the markup of entities within the text, the visualization of networks of connectivity between agents, the spatialization of geographical information, or the presentation of memoirs in a digital edition, the afterlife of the Moravian memoir is in flux, as is cultural memory—a flux that can counterbalance the (mis)uses of heritage. And it is this flux that will allow the digitized physical objects to be recontextualized, reclaimed, and reinterpreted and new acts of memoir to be performed.

Katherine M. Faull is professor of German studies and comparative humanities, Bucknell University, Lewisburg, Pennsylvania. Faull has several research interests, including Schleiermacher, feminism, and translation theory, but has for the past thirty years mainly worked with various aspects of Moravian history and has been researching, teaching, and collaborating in the field of digital humanities at both national and international levels. She is part of Moravianlives.org, a collaborative DH project with the Centre for Digital Humanities and the Departments of Literature and History at the University of Gothenburg, Sweden.

Notes

1. Smith, *Uses of Heritage*, 3.
2. See Böß, *Gottesacker-Geschichten*; Mahling, "Herrnhut Memoirs."
3. Vogt, "Spiritual Autobiography," 37.
4. Eakin, "Autobiography as Cosmogram," 24.
5. Assmann, *Das kulturelle Gedächtnis*, 55–56. Moving away from Jungian notions of a "collective unconscious" or a phylogenic inherited memory, Assmann defines collective memory as a product of culture and customs. According to this schema, communicative memory is the everyday memory of a community and is defined by and adheres to social codes. It is fed by individual memories that are socially mediated and in-group oriented. Communicative memory has a limited temporal horizon of perhaps eighty to one hundred years, or three generations. In contrast, cultural memory is distanced from the everyday in that it is an intentional construct of an objectivized history and moves toward a reconstruction of the past. See Assmann, "Collective Memory."
6. Haskins, "Between Archive and Participation," 401.
7. Vogt, "Spiritual Autobiography," 39.
8. Peucker, "Pietism and the Archives," 393–420.
9. Hughes, "Transmutability."
10. Haskins. "Between Archive and Participation," 401.
11. Cassel, Cassel, and Manning, "From Augustine of Hippo's."
12. Van Dijck, *Mediated Memories*, 18.
13. See "Addressing Our Histories of Colonialism and Historic Slavery," National Trust, accessed 1 March 2022, https://www.nationaltrust.org.uk/features/address ing-the-histories-of-slavery-and-colonialism-at-the-national-trust.
14. Assmann, *Religion and Cultural Memory*, 27.
15. Assmann, 94.
16. Benjamin, *Work of Art*.
17. Rockwell and Sinclair, "Thinking-through the History," 11.
18. Assmann, *Religion and Cultural Memory*, 108.

Bibliography

Assmann, Jan. "Collective Memory and Cultural Identity." *New German Critique* 65 (1995): 125–33.

Assmann, Jan. *Das kulturelle Gedächtnis. Schrift, Erinnerung und politische Identität in frühen Hochkulturen* [Cultural memory: Writing, memory and political identity in early high cultures]. Munich: Verlag C. H. Beck, 2007.

Assmann, Jan. *Religion and Cultural Memory.* Stanford: Stanford University Press, 2006.

Benjamin, Walter. *The Work of Art in the Age of Its Technological Reproducibility, and Other Writings on Media.* Edited by E. F. N. Jephcott, R. Livingstone, and H. Eiland, translated by M. W. Jennings, B. Dohety, and T. Y. Levin. Cambridge, MA: Belknap Press of Harvard University Press, 2008.

Böß, Stephanie. *Gottesacker-Geschichten: Eine Ethnographie zur herrnhuter Erinnerungskultur am Beispiel von Neudietendorfer Lebensläufen* [Stories from God's Acre: An ethnography on the Moravian culture of remembrance using the example of Neudietendorfer memoirs]. Münster: Waxmann, 2016.

Eakin, Paul John. "Autobiography as Cosmogram." *Storyworlds: A Journal of Narrative Studies* 6, no. 1 (2014): 21–43.

Faull, Katherine M., ed. and trans. *Moravian Women's Memoirs: Their Related Lives, 1750–1820.* Syracuse, NY: Syracuse University Press, 1997.

Cassel, Jean-Christophe, Daniel Cassel, and Lilianne Manning. "From Augustine of Hippo's Memory Systems to Our Modern Taxonomy in Cognitive Psychology and Neuroscience of Memory: A 16-Century Map of Intuition before Light of Evidence." *Behavorial Sciences* 3, no. 1 (2013): 21–41.

Haskins, Ekaterina. "Between Archive and Participation: Public Memory in a Digital Age." *Rhetoric Society Quarterly* 37, no. 4 (2007): 401–22.

Hughes, Jerald, and Karl Reiner Lang. "Transmutability: Digital Decontextualization, Manipulation, and Recontextualization as a New Source of Value in the Production and Consumption of Culture Products." *Proceedings of the 39th Annual Hawaii International Conference on System Sciences (HICSS'06)* 8 (2006): 165a.

Lost, Christine. *Das Leben als Lehrtext. Lebensläufe aus der herrnhuter Brüdergemeine* [Life as a text of teaching: Memoirs from the Moravian Brethren]. Herrnhut: Herrnhuter Verlag, 2007.

Mahling, Lubina, ed. "The Herrnhut Memoirs: 'The Wendish Brothers'; The Sorbian Everyday Life in the Herrnhut Memoirs of the Eighteenth Century. A Collection of Sources and Documentation." Sorabicon. Accessed 1 March 2022. https://www.sorabicon.de/en/the-herrnhut-memoirs/.

Peucker, Paul. "Pietism and the Archives." In *A Companion to German Pietism, 1660–1800*, edited by Douglas H. Shanz, 393–420. Leiden/Boson: Brill, 2014.

Rockwell, Geoffrey, and Stefan Sinclair. "Thinking-through the History of Computer-Assisted Text Analysis." In *Doing Digital Humanities: Practice, Training, Research,* edited by Constance Crompton, Richard Lane, and Ray Siemens, 9–21. London: Routledge, 2016.

Smith, Laurajane. *The Uses of Heritage.* London: Routledge, 2006.

Vogt, Peter. "Spiritual Autobiography and Ecclesiology: The Social Dimension of Individual Life Stories in 18th Century Pietism and the Moravian Church." In *Moravian Memoirs: Pillars of an Invisible Church*, edited by Christer Ahlberger and Per von Wachenfeldt, 35–57. Skellefteå: Artos Academic, 2017.

van Dijck, José. *Mediated Memories in the Digital Age*. Stanford: Stanford University Press, 2007.

Concluding Remarks and Perspectives

*Tine Damsholt, Marie Riegels Melchior, Christina Petterson, and
Tine Reeh*

"If only these walls could talk" is an expression frequently heard
at historic sites. The UNESCO World Heritage site of Moravian
Christiansfeld is such a place, with well-preserved buildings and a town
plan from the late eighteenth century. In this understanding of history,
walls and buildings are considered historic witnesses to the activities and
lives of the past. They form the tangible and material heritage, a relic that
has survived and now offers a point of entry into the now lost cultures
and experiences. This book, in contrast, has employed a more complex
understanding of history and heritage and how they are constantly created, negotiated, and recreated. Pasts are selectively recalled and used in
the present, as they are performed, experienced, and lived.

Already from the early days of its settlement, Moravian Christiansfeld
became a place to visit (see chapter 4, by Peter Hauge). However, these
visits did not concern the past. Instead, they addressed the future of the
Danish (and Norwegian) society and the relevance of learning better
practices from the Moravian Brethren, whether it was musical education, hymn singing, schooling of children, crafting skills, or industriousness. The positive legacy of Christiansfeld and its relevance for broader
society—the very possibility of heritagization—was inscribed from the
very start. From the eighteenth century onward, manifold actors have
taken part in an ongoing presencing of the past in the heritagization
processes. These actors cover a wide range, from the Danish kings and
the present Queen Margrethe II over public government officials, local
producers, and the Moravian Brethren themselves to the tourists who
visit the town every year and bring home honey cakes—the popular
materialization of Moravian heritage (see chapter 7, by Marie Riegels
Melchior).

From the perspective of the twenty-first century, it seems evident that the Moravian religious understanding of the individual and everyday practices of self were deeply entangled with the development of a new kind of subjectivity that was emerging in the modern welfare states: a religious as well as civic selfhood (see chapter 2, by Sigrid Nielsby Christensen, and chapter 3, by Tine Damsholt). These parts of the Moravian legacy within Danish society were not evident in the eighteenth-century context nor in the following centuries. This demonstrates how legacy and heritage are not stable objects. Instead, we select, negotiate, reconstruct, and perform the past in our ongoing lives through multiple and changing forms of past presencing.

However, with its unique and minority religion, Christiansfeld always constituted a crossroads between religious and secular practices and, as such, an ambivalent—or at least not straightforward—place-making in the Danish national discourse and historiography. Only the omission of more difficult parts allowed for a historiography of an almost unconditional positive legacy of Moravian Christiansfeld (see chapter 1, by Tine Reeh). Furthermore, the strong discourses and regimes of World Heritage also pose challenges for the local sites[1]—and for the Moravians, living one's everyday life within the World Heritage narratives is by no means unambiguous. Members of the congregation take part in an ongoing negotiation with tour guides' representations and visitors' expectations and try to authorize and control the stories about who the Moravians were and are (see chapter 6, by Rasmus Rask Poulsen). Also, it is questionable whether the heritagization processes enforced by the UNESCO designation will be able to sustain or even communicate the way the Moravian community structure continuingly generates specific relationships between present and past (see chapter 10, by Christina Petterson).

Finally, as heritage scholars have noted, the exclusion of so-called "dark heritage" is often a prominent part of heritagization processes.[2] In this sense, heritagization logics are also implied in the focus of this book, where we have mainly looked to the eighteenth century and the present, only briefly mentioning the more contested parts of the history of Moravian Christiansfeld during the nationalized nineteenth century as well as during the Second World War.

When UNESCO designated Christiansfeld a World Heritage site, the preserved buildings and the city plan were explicitly foregrounded, as they tell comfortable stories of a remote eighteenth-century origin, of architectural visions and aesthetic values recognizable in the twenty-first century. Following UNESCO's system of separate listings and categories of tangible and intangible heritage becomes problematic when it comes to religiosity, in that for Moravians, the intangible nature of their religious spirit is considered materially present in their buildings and town plan and as such is an equally important part of Moravian heritage (see chapter 9, by Jørgen Bøytler). This leads to several questions for the future of Christiansfeld as living World Heritage: Will distinct religious practices such as the writing of *Lebensläufe* (memoirs) survive and even grow in the future (see chapter 8, by Jill E. S. Vogt)? How will the digitization of Moravian source material affect the experience of Moravian heritage (see chapter 11, by Katherine M. Faull)? And how will the demography of the Christiansfeld congregation affect its sustainability as a living Moravian community (see chapter 5, by Margit Warburg)? These questions are not limited to Moravian Christiansfeld but permeate the field and queries of many heritage sites. How can we shape sustainable futures in the ways pasts are made present in our everyday practices?

In this book we have focused on the multiple ways the past is, or is made, present, whether implicitly—and taken for granted, materialized, performed, and experienced in everyday life—or valued and articulated verbally within various and changing heritage and historicity regimes.[3] Heritagization processes affect us all, from locals, professionals, and visitors to the religious and secular communities at large. We commemorate certain events and individuals and ignore others, and we continuously shape multidirectional relationships between past, present, and future in our daily lives and practices.[4] Within the UNESCO heritage regime, some aspects may be naturalized by various actors involved and, especially when it comes to religious heritage sites, the spiritual and intangible dimensions may be authorized and turned into unquestionable ideas about "how things really are or should be."[5] This may give rise to new concerns for tangible sites, where heritage tourism is experienced as a mixed blessing; it instrumentalizes and wears down the physical environment as well as transforming the local practices. The intention to protect buildings and sacred practices may be realized at the expense of other practices or may even destroy the very practices meant to be safeguarded, as has been discussed in the case of another site on UNESCO's World Heritage list: the "Camino" or the Routes of Santiago de Compostela in northern Spain.[6]

However, the protection of intangible heritage practices is no less problematic. The paradox of intangible heritage is that, as part of their safeguarding, cultural and religious practices have to be described, inventoried, and so forth. Thus, designations often imply the neat ordering, standardization, and even silencing and exclusion of those not fitting the official categories.[7] Safeguarding intangible heritage also risks freezing such living religious practices into petrified rituals devoid of meaning and lacking the inherent transformation always involved in lives lived.

Thus, the paradox of heritagization is that safeguarding—of either tangible or intangible heritage or both—may very well end up as destruction as well. It is still too early to tell whether this will be the case when it comes to Christiansfeld, the specific crossroads of heritage and religion we have dealt with in this book. While we write these concluding remarks, other Moravian settlements are already on the tentative lists and/ or preparing applications for inclusion on national as well as UNESCO World Heritage lists (e.g., Bethlehem in the United States, Herrnhut in Germany, and Gracehill in Northern Ireland). Which insights and experiences from Christiansfeld will they be able to develop and learn from? Heritage designation involves much more for a local community than preservation of old and beautiful buildings. A religious heritage site is a place where lives have been lived for better or worse and woven into the fabric of a religious community. But, to remain a living religious community and site, it is necessary to also involve and seek to shape possible and sustainable futures. Close scholarly examinations of pasts, presents, and their mutual entanglements are called for, to make it possible to sustain and enrich our understanding of the various ways of presencing pasts in the futures to come. The investigations and interpretations we have presented in this book may also shape the tales that the walls of Christiansfeld "will tell" in the future.

Tine Damsholt is professor of European ethnology at the University of Copenhagen. She has written extensively on national and patriotic discourses in eighteenth- and nineteenth-century Denmark and political rituals in contemporary Western countries based on cultural history and ethnographic fieldwork. Subjectivity, materiality, temporality, emotions, body, and gender are recurrent themes in her research. She is currently investigating the transformed everyday life during the COVID-19 pandemic and how it affects the ways we understand and practice pasts, present, and futures in daily life.

Marie Riegels Melchior is an associate professor in European ethnology at the University of Copenhagen. Her research interests concern mainly fashion and design culture, cultural history from the nineteenth century onward, and heritage and museum studies. She has written extensively on Danish fashion and design history in the twentieth- and twenty-first centuries as well as on museological issues when fashion enters museums. She is on the editorial board of the journal *Ethnologia Scandinavica: Journal of Scandinavian Ethnology*.

Christina Petterson is a visiting research fellow at the Australian National University and at the Department of Church History, University of Copenhagen. Her background is in theology (M.Th.) and cultural studies (PhD) and her research interests concern the relationship between Christianity and social history in the eighteenth century both in the colonies and Europe. She is on the editorial board of the *Journal of Moravian History* and recently published *The Moravian Brethren in a Time of Transition: A Socio-Economic Analysis of a Religious Community in Eighteenth-Century Saxony* (2021).

Tine Reeh is an associate professor in church history at the University of Copenhagen. Her scholarly focus has been on the nexus between religion and society in the Nordic countries. She has also worked with historiography, Luther reception, and secularization, and she is currently leading the interdisciplinary research project "Managing Melancholy: Dynamics of Theology and Medicine in 18th-Century Denmark-Norway," funded by the VELUX Foundations.

Notes

1. Bendix, Eggert, and Peselmann, "Introduction."
2. Thomas et al., "Dark Heritage."
3. Bendix, Eggert, and Peselmann, "Introduction"; Eriksen, *From Antiquities*.
4. Macdonald, "Presencing Europe's Pasts."
5. Sánchez-Carretero, "Heritagization of the Camino," 95.
6. Sánchez-Carretero, 113.
7. Hafstein, *Making Intangible Heritage*.

Bibliography

Bendix, Regina, Aditya Eggert, and Arnika Peselmann. "Introduction: Heritage Regimes and the State." In *Heritage Regimes and the State*, edited by Regina Bendix, Aditya Eggert, and Arnika Peselmann, 11–20. Göttingen: Universitätverlag Göttingen, 2012.
Eriksen, Anne. *From Antiquities to Heritage: Transformations of Cultural Memory*. Time and the World: Interdisciplinary Studies in Cultural Transformation, vol 1. New York: Berghahn Books, 2014.
Hafstein, Valdimar Tr. *Making Intangible Heritage: El Condor Pasa and Other Stories from UNESCO*. Bloomington: Indiana University Press, 2018.

Macdonald, Sharon. "Presencing Europe's Pasts." In *A Companion to the Anthropology of Europe*, edited by Ullrich Kockel, Máiréad Nic Craith, and Jonas Frykman, 233–52. Oxford: Wiley-Blackwell, 2012.

Sánchez-Carretero, Cristina. "Heritagization of the Camino to Finisterre." In *Heritage, Pilgrimage and the Camino to Finesterre*, edited by Christina Sánchez-Carretero, 95–119. Switzerland: Springer, 2015.

Thomas, Suzie, Vesa-Pekka Herva, Oula Seitsonen, and Eerika Koskinen-Koivisto. "Dark Heritage." In *Encyclopedia of Global Archaeology*, edited by C. Smith, 1–11. Switzerland: Springer Nature, 2019.

Index

Lightning Source UK Ltd.
Milton Keynes UK
UKHW022029200722
406152UK00003B/156

9 781800 735491